Nor stony tower, nor walls of beaten brass, nor airless dungeon, nor strong links of iron, can be retentive to the strength of spirit. But life, being weary of these worldly bars, never lacks power to dismiss itself...

My eyes close to dark...I dream...I fly...I am free as before...

—WILLIAM SHAKESPEARE, 1599

Letters
from
Alcatraz

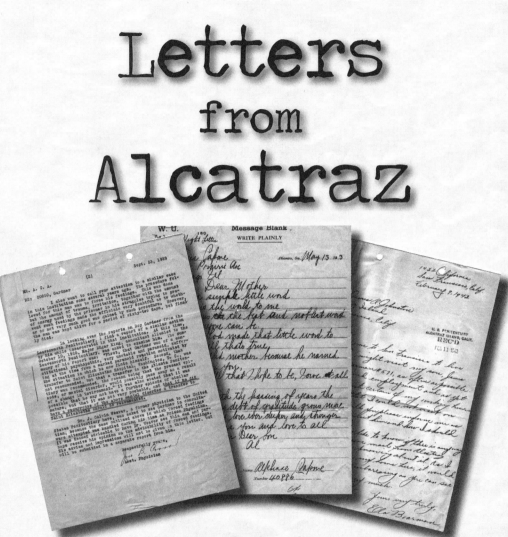

Michael Esslinger

OCEAN VIEW PUBLISHING
SAN FRANCISCO, CALIFORNIA

Letters from Alcatraz

By Michael Esslinger
Copyright © 2008

For information contact:

Ocean View Publishing
P.O. Box 222317
Carmel, CA 93922
CoastBooks@aol.com

First Edition, 2008

ISBN: 0-9704614-2-9
ISBN13: 978-0-9704614-2-1

Library of Congress Catalog Card Number: 2008934941

The principle letters in this collection are held as United States Public Records in the National Archives and Records Administration, United States Library of Congress, and the Bureau of Prisons. Several letters were also reprinted by permission from the Bob Baker Estate and the Alcatraz Alumni Association.

Narrative excerpts contained in *Alcatraz Island—the History* and select inmate biographies originally appeared in *Alcatraz—A Definitive History of the Penitentiary Years*, by Michael Esslinger, and is reprinted by permission from Ocean View Publishing.

All original source information is included in *Alcatraz—A Definitive History of the Penitentiary Years*.

No biographies or narratives within this book have been authorized or endorsed, implied or otherwise by those persons named or associated.

Book Design and Composition by John Reinhardt Book Design
Cover Design by Jim Zach

Printed in the United States of America

For Julie

Contents

Letters from Alcatraz

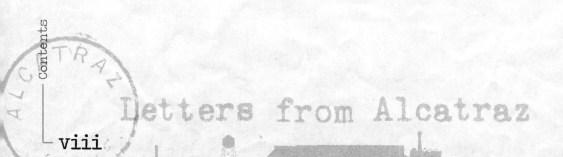

Alcatraz Prisoners Rules & Regulations

PRIVILEGES: You are entitled to food, clothing, shelter and medical attention. Anything else that you get is a privilege. You earn your privileges by conducting yourself properly. "Good Standing" is a term applied to inmates who have a good conduct record and a good work record and who are not undergoing disciplinary restrictions.

CORRESPONDENCE: Upon entrance to the institution, each inmate will be given a form to fill out, listing the persons with whom he wishes permission to correspond. After approval of the list, inmates may correspond only with the approved correspondents. You will refrain from discussing other inmates or institutional affairs. Violent or abusive letters will not be mailed. Correspondence is limited to two (2) outgoing and seven (7) incoming letters a week. All regular inmate mail will be collected by the evening watch Officer in the cellhouse. Writing materials are issued during the Tuesday P.M. bath line, at the supply table in the clothing room.

SEALED CORRESPONDENCE: As stated in Section 27, sealed correspondence may be addressed to certain Officials. Such letters may be sealed and placed in the special mail box which is located at the West End of the Cellhouse. You are not required to place any identifying information on the envelope and it will be forwarded to the Bureau without inspection.

SPECIAL HOLIDAY MAIL: In addition to your regular mail privileges you will be allowed to send your Mother an extra letter on Mother's Day. At Christmas time you will be allowed to mail (4) Christmas Cards. You may receive greeting cards only on the following occasions: Christmas, Easter, Father's Day and your birthday.

Inmates will not ask Officers, Officials or civilians to write or post letters for them or receive mail through Officers, Civilians or Officials except when acting in their official capacity.

Letters from Alcatraz

Letters from Alcatraz

X

Letters from Alcatraz

Letters from Alcatraz

Letters from Alcatraz

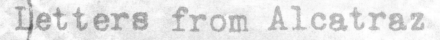

Letters from Alcatraz

Foreword

Larry L. Quilligan, Correctional Officer,
U.S.P. Alcatraz, 1949–1951

THE HALLMARK of Alcatraz was forged from its natural and manufactured isolation, paired against a strict and uncompromising set of rules and regulations. A sentence to Alcatraz translated to a life set in slow motion. The life of an inmate on the Rock was shaped by a firm and consistent regimen, day-in-day-out, year-after-year, decade-after-decade. Almost completely isolated from current events and the world outside, news seeped into the prison via letters from family members, magazines (with banned topics and articles removed), family visits, or an occasional classic movie. All served as his only link to the fast paced society in constant view just across the San Francisco Bay. On occasion, a new inmate would bring in news or stories from another prison or the outside, which quickly became a central discussion topic for inmates living inside the Alcatraz curtain.

My interest in Alcatraz stretches far into my youth. It would be in February of 1940 that I would make my first contact with the Alcatraz institution. While preparing an assigned high school civics class report, I wrote a letter to its first warden, James A. Johnston requesting material for use in my presentation. Amazingly, I received a timely letter back from Johnston, but his response brief and non-revealing:

February 6, 1940

Dear Sir:

Responsive to yours of February 1, 1940, I am obliged to say that I do not happen to have any printed material regarding the activities of the Island. Not knowing what your particular interest may be, I cannot undertake to write a description of the place or an account of the activities in a brief letter.

Sincerely,

J.A. Johnston

The Hollywood canvas of life inside Alcatraz was one of mystery and constant speculation. But life inside, as I knew it, wasn't glamorous or even remotely entertaining for those serving out their time. During my term, I came face-to-face with many of the more infamous inmates, including Robert Stroud "Birdman of Alcatraz," Alvin Karpis, and George "Machine Gun" Kelly. On Alcatraz, without exception, every man was treated equal. Young or old, infamous, famous or unknown, murderer or counterfeiter, their conduct was the only compass for the few earned privileges allowed, or alternately taken away. Celebrity status or notoriety in the free world had no merit on the Rock.

The officers spent their work hours under the same roof and in principal endured the same regimen of those they supervised. Even for officers, Alcatraz proved it could be a very dangerous place when living and working along men who became desperate to escape. While officers governed the frequent counts and structured movements of the inmates, they enforced a set of rules and regulations that endured only minor changes over the course of nearly three decades of Alcatraz's history. The letters in this collection begin to chip away the myths surrounding the Rock, and represents life inside and out of Alcatraz, in the words from many of America's most well known incorrigibles. Most of these letters only represent the inmates' viewpoint, but still shed light on the issues that dominated the thoughts and opinions of those who served time both on and off Alcatraz.

For me it's been well over fifty years since I patrolled the cellblocks and gun towers of Alcatraz. The sounds and imagery are still crisp in my mind as I think back to those experiences. I remain intrigued about the history and inter-workings of Alcatraz, even with my direct link to its past. As mentioned previously, the letters in this collection primarily make-up the experiences of the inmates as illustrated in their personal correspondence. However, there is little doubt; life for these men wasn't easily spent from inside their five by nine foot cell. And these letters, many presented through a singular lens, often represent the hardship and isolation these inmates endured as part of the Alcatraz regimen. The late James V. Bennett wrote in a perspicacious and contrasting observation:

"…this was the place where the legend of the big house in the annals of crime would live the longest and die the hardest. Alcatraz was never without a sense of fantasy."

Foreword

Letters from Alcatraz

Those words, especially the operative nouns, legend and fantasy, echo my studied conclusions following a lifetime of interest with the U.S. Penitentiary Alcatraz, and a subsequent lifetime career in prisons, jails, probation, parole, and criminal justice planning. In the end, the legacy of Alcatraz will endure as a prominent icon of the 20th Century. Through these letters, hopefully, the realities of doing time and the living wages of crime paid by these inmates help bring into focus, a heritage of awareness and redemption.

ALCATRAZ

Letters from Alcatraz

Preface

THE INSPIRATION for this book came from a very unexpected source. During the filming of an interview I did for a National Geographic documentary, the journalist posed to me a deeply rooted question off camera: Were there any stories that in retrospect I wish had been included in my first book on Alcatraz but were lost to the editor's pen? This one simple question struck a profound chord that resonated for several weeks. During the course of researching and writing my first book on Alcatraz, I had come across numerous letters that provided a haunting glimpse of the emotive pain and separation that inmates experienced while incarcerated both on and off the Rock.

There was also another letter written by the widow of one of the officers killed during the Battle of Alcatraz that has haunted me ever since reading it. Written only a couple weeks following the tragedy, it showed a very brave young woman who was optimistic about an uncertain future for her and her children. It was a powerful reminder that behind the sensationalized stories and media publicity, these were real people who had faithfully

served the public and in doing so made the ultimate sacrifice, and in some cases their families suffered immensely. I was profoundly affected by her letter and always felt that it was important to humanize rather than glamorize the events and associated history of Alcatraz.

Originally, these had been intended to be published in the first book, but sadly, because the letter topics were fragmented and without much consistency in their themes, the majority wound-up on the cutting room floor. There was also a competing space dilemma. The book on the Rock had now been termed "the Brick" since it weighed as much and simply had to be reduced to reasonable size. Despite this, I had long felt that many of these letters couldn't be simply lost to history.

Throughout its tenure, Alcatraz endured the scarred and horrid status as America's Devil's Island. It is the most famed prison in American history and its design was to break the spirits of America's most legendary crime moguls. There is no prison with more notoriety. Speculation of human torture and deprivation frequently emerged in newspapers and newsreels during its era of operation. The zenith of this reputation was realized during the famed murder trial of Henri Theodore Young in 1941, where Alcatraz was put on-trial for the confinement practices imposed on inmates. The final verdict of involuntary manslaughter and overt implications that the conditions of Alcatraz was a contributor, locked-down its reputation for life.

In candor, if you exclude the era of the silence rule and working period of the primitive dungeon cells located in the cellhouse basement, most of the former inmates I interviewed and further written in many of their own personal autobiographies, describe Alcatraz as being one of the best and cleanest institutions within the federal prison system. It was a turning point, rather than a dead-end. The industries and work programs offered structure and job skills that were essential to meaningful employment in free society. In-fact, numerous Alcatraz alumni integrated back into society assuming very productive roles. While inmates despised the rigid structure and hard stone regulations, several later acknowledged that it helped them adapt when finally released. Inmate morale at Alcatraz was better than at most other federal institutions. Most agreed that the officers while not friendly were generally respectful if you followed the rules, the food was better than any other prison (state or federal), and single cells (even-though small and inherently cold) offered privacy and other advantages not enjoyed at other institutions.

As one of numerous examples, former Alcatraz inmate Henry Hawk described Alcatraz to an Associated Press reporter following his release:

> "I soon found out Alcatraz is a really swell place. You get good food. You have pleasant work to do. The real difference between it and any another one is that they really keep their eyes on you, and enforce discipline. Escape? No sane man ever thinks about it."

This is not to assert that every inmate released from Alcatraz fared well. There was still a notable population of inmates that once released walked a quick path back to prison, and in some cases even back to Alcatraz. Case in point, Theodore Audett stood alone in his class. Once released, he continued his crime parade, landed back in federal prison and served three completely separate terms on Alcatraz under three separate register numbers.

Alcatraz was designed under strict rule concepts and was intended to be a harsh prison. It was one of the toughest in the federal system and it was meant to be uncompromising. It was the pioneer of the super-max prison concept; engineered to harbor the worst criminal element and to break the most incorrigible, violent and escape prone inmates within the federal system. Strict rule and harsh discipline set the tone for those who had reined control in other federal institutions. However, the torture experienced by inmates was much more psychological than physical. Many of the inmates had reconciled themselves to long sentences and abandoned any hope of being released. The remote and isolated conditions created by its native surroundings of freezing bay waters, provided a natural deterrent for escape. The reputation and lore of Alcatraz in other institutions demanded a yield to defeat. The rigid and relentless prison regulations offered little opportunity for individualism and forced uniformity. Surviving Alcatraz was to walk straight and follow the rules. The ultimate punishment for those who strayed was banishment to a cold and pitch dark isolation cell with steel floors, where all external elements of sound and light were expelled. As Warden Paul Madigan would later emphasize, Alcatraz was established to teach criminally minded men the importance of good character, not necessarily intellect.

MY INTRIGUE WITH ALCATRAZ has endured for well-over three decades. Following the publication of my first book on Alcatraz, a comprehensive study of the prison, I thought it would sullen my interest and put Alcatraz to rest. I miscalculated, as this couldn't be farther from the truth... The stories still intrigue, the history forever fascinating, and the human drama of living in the extreme still grip me. In the time since the publication of my first work, I've returned to Alcatraz numerous times. I've spent many of the early morning hours walking the empty and silent cellblocks before the waves of visitors swarm the island; the silence broken only by the occasional screech of a passing seagull or the fog horn of a passing ship. To me, the abandoned prison is still very much alive with history. Within its walls, the voices still remain.

One of the most poignant stories that emerged from the cutting room floor was that of former Alcatraz inmate Dale Stamphill, my very first formal interview over two decades ago. Dale had been shot by prison guards during a thwarted escape

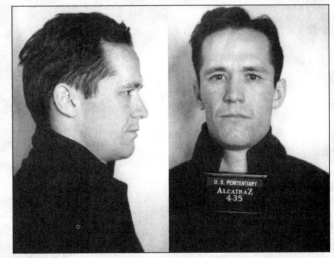

Dale Stamphill

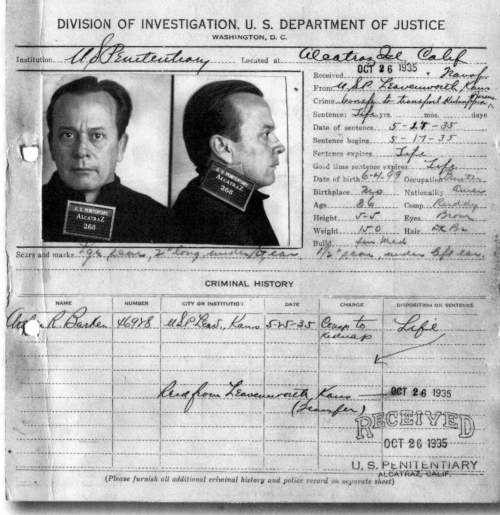

DIVISION OF INVESTIGATION, U. S. DEPARTMENT OF JUSTICE
WASHINGTON, D. C.

Arthur "Doc" Barker

attempt with famed inmates Doc Barker, Henri Young, Rufus McCain and Ty Martin in January of 1939. He arrived at Alcatraz in January of 1938, following a series of escape attempts at other institutions and a history of kidnapping and robbery. Stamphill would play a key part in their meticulously planned escape attempt which originated inside what was thought to be one of the most secure areas of the prison (despite not yet having been walled-off from other sections of the penitentiary).

The cells in the segregation unit (D-Block) had escaped the tool-proof bar retrofit initiated during the prisons formal transfer from the military to the Bureau of Prisons in 1934, retaining the original soft flat-iron bars. Using contraband tools, the inmates were able to break free from their cells using hacksaw blades, climb through a barred window of the cellblock using a makeshift bar-spreader, and into the freedom of night under a silent sky.

In the dim early hour of their escape,

all that was present were the sounds of the ocean as a heavy fog stood as a dark curtain blackening the vibrant vistas of the San Francisco shoreline. Sadly, the escape ended almost as quickly as it began. As the inmates descended into a barren cove to embark on their mile and a quarter swim to shore, searchlights and escape sirens assaulted the silence after an alert guard discovered the men missing from their cells while conducting a routine count.

As prison officers and searchlights converged over the fog shrouded cove, hazy human figures plunged into the water to a rush of freedom. The dark of night and high tide masked the teeth-sharp rocks which demanded slow and careful passage. After a terse and snubbed warning to halt, officers unleashed a raining hail of gunfire, ending their dream of escape. Young and McCain were found stripped of their clothing and shivering violently from the freezing bay waters. Martin was found in the same condition bleeding from numerous cuts, pleading for leniency. Stamphill and Barker fared the worst while unsuccessfully attempting to find cover from behind a rock. Stamphill suffered serious injuries to his lower extremities from the explosive bullet wounds delivered by the officer's rifles. Barker was found with a bullet wound to the head and both men were so incapacitated that a small boat was launched to recover them from the waters cove. Barker later died from his bullet wound and in the prison hospital his last recorded words spoken: "I was a fool to try it. I'm all shot to hell...."

The aftermath of the escape left tensions between some of the inmates at a soaring high. Following his release from isolation, a classification imposed as punishment for the escape attempt, Young fatally-stabbed McCain inside the prison industries building on Alcatraz. The murder resulted from what Young testified during his trial as "a conflict that arose from the failed escape." Some later alleged that the animosity stirred when McCain announced that he didn't know how to swim once he reached the water's edge, with Young ultimately blaming McCain for the plots failure. Young's trial would become one of the most famous events in Alcatraz history.

Stamphill's wounds were serious but not fatal. He was hospitalized for a brief period and then placed in isolation until August of 1940. He integrated back into the general population and was given a new work assignment. From this day forward, he would walk a straight line and become a model inmate. He remained in the general population for another ten years before being released from Alcatraz and finishing out his prison sentence at Leavenworth.

His escape, however, was not the story that intrigued me most. During my interview, he closed with a profound story of how he escaped mentally from Alcatraz. Before sharing his very personal story, he prepared me by stating it was "a lot of sappy bullshit" but it was the truth of what he had dreamed about, and how it contributed to his survival of another ten years on the Rock.

As a result of his injuries suffered during his failed escape, Stamphill had made frequent follow-up visits to the prison hospital situated above the mess hall. During one of his appointments, he covertly slipped into his cuffed sleeve and smuggled out a small empty pharmaceu-

Preface

Letters from Alcatraz

Clark Howard (left), crime novelist and author of Six Against the Rock, former Alcatraz inmates Willie Radkay (middle) and Dale Stamphill (right) in 1976 at Radkay's home in Prescott Kansas.

tical bottle used to store medications in the prison pharmacy. He began to fill the bottle with strands of his own hair, along with a small torn piece of paper that only included his name. He recalled that the paper had a mild scent of perfume. A fellow inmate had torn a piece of a letter written by his wife which had made it past the mail censor. It became an emblematic capsule of terms. Using a dense piece of rubber acquired from a friend working in the mat shop, he tightly corked the bottle to assure a permanent seal. In his cell he conducted mini buoyancy tests by floating the bottle in his toilet and submerging it to assess whether it could withstand a long toss into the bay and still float.

On what Stamphill described as a "crisp-clear-day" during his walk down the path to the prison industries, he pulled the concealed bottle from under his cloth-ing and threw it with the able skill of a major league baseball player, far over the barbwire fence and into the bay waters. He confidently, if not proudly explained that its fall into the water was no less graceful than a bird's winged landing. He stated that he slowed his walk, and then looked around to affirm the officers didn't see the toss. He glanced over his shoulder just in time to see it bobbing in the far distance and safely clear of the rocky shore. He thought to himself that escape had come at last... On that very evening, he claimed a vivid memory. At lights out in the cellhouse, he commenced the first leg of his long private journey. By closing his eyes and dreaming of the bottle's voyage, he could see farther than he'd ever seen before....

For the next decade, Stamphill alleged that that sealed bottle had become a symbolic method of escape. He would lie in his cell bunk at night, dreaming of how far the bottle traveled and what exotic places that part of him had traveled to. He became obsessive reading travel books from the Alcatraz library and studying world geography. Every night for nearly a decade, his escape successful...

Dale's story stayed with me for nearly twenty years, long after him suffering a debilitating stroke. It represents the painful and fragile string of choices that landed him and so many other inmates on Alcatraz, and their yearning for freedom. Their letters and general correspondence was an important part of the island's history and couldn't be left to fade and disappear into the shadows of time.

There is no better insight to the human condition of the inmates than reading their letters, written in their own words. They represent the authentic thoughts and ideas with many written from inside their small cold cells at Alcatraz and at other prisons. This book offers a glimpse of that experience. Most of these letters were never intended for a mass audience. Some chronicle their hope for life and yearning to get out of prison. Others still show hope when release is a distant reality. Others communicate frustrations with the harsh prison rule and their demands for better conditions. This was all they had on Alcatraz; their thoughts, dreams and hope for something to change. Everything else was regulated.

> San Francisco news
> San Francisco Cal
>
> Please investigate criminal cruelty practices on prisoners at Alcatraz Prison. A few of the cases are (1) Edgar Lewis, age 28, serving 3 ys sentence, kept in dungeon for a total of more than 6 wks, starved, shot in face with gas gun, beaten over head with clubs by three guards (names will be given to investigating committee). He is how insane and is kept in a cage in the hospital. No hope for his recovery. His family lives at Los Banos, Calif. They don't know about it yet. The warden naturally wont give out information that will hang himself, but if an investigation is made and the inmates are questioned you will get the evidence. Another case is Jos. Bowers also insane from same cause, but not as bad condition as Lewis. James Grove is also insane and is under mental observation. John Stadeg is

In an effort to stay true to the historical ingredients of these letters, and after months of self debate, I chose to refrain from any significant editing. The grammatical elements remain mostly as originally written. As a final point to reiterate, it is crucial to recognize that my goal of presenting these letters was to only humanize the experience, and not in any way glamorize the crimes of these men. It was important to represent this history in its purest form. I felt it was important to present these letters without additional censoring. As one example, I personally struggled with the racial comments and the associated content produced in letters by Donnis Willis, Ralph Roe, and a couple of others. I felt the comments and opinions in these letters, regardless of the era from which they were written, contained harsh racial comments which were demeaning and spiteful in nature. However, my role was to maintain the historical integrity of original content, without censoring due to my personal objections of the material.

After spending hours navigating the personal thoughts and letters of these inmates, one can't help but feel a sense of sadness through the desperation of some of their writings. Even still, there were victories for some who did their time on Alcatraz, and integrated back into society.

It is here where the past collides with the present and the true essence of Alcatraz comes to life.

"Alcatraz is a necessary part of the government's campaign against predatory crime. Certain types of prisoners are a constant menace. They create an atmosphere of tension and unrest wherever they are confined. They break-down the morale of the more promising inmates and are constantly plotting violence, riots, or escape.... We are looking forward to great things from Alcatraz."

—HOMER CUMMINGS, United States Attorney General, 1934

Letters from Alcatraz

Alcatraz Island: The History

TOOL STEEL that no file can scratch; locks that can be opened electronically and mechanically only by two men separated posts; forty veteran guards hand-picked from other federal prisons, armed with automatic pistols, rifles, and machine guns; tear gas; electric instruments that reveal the presence of hidden pistols or knives on the persons of prisoners or visitors; barbed-wire entanglements; one and one quarter miles of water whose current defies all but the strongest swimmer; patrol boats of penitentiary and coast guard prison radio that can summon 200 police cars to the shores of San Francisco in five minutes. This was how

Popular Science Magazine introduced the ultimate escape-proof prison to the intrigued public.

From 1934 through 1963, Alcatraz Federal Penitentiary served as America's most notorious prison. Shrouded by fog and secrecy, it was designed to house the most legendary crime figures that tore at the very fabric of American society. These men had pushed their crimes to the outer limits. Designed as a maximum custody, minimum privilege federal prison, Alcatraz was the defining solution to the lawless rein that gripped America during the Prohibition Era. Its reputation for impregnability and harshness was deliberately encouraged by an American government intent on a show of strength to discourage criminal activity.

High profile and powerful crime magnates had presented the government with unique confinement dilemma. Gangsters of the era like ace enemies Al Capone and Machine Gun Kelly who had become household names, were glamorized by the press. The resulting fame and the elite status ultimately created a surge of followers.

Alcatraz was born from the concept of housing public enemies who had resisted reform while incarcerated, and continued to facilitate corruptive activities from within the federal prison system. These high profile criminals would be housed under a single roof and completely isolated from the public eye. The Federal Bureau of Prisons (BOP) was established in 1930 under the direction of President Herbert Hoover, as a branch of the Department of Justice (DOJ). In 1933 when the Federal Bureau of Investigation (FBI) was formed under the leadership of Director J. Edgar Hoover, he moved America to wage a public war against societal enemies.

In an unpublished commentary entitled *The Rock of Remorse* written by former inmate Roy Gardner who later committed suicide years following his release, recorded his personal views of life as an inmate during the early years on Alcatraz:

The easiest way to get a clear mental picture of Alcatraz is to imagine a large tomb situated on a small island and inhabited by corpses who still have the ability to walk and talk. In other words, a mausoleum holding the living dead. The phrase "the living dead" is in no way an exaggeration, because 75% of the men incarcerated on Alcatraz are doomed to die there, and they know it.

The prison is similar to many other prisons throughout the county, cellblocks, dining room, work shops & etc, but the management of the prison is surely different. Alcatraz was designed to break "hard guys," and it is surely accomplishing what it was designed for. The writer of this article was until very recently, an inmate of Alcatraz, and my knowledge first-hand.

The system on Alcatraz changes desperate public enemies into listless, lifeless automans, walking around apparently waiting for death to release them and not caring how soon it comes. The breaking of desperate men on that Rock is all mental. There is no brutality or physical violence practiced or permitted by the prison officials, however, the mental torture is much worse than any physical torture could possibly be. Of course, it is necessary if society is to be protected, to break public enemies such as gangsters and snatchers, and the system on Alcatraz is surely clicking 100%

The daylight hours on Alcatraz are not so bad because the prisoners have something to occupy their minds, but the hours between 5PM and 7AM are the hours that seer mans' souls and break their spirits.

Seventy-five percent of the prisoners there know they will never again experience the rapture of a woman's kiss. They will never again shake the hand of a true friend. Never again enjoy an hour of freedom.

During the first year of imprisonment they spend many sleepless hours looking at the ceiling and wondering who is kissing her now. Some of them go raving mad and awaken the entire cellblock with their insane screams. Others suffer in silence, and the only indication of their suffering in their bloodshot eyes in the morning.

Prisoners usually refer to those sleepless nights as "pay nights" and they all know what pay nights are, yet I have never heard a pay night adequately described. It seems there are no words that can actually describe those terrible nights. During many years of imprisonment I have experienced many pay nights, yet I am unable to draw a word picture of those nights. Let's just call them hell-nights and let it go at that.

Most of the doomed men on Alcatraz will die in bed, while others will die under guns of guards or in the icy waters of the San Francisco Bay. The fact that there is no escape leaves death as the only alternative for most of the inmates. Some of them actually realize that fact and linger on and let nature take its course. Watching those hopeless men walking around and existing from day to day is a pitiful sight.

An indescribable something prevails on Alcatraz that is not felt in any other prison. It seems to be a mixture of hopelessness, hatred, self-pity and cowardice. Most of the long timers

lose hope after about a year a year and begin felling sorry for themselves. The next step is to become suspicious of his fellow prisoners, and then hatred develops. When he gets to that stage he usually sits off by himself and broods, always blaming others for his troubles. If you remind him that he himself is responsible for his trouble, you are liable to have to fight him, because he is usually ready to back up his arguments with his fists.

Of course the men confined there can expect no sympathy from society because 90% of them are habitual criminals, and probably 50% are murders. That type of criminal has forfeited all claims to consideration by society, and theoretically dug his own grave. He would have been much better off had he committed suicide, and let others dig his grave.

It seems that rules governing Alcatraz were designed to dovetail together and focus on the one object, that object being to break desperate men. The rule forbidding radio and newspapers effactually cuts off the prisoners contact with the outside world. The rules governing correspondence are so strict that no public news of any kind can possibly filter through. An example of that censorship occurred with the dirigible Macon (a military airship) broke up. Although it happened on the Pacific Coast we knew nothing of it for 10 days after.

No guard dares tells an inmate that is published in the newspapers. His job wouldn't be worth a dime if he did incidentally, guards are watched just as closely as the prisoners, and when any news gets into the prison, every effort is made to find the source, and if the source is found that guard joins the ranks of the unemployed.

Alcatraz is the last stop for big time

Alcatraz Island: The History

criminals, and there is no chance to detour past it, once the "G" men get their hands on you. Alcatraz will not stop crime, but it has already put an awful crimp in it. The public enemies of 1932 and 1933 are all buried, some dead, some alive on Alcatraz, but buried just the same. A strange condition now prevails in the underworld; there are none who care to assume leadership, as the suicide title of "public enemy." Public enemy is just another way to spell Alcatraz, but it means the same thing.

In order to discourage or prevent organized resistance, the prisoners are not permitted to assemble in groups of more than three. When four or five get their heads together, it is a bad sign and they get orders to scatter. The dangerous men are all well known to the guards, and when two of them are seen constantly together, talking in low tones, they are either separated or a special watch is placed on them.

Probably the most effective machines ever installed in any prison are the magnetic searchers now in use on Alcatraz. It is impossible to carry a gun or knife, or any metal object through that frisker without detection, and the prisoners are sent through four times daily. It is impossible for a prisoner to enter or leave the cellblock without passing through the searcher, and if he has a weapon of any kind concealed on his person he is sunk, because that frisker never misses. Alcatraz is rock solid…

The early origins of Alcatraz date back hundreds of years into early California history. It received its name in 1775 when Spanish explorer Juan Manuel de Ayala charted the San Francisco Bay, and named this tiny wind-swept island La Isla de los Alcatraces, which translated to *Isle of the*

Pelicans. The small uninhabited island had little to offer, with its swift currents, craggy cliffs, bleak vegetation struggling for survival, and a stark unsoftened landscape.

Seventy-two years later in 1847, the U.S. Army took notice of Alcatraz Island for its strategic value as a military fortification. Topographical engineers began conducting geological surveys, and by 1853, U.S. Army Engineers had started constructing a military fortress on the island, along with the Pacific Coast's first operating lighthouse. Earlier in 1848, the discovery of gold along the American River in California brought shiploads of miners from around the world to the West Coast in search of the precious metal. The once sleepy little village had transformed overnight into a thriving harbor with transcontinental ships pouring in from around the world. Prior to the discovery, the Bay had been used primarily for the transportation of hides and other provisions between the various Missions spread around the Bay. As word spread around the globe of abundant wealth in California, the United States Government would invoke security measures to protect its land and mineral resources from seizure by other countries. One early survey report described the San Francisco Bay in the 1850s as a "vast forest of ship masts, waving back the crews who abandoned their vessels in search of Gold."

After several years of laborious construction and various armament expansions, Alcatraz was established as the United States' western symbol of military strength. The new military fortress featured long-range iron cannons and four massive, 15-inch Rodman guns, which were capable of sinking mammoth hos-

This photograph is from an early Stereograph with Fortress Alcatraz clearly visible in the distance. The photo was taken following the Civil War from the army wharf at Point San Jose in 1864 by Eadweard Muybridge. The 15-inch cannon balls seen in the foreground each weighed over 400-pounds and was capable of sinking hostile ships at a distance of three miles. Alcatraz was America's premier harbor defense post and a symbol of military strength during this era.

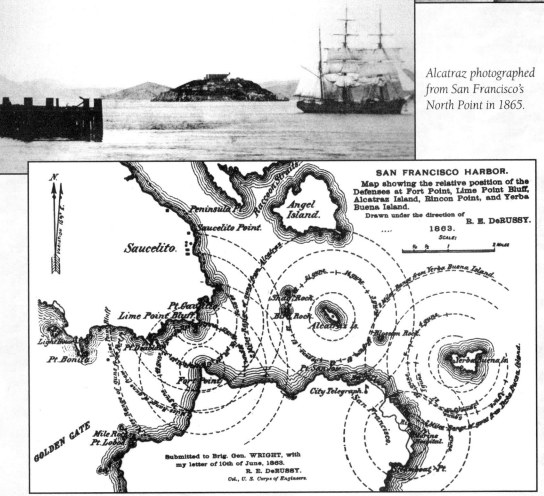

Alcatraz photographed from San Francisco's North Point in 1865.

A military defense map from 1863 representing cannon firing ranges. Fortresses located at Alcatraz, Lime and Fort Points created a triangular defense blueprint. As enemy ships progressed in the San Francisco Bay, they would navigate straight into the firing ranges of these heavily armored fortifications.

Alcatraz Island: The History

Letters from Alcatraz

tile ships three miles away. The guns of Alcatraz could fire 6,949 pounds of iron shot in one barrage. Though the fortress would eventually fire only one 400-pound cannon round at an unidentified ship and miss its target, the island had lived up to its self-made reputation as an icon of U.S. military power. But within a few decades the island's role as a military fortress would start to fade away and its defenses would become obsolete by the standards of more modern weaponry.

Because of its natural isolation, surrounded by freezing waters and hazardous currents, Alcatraz would soon be considered by the U.S. Army as an ideal location for holding captives. In 1861 the island began receiving Civil War prisoners, and in 1898 the Spanish-American war would bring the prison population from a mere twenty-six to over four hundred and fifty. Then in 1906, following the catastrophic San Francisco Earthquake, hundreds of civilian prisoners were transferred to the island for safe confinement. By 1912 a large cellhouse had been constructed on the island's central crest, and by the late 1920's, the three-story structure was nearly at full capacity.

Alcatraz was the Army's first long-term prison, and it was already beginning to build its reputation as a tough detention facility by exposing inmates to harsh con-

One of the prime objectives of Alcatraz as a military fortress was protecting California's mineral resources from hostile foreign powers. Heavy armaments of long, medium and short range cannons were strategically targeted to protect San Francisco from enemy ships entering the Golden Gate. Early fortifications included massive 15-inch Rodman cannons with a barrel weight of nearly 50,000 pounds, and smaller varieties of Howitzer, Columbiad and Mortor cannons.

Letters from Alcatraz

*An early illustration of the original
island structures in 1883.*

*The Alcatraz Citadel as it appeared in
1893 following the Civil War. Note the
cannon balls used around the perimeter
as decorative border pieces. The building
was later converted in apartments for
married officers until construction on the
new cellhouse began in 1909.*

*A circa 1902 photograph of the main roadway leading to the Citadel. Note the smoothbore Columbiad
cannon buried muzzle-first as road bumper as referenced in the original caption.*

Alcatraz Island: The History

Letters from Alcatraz

Alcatraz Upper-Prison, circa 1903.

Prisoner line-up and count at the upper-prison in 1903. Numerous counts were performed daily. Dual line-ups as seen in this photo were referred to by prisoners and guards as "nuts and butts." Armed sentries patrolled the perimeter wall and regulated activities within the stockade walls.

The only known surviving photograph of the upper-prison interior, circa 1902. Clearly visible under close examination are personal photographs and other items visible in the cells. The upper-prison faculties could house 307 prisoners.

Letters from Alcatraz

A panoramic photograph showing the devastating aftermath of the San Francisco Earthquake in 1906 from Russian Hill to Telegraph Hill. Alcatraz seen in the distance, received 176 prisoners from various local jails for more secure housing, and suffered only minor damage.

finement conditions and ironhanded discipline. The prisoners were separated into three classes based on their conduct and on the crimes they had committed, and each class held distinct levels of privilege. For example, prisoners in the third class were not allowed to have reading material from the library or visits and letters from relatives, and a strict rule of silence was rigidly enforced at all times. Prisoners who violated these rules faced strict disciplinary measures. In addition to losing their earned class rankings, violators were assigned punishments that included but were not limited to working on hard labor details, wearing a twelve-pound ball and ankle chain, and enduring solitary lock-downs with a severely restricted bread and water diet.

The average age for law-offending soldiers was twenty-four years, and most of the prisoners were serving short-term sentences for desertion or lesser crimes. However, it wasn't uncommon to find soldiers serving longer sentences for the more serious crimes of insubordination, assault, larceny and murder. One interesting element of the military order was that prisoners' cells were used only for sleeping, unless the inhabitant was in lock-down status. All prisoners were prohibited from visiting their cells during the day. Inmates with first or second class rankings were allowed to go anywhere about the prison grounds, except for the guards' quarters on the upper levels.

Despite the stringent rules and harsh standards for hardened criminals, Alcatraz primarily functioned in a minimum-security capacity. The types of work assignments given to inmates varied depending on the prisoners, their classification, and how responsible they were. Many inmates worked as general servants who cooked, cleaned, and attended to household chores for island families. In many cases, select prisoners were entrusted to care for the children of staff members. Alcatraz was also home to several Chinese families, who were employed

Alcatraz Island: The History

North end, showing structural
steel to carry water tanks, and mess hall
and basement.

West side

Alcatraz Island: The History

The Alcatraz Military
Prison cellhouse began
construction in 1909 was
completed in late 1911.
The new cellhouse opened
in February of 1912 and at
the time of its completion,
it was the largest steel-
reinforced concrete
structure in the world.

as servants, and made up the largest segment of the island's civilian population. The lack of a strict focus on prison security favored some inmates who hoped to make a break to freedom. But in spite of their best efforts, most escapees never made it to the mainland, and usually turned back to be rescued from the freezing waters. Those who were not missed and failed to turn back eventually would tire and drown. While inmates could conceptually escape the watchful eye of a sentry, scale a fence or evade gunfire; the strong and rushing tides were constant and unforgiving, even for the most adept and athletic escapees. Despite the San Francisco shoreline only being 1¼ miles south and the Marin shores three miles north, Alcatraz was isolated from both as if it were in the middle of the Pacific Ocean. The Bay waters were ultimately the foremost deterrent and key to the prison's historic success.

THE PUBLIC DISLIKED having an Army prison as a sterile focal point in the middle of the beautiful San Francisco Bay, so the Military made arrangements to have soil from Angel Island brought over, and it was spread throughout the acreage of Alcatraz. Several prisoners were trained as able gardeners, and they planted numerous varieties of flowers and decorative plants to give the island a more pleasing appearance from the mainland. The California Spring and Wild Flower Association contributed top-grade seeding, ranging from rose bushes to lilies. The island residents enjoyed tending their gardens, and it was said that the landscape work assignments were among those most favored by the prisoners.

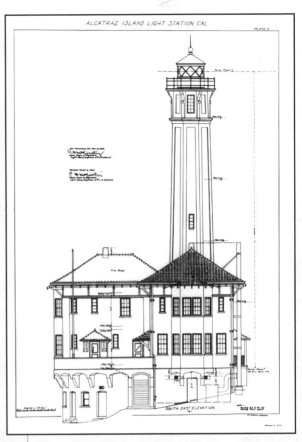

ALCATRAZ ISLAND LIGHT STATION, CAL

SOUTH EAST ELEVATION

The original lighthouse built in 1854 used a powerful optical lens to amplify the luminance of a whale-oil burning lamp. It was replaced in 1909 with a modern electric eighty-four-foot concrete tower with adjacent living quarters and was lit with a smaller fourth-order lens.

Over the decades the prison's routine became increasingly more relaxed, and recreational activities grew more prevalent. In the late 1920's prisoners were permitted to build a baseball field, and were even allowed to wear their own uniforms. On Friday nights the Army hosted "Alcatraz Fights" that featured boxing matches between inmates selected from the Disciplinary Barracks population. These fights were quite popular and often drew visitors from the mainland who had managed to finagle an invitation.

Alcatraz Island: The History

Letters from Alcatraz

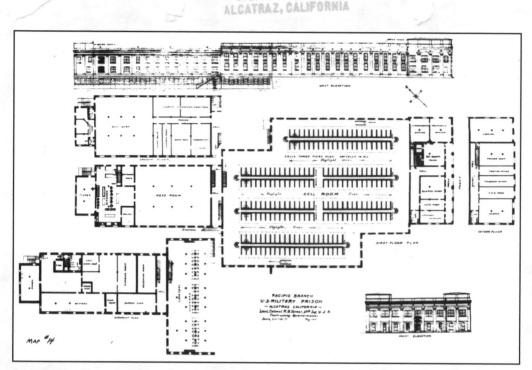

A cellblock architecture drafting from Lt. Colonel R.B. Turner, Constructing Quartermaster, May, 1908, and an early military map of Alcatraz drafted by the U.S. Army Quartermaster in January of 1928. Many of the original structures remained in use during the federal prison years.

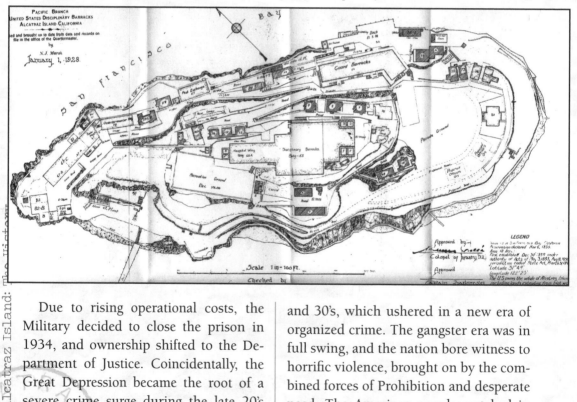

Due to rising operational costs, the Military decided to close the prison in 1934, and ownership shifted to the Department of Justice. Coincidentally, the Great Depression became the root of a severe crime surge during the late 20's and 30's, which ushered in a new era of organized crime. The gangster era was in full swing, and the nation bore witness to horrific violence, brought on by the combined forces of Prohibition and desperate need. The American people watched in

A military prison sentry paroling A-Block in 1932.

Alcatraz Federal Penitentiary.

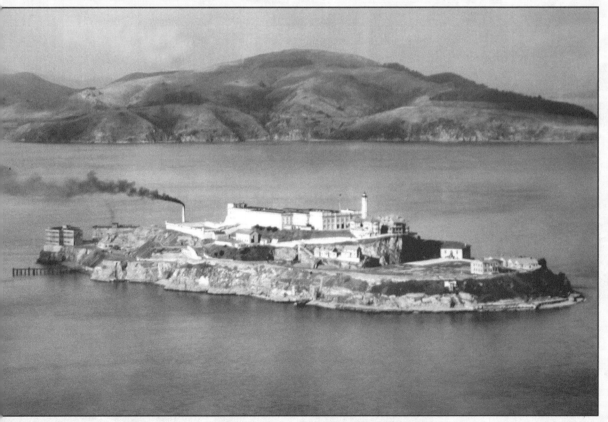

fear as influential mobsters and sharply dressed public enemies exerted heavy influence on metropolitan cities and their authorities. Law enforcement agencies were often ill-equipped to deal with the onslaught, and would frequently cower before better-armed gangs in shoot-outs and public slayings.

A public cry went out to take back America's heartland, and so the die was cast for the birth of a unique detention facility—one so forbidding that it would eventually be nicknamed Uncle Sam's Devil Island.

Alcatraz was the ideal solution. It could serve the dual purpose of incarcerating public enemies while standing as a visible icon, a warning to this new and ruthless brand of criminal. Sanford Bates, the head of the federal prisons, and Attorney General Homer Cummings led the project, and they kept a hand in the finely detailed design concepts. One of the nation's foremost security experts, Robert Burge, was commissioned to help design a prison that was escape-proof as well as outwardly forbidding. The original cellblock, built in 1909, would undergo extensive upgrades and renovations.

In April of 1934 work was begun to give the military prison a new face and a new identity. The soft squared bars were replaced with modernized tool-proof substitutes. Electricity was routed into each cell, and all of the utility tunnels were cemented to completely remove the possibility that a prisoner could enter or hide in them. Tool-proof iron window coverings would shield all areas that could be accessed by inmates. Special gun galleries would transverse the cellblock perimeters, allowing guards to carry weapons while protected behind iron rod barriers.

These secure galleries, which were elevated and out of reach of the prisoners, would be the control center for all keys, and would allow the guards the unique ability to oversee all inmate activities.

Special teargas canisters were permanently installed in the ceiling of the Dining Hall, and they could be remotely activated from both the Gun Gallery and the outside observation points. Guard towers were strategically positioned around the perimeter, and new technology allowed the use of electromagnetic metal detectors, which were positioned outside of the Dining Hall and on the Prison Industries access paths. The cellhouse contained a total of nearly 600 cells, with no one cell adjoining any perimeter wall. If an inmate managed to tunnel their way through the cell wall, they would still need to find a way to escape from the cellhouse itself. The inmates would only be assigned to B, C, and D-Blocks, since the primary prison population would not exceed 302 inmates. The implementation of these new measures, combined with the natural isolating barrier created by the icy Bay waters, meant that the prison was nearly ready to receive the nation's most incorrigible criminals.

But even during its tenure as a military prison, Alcatraz had carried the reputation as being dark, poorly ventilated and barbaric. The future Warden would later write that Alcatraz was modernized to break this reputation, and would be maintained as such over its history. He wrote:

> Standing where we could see the side walls and look down the length of the corridor I called attention to the forty six windows on one side and fifty two windows on the other side and directing a glance upward to the roof

with 372 feet of 4½ foot-wide sky-lights I said "I remember going over the amount of daylight with our Superintendent of Construction, when we putting in some new windows and his measurements showed me that we have about 3,800 square feet of light space in the cellhouse. We have ample cross ventilation as well as motor operated exhaust fans for pulling smoke and bad air out and we are insistent on cleanliness, so that's why you don't get any prison smell such as you say you expected.

Alcatraz was designed with some of the most sophisticated security features of its era. Officers could control individual or groups of cells remotely using pull levers located at the end of each cellblock.

View of Broadway from the East Gun Gallery.

Letters from Alcatraz

James Aloysius Johnston, a progressive minded reformer, served as Alcatraz Warden from 1934 to 1948.

THE BUREAU OF PRISONS selected James Aloysius Johnston as the new Warden of Alcatraz. Johnston was an ideal choice, with his strict ideals and humanistic approach to reform. He came to the position with a broad-based background in business, and more than twelve years of experience in the California Department of Corrections. James Johnston had been appointed as the Warden of San Quentin Prison in 1913, and had also served a brief appointment at Folsom Prison. He had become well known for the programs he implemented in the interest of prisoner reform. He didn't believe in chain gangs, but instead thought that inmates should report to a job where they were respected and rewarded for their efforts.

Nicknamed the "Golden Rule Warden" at San Quentin, Johnston was praised in newspapers for improvements made in California highways, many of which were graded by prisoners in his road camps. Although inmates were not compensated for their work monetarily, they were rewarded with sentence reductions. Johnston also established several educational programs at San Quentin that proved successful with a good number of inmates. But despite his humane approach to reform, he also carried a reputation as a strict disciplinarian. His rules of conduct were among the most rigid in the correctional system, and harsh punishments were meted out to inmates who defied prison regulations. During his tenure at San Quentin, Johnston oversaw the executions by hanging of several inmates, and he was not unfamiliar with the challenges of managing the most vicious rogues of society.

As Warden of Alcatraz, Johnston was given the authority to handpick his correctional officers from the entire federal prison system. Working together with Federal Prisons Director Sanford Bates, the new Warden devised new guiding principles under which the prison would operate. To begin with, it was established that prisoners would have to "earn" their transfer to Alcatraz from other prisons, and no one would be directly sentenced to Alcatraz from the courts. Inmates who sought an attorney to represent them while incarcerated at Alcatraz would have to do so by direct request to the Attorney General. All privileges would be limited, and no single inmate, regardless of his public stature, would be allotted special rights or freedoms.

Alcatraz Island: The History

Letters from Alcatraz

In 1947 the library at Alcatraz contained a catalog of 9,243 titles of fiction and non-fiction works which grew to approximately 12,000 by 1962. Titles ranged from travel to technical, greatest classics to modern; the inmates Alcatraz were typically very well read. The average inmate in the general population would read seventy-five to a hundred books a year, not including periodicals and magazines.

Books held in the Alcatraz Library were given a special catalog number and a mimeographed catalog was distributed to each cell. Inmate numbers were used in lieu of library cards for checkout records. Paperbacks were generally removed from their original binding and bound with new boards. Bibles were the only book allowed to be kept by inmates in their cell indefinitely. Former inmate Robert Gilford described the process for checking books out of the library: "You had a library card ... full of numbers. And you was supposed to keep 20-numbers on there. The numbers would correspond with the titles of the book [in the catalog] and each day you put your card up there when you go to work and one of the guys that worked in there would come and pick the cards up and then they'd go in there and they'd look and try to get the book, the number one choice. If they couldn't, they take the number two choice and deliver them to your cell."

Reading materials at Alcatraz were heavily censored, and the subjects of sex, violence and crime were strictly forbidden. The exception to this rule was war themed, old western and some adventure material. War titles spanned from the Civil War through World War II. War titles were believed to inspire patriotism and higher industry production for the military. Adventure books were among the most popular and sometimes the violent elements were overlooked if administrators and the Chaplain felt "good over evil" elements improved morale, or even in some cases create fear of the environmental elements to discourage escapes. The resident Chaplain, who was also responsible for the content of the reading materials, generally supervised the prison library. The prison featured its own bookbindery, and utilized a special catalog system. The library also included a music collection of nearly 1,000 records.

Visitation rights would have to be earned by the inmates, and no visits would be allowed for the first three months of residence at Alcatraz. All visits would have to be approved directly by the Warden, and their number would be limited to only one per month. Inmates would be given restricted access to the Prison Library, but no newspapers, radios, or other non-approved reading materials would be allowed. Receiving and sending mail would be considered a privilege, and all letters both in-coming and out-going were to be screened and typewritten after being censored by prison officials. Work was also seen as a privilege and not a right, and

Alcatraz Island: The History

Letters from Alcatraz

consideration for work assignments would be based on an inmate's conduct record.

Each prisoner would be assigned their own cell, and only the basic minimum life necessities would be allotted, such as food, water, clothing, and medical and dental care. The prisoners' contact with the outside world was completely severed. Convicted spy Morton Sobell would later state that this policy was so rigidly enforced that the inmates were never even allowed to explore the cellhouse. They would be marched from one location to another, always in a unified formation. The prison routine was rigid and unrelenting, day after day, year after year. As quickly as a given privilege could be earned for good behavior, it could be taken away for the slightest infraction of the rules.

Wardens from the various federal penitentiaries were polled, and they were permitted to send their most incorrigible inmates into secure confinement on the Rock. The prison population at Alcatraz was thus made up of inmates who had histories of unmanageable behavior or escape attempts, and high-profile inmates who had been receiving special privileges because of their public status and notoriety. In July of 1934, there were

Alcatraz was designed to lockdown America's most notorious inmates. The first groups of prisoners were sent via special train cars designed specifically for the transportation of high-risk escape-prone inmates. As the trains traveled across the nation, the public gathered to get a glimpse of the inmates being transferred to America's Devil Island. Upon their arrival in San Francisco, no security risks were taken and the train cars were loaded onto barges and transported directly to the island.

U. S. PENITENTIARY
ALCATRAZ, CALIFORNIA

A group photograph of the Alcatraz Federal Penitentiary personnel, taken on June 4, 1936. Warden James Johnston is seen sitting in the middle. To his left is Deputy Warden C.J. Shuttleworth, and to his right is future Deputy Warden E.J. Miller. Various other prominent officers are pictured who have historical ties to key events. Most notably Royal Cline, second officer on right in back row. Cline was murdered during the May 23, 1938 escape attempt by Rufus Franklin. Captain Henry Weinhold, (seated four down from Johnston on his immediate right) was critically injured when he was shot in cold blood by Joseph Cretzer during the May 1946, Battle of Alcatraz.

only thirty-two military prisoners who had been left to serve out their sentences on Alcatraz. By August of the same year, Alcatraz had begun to receive inmates from McNeil Island in Washington State (eleven inmates), Atlanta Federal Penitentiary (fifty-three inmates), and Leavenworth in Kansas (one hundred and two inmates). Among the first to be sent to Alcatraz were Al Capone, Doc Barker (the last surviving son from the famous Ma Barker Gang), George "Machine Gun" Kelly, Robert "Birdman of Alcatraz" Stroud, Floyd Hamilton (a gang member and driver for Bonnie and Clyde), and Alvin "Old Creepy" Karpis. Inmates arriving at Alcatraz were driven in a small transfer van to the top of the hill. They were processed in the basement area, and were then provided with all of their basic amenities and allowed a brief shower.

Roy Gardner, wrote about his arrival at Alcatraz and offered personal reflections on the iron rule concept:

When we were all checked in we were marched into the mess hall and Warden Johnston got up and told us plainly what we were up against. "The rules have been laid down by the government in Washington," he said, "and there will be no deviation. I did not make the rules, but as long as I'm here I will enforce them." He sat down — and we all knew he meant every word, but we didn't know, or dream what the words really meant.

A bare idea of what they came to mean to us may be gleaned from a few factors which add to the fuel of "Hellcatraz":

1. Lost hope. The backbone of the hardest con melts to jelly under the lash of discipline without hope.
2. The rule of silence/ No talking in the cellhouse or in the mess hall; mute men alone with their thoughts.
3. Complete isolation from the outside word. No newspapers, radio or any other means of knowing what's going on outside.
4. The brand of hatred- a hatred peculiar to one small rock alone- that brews in the minds and hearts of men thus shut up.
5. Over and above all, discipline. Rigid, severe, unrelenting. Rules on Alcatraz, like the bars, are steel. Both are inflexible; nether bends.

When Al Capone arrived on the island, he quickly attempted to flaunt the power he had enjoyed at the federal penitentiary in Atlanta. Capone had taken advantage of many of the leniencies allowed in the other prison. In fact, he had constantly solicited guards to work for him, belittling their low wages and attempting to get their help in running his rackets from inside the prison. Capone, however, was unlike most of the other new inmates who had come to Alcatraz with long criminal records, as veterans of the penal system. Capone had only spent a short time in prison, and his stay had generally been much different from that of the other convicts. Capone had enjoyed the ability to control his environment by getting Wardens to arrange unlimited visits from family and friends, and he was even believed to have had booze smuggled into his cell, along with special uncensored reading materials.

Warden Johnston had a custom of meeting the new inmates when they first arrived at Alcatraz, and he usually participated in their brief orientation. Johnston wrote in a personal memoir that he had little trouble recognizing Capone as he stood in the lineup. Capone was grinning, and making quiet smug comments from the side of his mouth to other inmates. When his turn came to approach Warden Johnston, it appeared that he wanted to show off to the others by asking questions on their behalf, affecting a leadership role. Johnston quickly gave him his AZ prison number, and made him get back in line with the other convicts. During Capone's time at Alcatraz he made several attempts to persuade Johnston into allowing him special privileges, but all were denied. Johnston maintained that Capone would not be given any special rights, and would have to follow the rules like any other inmate.

Capone eventually conceded defeat, and one day he would comment to Johnston, *"It looks like Alcatraz has got me licked."* Capone spent four and a half years on Alcatraz, and during this time he held a variety of jobs. Capone's term at Alcatraz was not easy time, and he had to cope with his share of trouble as well. For example, he once got into a fight with another inmate in the recreation yard, and was placed in isolation for eight days. Then while Capone was working in the prison basement, an inmate who was standing in line waiting for a haircut exchanged words with him, and stabbed him with a pair of shears. Capone was admitted to the prison hospital with a minor wound, and was released a few days later. He eventually became symptomatic from syphilis, a disease he had evidently been carrying for years. In 1939 he was transferred to Terminal Island Prison in Southern California to serve out the remainder of his sentence.

George "Machine Gun" Kelly was also in the first group of inmates to arrive at Alcatraz in August of 1934. Kelly's time on the Rock would be far less eventful than Capone's, and he was said to be a model prisoner. Kelly worked in the Industries, lived on the second tier of B-Block, and quietly transferred back to Leavenworth in 1951 after spending seventeen years on the Rock. Alcatraz would continue to be a magnet for many famous gangsters throughout its tenure as a federal penitentiary. Most followed the stringent routines with little or no defiance, and their public identity on the outside was completely erased once they arrived on the Rock.

George "Machine Gun Kelly" being escorted under heavy guard to prison. Kelly would arrive with one of the first groups transferred by train to Alcatraz in 1934.

A group of correctional officers standing inside the main entrance to the prison cellhouse.

Letters from Alcatraz

A contemporary view of "Broadway" as seen while standing inside the Alcatraz Dining Hall doorway.

Inmates filing into the Dining Hall, termed the "Gas Chamber" by prisoners, circa 1950. Special fixed teargas canisters were installed throughout the dining area, and could be activated remotely in the event of any mass disturbance.

Alcatraz Island: The History

Letters from Alcatraz

A solitary officer supervises prisoners while locked in their cells on Broadway, circa 1940. Officers were not allowed to carry firearms inside the perimeters of the cellhouse. Their only leverage was an officer located inside the gun galleries situated at each end of the cellblock. The gallery officers carried high-powered rifles and were a constant presence while watching over inmates.

B-Block as seen from the second tier looking toward the East Gun Gallery.

THE INMATES' DAY BEGAN when they were woken at 6:30 a.m., and they were given twenty-five minutes to tidy their cells and stand to be counted. At 6:55 a.m. individual tiers of cells would be opened one by one, and the inmates would march in single file into the Mess Hall. They would be given only twenty minutes to eat, and then would be marched out to line up for their work assignments. The methodical cycle of the prison routine was unforgiving and utterly relentless. It never varied through the years, and was as precise and reliable as clock-

A contemporary photo looking down the "Broadway" corridor towards "Times Square."

An officer seen patrolling the C-Block corridor, an area known to inmates as "Park Avenue" in March of 1956.

Letters from Alcatraz

Standard Alcatraz cell.

second tier of B-Block, and were placed in quarantine status for the first three months of their imprisonment on the Rock.

There was a ratio of one guard to every three prisoners on Alcatraz, as compared with other prisons, to which the ratio exceeded one guard to every twelve inmates. With the gun galleries at each end of the cellblocks and the frequent inmate counts (twelve official counts per day), the guards were able to keep extremely close track of each and every inmate. Because of the small total number of prisoners at Alcatraz, all of the guards usually knew each inmate by name.

In the early years at Alcatraz, Warden Johnston maintained a grim silence policy that many inmates considered to be their most unbearable punishment. Silence was mandatory in the cellblocks and in general formation. Inmates were permitted to talked quietly only during meals when seated, and at their work post when it didn't interfere with their assigned tasks. There were reports that several inmates were being driven insane by the severe rule of silence on Alcatraz. One inmate, a former gangster and bank robber named Rufe Persful, went so far as to take a hatchet and chop off the fingers of one of his hands while working in one of the shops. This event was later inaccurately depicted in the

work. Monotony was the Alcatraz theme and dominated the life of inmates.

The main corridor of the cellhouse was christened "Broadway" by the inmates, and the cells along this passageway were considered the least desirable in the prison. The cells on the bottom tier were inherently colder because they stood against the long slick run of cement, and they were also the least private, as inmates, guards, and other prison personnel frequented this corridor. Newer inmates were generally assigned to the

movie *Escape from Alcatraz* starring Clint Eastwood, which chronicled the 1962 escape attempt by Frank Lee Morris and the Anglin Brothers. The silence policy was later relaxed, but this was one of only a few policy changes that occurred over the prison's history.

The sinister mythology surrounding life on Alcatraz was created primarily out of a lack of reliable information, and because of the negative publicity, Alcatraz became known to the public as "Devil's Island." Warden Johnston had done a good job of keeping the media at a distance and this resulted in the publication of several misleading stories. The fact that inmates were rarely directly paroled from Alcatraz only added to the mystique. The media had a difficult time finding men who had lived on the inside, because when they were released from Alcatraz, they were sent on to other prisons to finish out their sentences. When the press would talk with former inmates, the ex-

Hollywood was one of the primary architects in helping shape the myths and lore surrounding Alcatraz. The media was strictly isolated from the inter-workings of the prison. Hollywood film sets designed during the same era relied mainly on second hand descriptions and early press release photos that offered only limited views of the interior sections. Alcatraz Island was released by Warner Brothers in 1937 and was the first motion picture to spotlight the island on screen, a tradition that would continue into the next century. Actor John Litel is seen here during the filming of Alcatraz Island on a Hollywood sound stage.

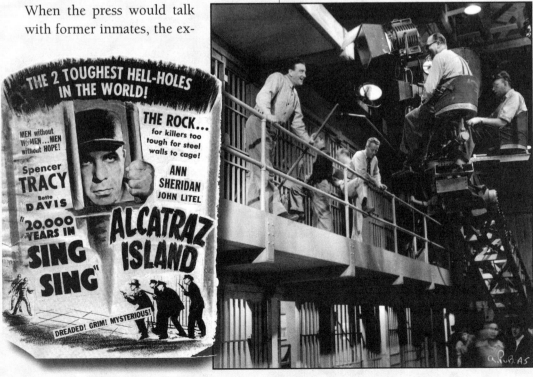

prisoners usually depicted horrific scenes about the brutalities they had experienced while incarcerated there. Most of these portrayals were flawed, but the stories of horrid beatings, rigid disciplinary measures, and extreme isolation nevertheless fueled the public's interest.

Following the famed and controversial Henri Young trial in 1941, although not necessarily to coincide, the Treatment Unit (D-Block) underwent a complete renovation. This unit was comprised of forty-two cells that provided varying degrees of security and isolation. The most serious offenders of prison rules could be confined to the "Strip Cell." This cell was by all accounts the most severe punishment that any prisoner could endure, as it ensured complete sensory deprivation.

The strip cell was a dark steel-encased cell with no toilet or sink. There was only a hole in the floor for the inhabitant to relieve himself, and even the ability to flush the contents was controlled by a guard. Inmates were placed in the cell without clothing, and were put on severely restricted diets. The cell had a standard set of bars with an expanded opening through which to pass food, and a solid steel outer door that remained closed, leaving the inmate in pitch-black darkness. Inmates were usually subjected to this degree of punishment for periods of only one to two days. The cell was cold, and the sleeping mattress was only al-

June 1, 19/1
ALCATRAZ
Cell Block "D" (completed)

Alcatraz Isolation Unit (D-Block). This section of the prison consisted of forty-two isolations cells, with six, having closed front heavy gauge steel doors to punish hardcore offenders. Inmates held in this section of the prison were confined to their cells 24-hours a day, with a limited once per week visit to the recreation yard and shower (located at the end of the cellblock).

lowed during the night, and was taken away during the daylight hours. This was considered the most invasive type of punishment for severe violations and misconduct, and it was genuinely feared by the general population inmates.

"The Hole" was the nickname given to a similar cell-type that made up the remaining five dual-door cells on the bottom tier. These cells contained a toilet as well as a low-wattage light bulb. Inmates could spend up to nineteen days in this level of isolation, which was also considered to be a severe form of punishment

Serious violators of the prison rules were locked in a pitch-black strip cell with no clothing or blankets during the day, where they could only sit or lie on cold steel flooring. There was a hole in the floor for the inmate to relieve himself, and the contents could only be flushed remotely by a guard. The maximum duration permitted for confinement in full darkness was nineteen days. At night, inmates were provided with a mattress and a set of blankets. These were removed immediately at daybreak.

Ceramic isolation cell located in the prison hospital ward.

An interior view of one of the six solitary confinement cells with the heavy- gauge steel door in the closed and locked position. The door design allowed for complete sensory deprivation, with no light and only muffled audible sounds seeping in from outside. The cell was box-steel and inmates enduring severe punishment were provided only a blanket during night time hours.

Alcatraz Island: The History

Letters from Alcatraz

by general population inmates. The mattresses were taken away during the day, and the inmates were left in a state of constant boredom and severe isolation. Officers would sometimes open the small window in the solid steel outer door, to allow in a little light for inmates who were serving their time in solitary peacefully.

The remaining thirty-six segregation cells were similar in form to the cells of the general prison population although significantly larger. Inmates being held in basic segregation were allowed only one visit to the recreation yard per week, and two showers. The prisoners spent the remaining time in their cells. Even meals were served in the cells, and the inmates' only means of psychological escape was through reading. The city views from the upper tiers were also considered by prisoners to be a form of torture, because the sounds and sights of freedom were so near, yet so far.

During the twenty-nine years of the prison's operation, there were over fourteen attempted escapes from Alcatraz, in which thirty-four different men risked their lives to flee from the Rock. Almost all of the escapees were either killed or recaptured, but of all the attempts, two were especially significant to the island's history. In 1946 an inmate named Bernard Coy managed to fashion a makeshift bar-spreader, and climbed up to break into one of the gun galleries. Coy overpowered an unsuspecting guard, took his weapon, and dropped additional firearms down to several waiting accomplices. Led by Coy and fellow inmate Joseph Cretzer, the inmates had devised a plan to blast out of the prison using the stolen firearms, but they were unable to locate the key that would give them access to the prison recreation yard. The desperate convicts eventually took several guards hostage, and proceeded to wage a violent war against Alcatraz.

Thousands of spectators watched from the San Francisco shores while U.S. Marines rushed the island, barraging the cellhouse with mortars and grenades. Inmates inside the cellhouse took refuge behind water-soaked mattresses, and lay helplessly trapped while bullets whizzed around them. The convicts had realized that all hope of escaping was gone, and so Alcatraz inmates Bernard Coy, Joe Cretzer, and Marvin Hubbard, Sam Shockley, Miran Thompson, and Clarence Carnes decided to wage a violent battle.

Warden Johnston was unable to get a full assessment of the number of inmates involved, and he believed that there was a potential threat to the city of San Francisco. With the entire prison under siege, Johnston called for aid from the Navy, the Coast Guard, and the Marines. Meanwhile Cretzer became desperate, realizing that the hostages, all of whom were prison correctional officers, would probably credit him with plotting and executing his second escape attempt. Coldly and methodically, he pointed his pistol into the crowded cell where the officers were being held, and opened fire.

The fighting lasted two full days, and finally with no place left to hide from the ceaseless gunfire, Cretzer, Coy, and Hubbard retreated to a utility corridor for shelter. The rest of the accomplices returned to their cells in the hope that they would not be identified as direct participants in the break attempt. In the final shootout, Cretzer, Coy, and Hubbard were killed in the corridor by bullets and shrapnel. One officer named William

Miller died from his injuries, and a second officer, Harold Stites, was shot and killed during an attempt to regain control of the cellhouse. Inmates Thompson and Shockley were later executed together in the gas chamber at San Quentin for their role in the murder of Officer Miller, and Clarence Carnes received an additional ninety-nine-year sentence.

Members of the press view the Battle of Alcatraz from a barge in May of 1946.

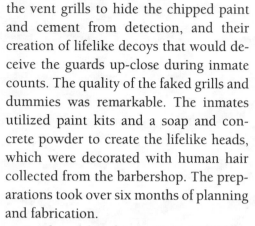

THE MOST FAMOUS ATTEMPT at escaping from Alcatraz was carried out by Frank Lee Morris and brothers Clarence and John Anglin. Their escape would trigger one of the most intensive and lengthiest manhunts in United States history. In 1962, a fellow inmate named Allen West helped the trio to devise a clever plan that involved constructing a raft and inflatable life vests to navigate the Bay waters, along with human decoys to fool the guards during the routine counts. Over the course of a several months, the inmates used special tools stolen from various prison work sites to chip away at the vent covers in their cells, meanwhile carrying on with the creative fabrication of the dummies and decoys.

The vents were located at the rear of each cell, and were covered with ten by six inch thatch-patterned metal grills. The true ingenuity of the plan lay in the prisoners' methodical camouflaging of the vent grills to hide the chipped paint and cement from detection, and their creation of lifelike decoys that would deceive the guards up-close during inmate counts. The quality of the faked grills and dummies was remarkable. The inmates utilized paint kits and a soap and concrete powder to create the lifelike heads, which were decorated with human hair collected from the barbershop. The preparations took over six months of planning and fabrication.

On the night of June 11th, 1962, immediately following the 9:30 P.M. count, Morris and the Anglins scaled the utility shafts to reach the roof. Allen West, whom the FBI would later suspect of masterminding the whole plot, had spent the majority of his time over the past six months in building the decoys, and hadn't been able to make as much progress as the others in widening the concrete vent opening in his cell. His accomplices therefore had no choice but to leave him behind. Once they reached the roof, they climbed through a ventilator duct where they had spread apart the thick metal bars, and made their way to the edge of the roof.

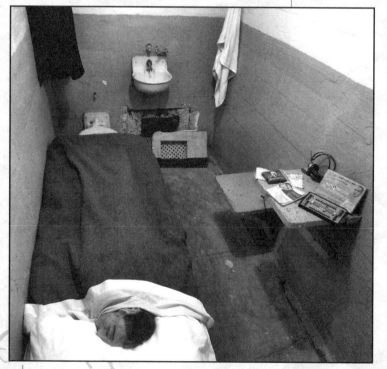

Four inmates spent several months acquiring materials to make a raft, life jackets and dummy heads which were left in their beds and used as decoys to trick prison guards. After tunneling through concrete and ceiling vents, three of the inmates vanished and were never seen or heard from again. Their whereabouts remain unknown.

U. S. PENITENTIARY
ALCATRAZ, CALIFORNIA

WANTED BY THE FBI

ESCAPED FEDERAL PRISONERS— BANK ROBBERS

After descending utility pipes attached to the cement cellhouse wall, all three scaled a fifteen-foot fence, and hurried down to the island shore where they inflated their raft and life vests. The inmates ventured out into the freezing Bay waters, and were never seen or heard from again. Back at the cellhouse during the morning count, a guard probed his club into one of the inmates' cells, and the dummy head rolled off the bed and onto the floor.

Decades later, it is still unknown whether the inmates ever succeeded in making their escape. The story was dramatized in several books, and in the famous motion picture *Escape from Alcatraz*, starring Academy Award® winning actor Clint Eastwood. The FBI actively pursued the case for several years, but never came across any effectual leads. They did, however, make a final determination that the attempt had been unsuccessful.

Alcatraz Island: The History

Letters from Alcatraz

Perhaps one of the greatest ironies of Alcatraz was that the frigid and treacherous waters of the San Francisco Bay, which had proved to be the ultimate deterrent to escape for nearly three decades, would eventually contribute to the downfall of America's super-prison. Following the escape of Morris and the Anglins, the prison fell under intense scrutiny due to its deteriorating structural condition and the diminishing security measures that had resulted from governmental budget

On March 21, 1963, U.S.P. Alcatraz closed after twenty-nine years of operation. It had housed some of America's most legendary crime figures, and in the opinions of many government officials had accomplished its mission. Robert Stroud, the famed "Birdman of Alcatraz," would serve seventeen years on Alcatraz, all in an isolation status. George "Machine Gun" Kelly would spend eighteen years on Alcatraz and was considered a model inmate by prison guards. Al Capone would

cuts. However, this development should not be credited entirely to the escape, since many of these decisions were already in process before the attempt was made. The corrosive effects of the saltwater, combined with the exorbitant cost of running the prison ($10.10 per prisoner per day, as compared with $3.00 at U.S.P. Atlanta, not including the estimated five million that would be required for restoration), provided U.S. Attorney General Robert Kennedy with grounds for closing the prison.

spend over four years on Alcatraz, all under strict confinement conditions with no special privileges. Alvin "Creepy" Karpis would hold the record for time served on Alcatraz. He would serve nearly twenty-six years on the Rock. His summation of over a quarter century spent on Alcatraz Island was simply stated:

"A quarter of a century in Alcatraz has been an empty, futile experience."

—Alvin Karpis

An Introduction to this Collection

"There is so much suffering here...so much agony."

—ROY GARDNER

FOR THE majority of inmates serving time on Alcatraz, the ability to escape was not a cleaver scheme or even a plot to acquire tools and break-free from the cellhouse. For most, their escape was a movie in the upstairs theatre, a book, a magazine, or in the later period, a radio show that allowed them for one brief moment... to forget. Mail from a loved one was always a welcome escape of sorts.

The letters in this collection represent a wide-spectrum of people, their ideas, their sufferings, their frustrations about prison conditions, disappointments, their hopes, and in some cases their victories. Not all are from inmates. This collection doesn't draw from any specific theme or thread. They were not all written while at Alcatraz. Some letters seem more trivial than others, and some contain sharp words that cut at the spaces on the paper they were written. But all of the inmate letters share one common ingredient. They either were written inside a cold cell on Alcatraz, on their way to Alcatraz, or maybe just released from Alcatraz to an-other prison, or finally free from all prisons. The mark of Alcatraz is what binds these men in history. Their right of passage to freedom or a life condemned was like no other. Their letters range from seemingly unimportant requests to the administration, a request for a new job assignment, or a letter reflecting an inmate's deep feelings of sorrow when contemplating the reality of their situation. Sometimes they are profound; sometimes a sense of humor evident.

Nothing was ever more important to an inmate on Alcatraz than his mail. In many cases the mood of the inmates changed with the frequency of letters received during mail call. As former Correctional Officer Cliff Fish would later comment, "Every inmate knew who was receiving mail and who had been forgotten." For those who were lucky enough to receive mail it was a brief journey to forget their plight. For those forgotten, it was sometimes agony with no outside contact. The mail system on Alcatraz and other federal prisons served as a lifeline to the outside world. For many, especially during the early federal years, time

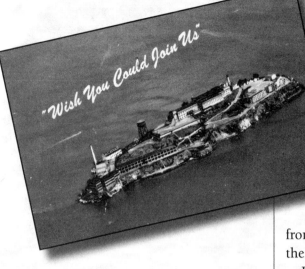

"Wish You Could Join Us"

ful issues for inmates. Some letters told of a wife's decision to divorce and remarry, others communicated the dreaded death of a parent or sibling. Most lifted spirits. There was no information considered trivial to an inmate isolated on Alcatraz. The inmates were eager to read anything anyone had to say and to hear any news from the outside world. Many of the men were far away from home and their families didn't have the financial means to visit.

Inmate correspondence was intensely governed, and rules didn't allow for inmates to discuss issues and conditions shielded by the prison curtain. If the letter required censoring, the original would be transcribed and surgically edited of any suspect material before being mailed. The originals would be sealed in their inmate files and lost to passing time. Regardless, their words were carefully crafted to minimize censoring. Each letter was written on specially issued Federal Bureau of Prisons stationary, and envelopes bearing the infamous Alcatraz postmark.

As dictated under regulation, many of these letters never escaped from Alcatraz. Some of the content would be deemed in violation of regulations, censored and then typewritten before being mailed to the addressee. Several were sealed in their inmate files and forgotten for several decades. These letters remind us of who these men were; their voices in prose, and a reminder of personal struggles of life inside the walls of Alcatraz and other federal prisons to which they resided.

slowed without ready access to the events and tribulations of home.

An excellent example of this was illustrated by Warden Johnston with a letter he reprinted in his personal 1949 memoir. The letter dated February 16, 1946, read in part:

Dear Mother and All:
Your last letter was received about Christmas time and since that time I've expected a letter each day as our mail man makes his rounds but so far no letter from home. There is a song around here called, "No letter today" — I expect it may be a good idea for me to begin to learn the words of this song because the mail man always says — no letter today! At any rate I expect you folks will get around to writing soon now. I hope!

Inmates were known at times to share their mail with others who were considered close friends. These letters sometimes communicated very personal and pain-

Alcatraz Officer
Larry Quilligan

UNITED STATES PENITENTIARY
ALCATRAZ, CALIFORNIA
December 21, 1948
Mr. Lawrence L. Quilligan
Canton, Ohio

Dear Sir:

You are offered Probational Appointment for the position of Correctional Officer, CPC-7, $3024.96 per annum, and are requested to report for duty not later than 8:00 a.m., January 10, 1949.

Upon reporting for duty you will be given a medical examination by a Federal Medical Officer to conform to the physical requirements for the position as outlined in the Correctional Officer Examination Announcement. YOU MUST PASS THIS EXAMINATION BEFORE YOU CAN BE ENTERED ON DUTY, so you should feel reasonably sure of being able to pass it before accepting this appointment.

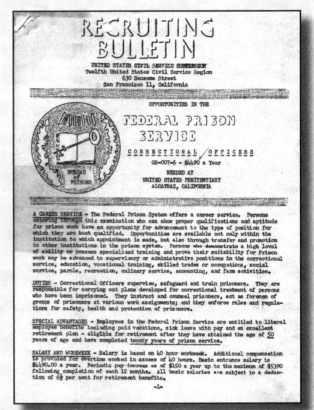

RECRUITING BULLETIN

UNITED STATES CIVIL SERVICE COMMISSION
Twelfth United States Civil Service Region
630 Sansome Street
San Francisco 11, California

OPPORTUNITIES IN THE

FEDERAL PRISON SERVICE

CORRECTIONAL / OFFICERS

CS-007-6 - $4490 a Year

NEEDED AT
UNITED STATES PENITENTIARY
ALCATRAZ, CALIFORNIA

A CAREER SERVICE - The Federal Prison System offers a career service. Persons entering through this examination who can show proper qualifications and aptitude for prison work have an opportunity for advancement to the type of position for which they are best qualified. Opportunities are available not only within the institution to which appointment is made, but also through transfer and promotion to other institutions in the prison system. Persons who demonstrate a high level of ability or possess specialized training and prove their suitability for Prison work may be advanced to supervisory or administrative positions in the correctional service, education, vocational training, skilled trades or occupations, social service, parole, recreation, culinary service, accounting, and farm activities.

DUTIES - Correctional Officers supervise, safeguard and train prisoners. They are responsible for carrying out plans developed for correctional treatment of persons who have been imprisoned. They instruct and counsel prisoners, act as foremen of groups of prisoners at various work assignments; and they enforce rules and regulations for safety, health and protection of prisoners.

SPECIAL ADVANTAGES - Employees in the Federal Prison Service are entitled to liberal employee benefits including paid vacations, sick leave with pay and an excellent retirement plan - eligible for retirement after they have attained the age of 50 years of age and have completed twenty years of prison service.

SALARY AND WORKWEEK - Salary is based on 40 hour workweek. Additional compensation is provided for overtime worked in excess of 40 hours. Basic entrance salary is $4490.00 a year. Periodic pay-increase as of $150 a year up to the maximum of $5390 following completion of each 12 months. All basic salaries are subject to a deduction of 6½ per cent for retirement benefits.

-1-

The twelve-month period of probation for this position is considered part of the examination. If your services are not satisfactory during this probationary period, you may be separated at any time during the period by a letter notifying you accordingly.

Your appointment will be subject to a check of records and to a CHARACTER INVESTIGATION now being conducted by the Federal Government, and your retention in the Service will depend upon such investigation's proving satisfactory to the Government.

Please bring with you a photostatic copy of your honorable discharge to establish date of birth.

No family quarters are at present available on Alcatraz, but a limited number of single rooms in bachelor quarters are available, together with some dormitory style space for temporary usage.

If entered on duty on January 10th your first pay period would run January 10th to January 22d, 1949, and would actually be paid on February 4, 1949. Thereafter, you would be paid ever other Friday. Upon reporting for duty, board the Alcatraz launch at Dock 4, Fort Mason (foot of Van Ness Avenue, San Francisco). Present this letter to the duty officer on the launch for identification. For boat schedule, telephone Ordway 3-1437 upon you r arrival in San Francisco.

You may accept or reject this offer of appointment by filling in the "Availability Statement" attached and mailing it to this office. It is requested that you reply immediately. Failure to reply to this offer of appointment will result in the removal of your name from the register of eligibles until such time as you request restoration and furnish the information asked for in the "Statement of Availability."

For your further information, we attaching a mimeographed statement designed to provide the answers to the questions most often asked regarding the position, conditions on Alcatraz, etc.

Sincerely,

E.B. Swope
WARDEN

Ervie Walters

January 24, 1936

The U.S.A. Attorney General
The Honorable Homer S. Cummings

Dear Sir:

I am one of the original "32" soldier prisoners that was turned over to this Federal Institution on June the 19th, 1934, and at that time I couldn't see why we was being left here for most of us was first time losers, and we understood that this place was to harbor nothing but the toughest kind of convict, which is "true," that is why I'm writing this letter, asking you to have me transferred, because I don't belong here, and I know that those of the "32" that are here with me now, are all of the same frame of mind, but I am speaking for myself, for they have the same writing privileges that I have.

My record is "very good," as I haven't caused any trouble in the 5 years that I have been confined, and I'm doing my best to keep it that way. Sir, if you think I deserve a transfer and give it to me, I will certainly appreciate it, for I sure want to get away from this place. I thank you.

Respectfully Yours,

Ervie R. Walters
#28

Richard Franseen

Convicted counterfeiter Richard Franseen, AZ-387, (registered under the name of Franzeen) provided a seemingly optimistic insight to his new residence at Alcatraz. Excerpts from this letter were originally printed anonymously in Warden Johnston's Alcatraz memoir. Franseen would later become close friends with inmate Elliott Michener, who provided updates to Warden Swope on their successful transition to freedom once released from prison.

Alcatraz, March 19, 1937

Mrs. Roy Conner
Box 123
Cromwell, Minnesota

Dear Tillie:
  When you write to me, you will be permitted to write on three sheets of paper; but on only one side. You may, I believe, write as often as you wish. When you mention any person, use the full name, not the nickname or initials. My only correspondence, are to be blood relations, and so I would like to get Oscar Franseen's address. Without his address I can't get his name on the mailing list. As yet, I have haven't been assigned to any work. I have no preference, except that I would like to be placed on one of the jobs on which "industrial good time" is given. This amounts to two days a month, and would cut more than a year from the time I must serve.
  This is my fourth day in the institution, and though it is much too soon to make a prediction, I think that I am going to like this place. The living conditions are better here than in any other institution in which I've been. The cell house is clean, so clean that the fl oors re fl ect light. They are of concrete; literally they are being cleaned continuously that they

are polished until they show reflection. The same is true of railings and of everything else.

The food is first-class. Better far than that of Leavenworth. We get variety, usually three or four dishes. For breakfast we get fruit with hotcakes, hot buns, or cereal. For dinner and supper we get meats, greens, salads, cauliflower, creamed cod, as well as ice cream, pie, cake, and puddings. And I've only been here four days.

The publicity that this institution has received has been very unfair. The picture portrayed by the papers and by rumor is of an institution run by beetle-browed guards, whose only delight is to drive the prisoners, a broken down group who have given up all hope of ever leaving this prison except in straight jackets or in coffins, with clubs, while backed up by sub-machine guns and tear gas. I'm ashamed that I partially believed such reports.

I have never before seen a group of prisoners that is as neat as this. They are clean shaven. When they come into the dining room, every head has been combed and I believe that every face has been washed. We wear coveralls with six buttons down the front, and as yet I haven't seen a single button gone or unbuttoned. I've seen several of these men in other prisons, and even those that were the crumbiest now looks like a new clothespin. It is true that most of the faces are expressionless, but I've only seen them in the dining room, and since a "silent-system" is in effect the men are inclined to be serious.

Another thing of which I approve highly is that the guards and the prisoners are not allowed to fraternize together. This does away with having to meet one another socially even though the two groups can have nothing in common, and does away with a great deal of friction with which most other prisons must contend.

The guards, too, have affected me favorably. I expected to meet a group of martinets that cracked the whip instead of using their brains. So far they have been extremely polite and have used patience and instructions instead of the orders and growls one would expect. They are as neat as a group chosen to represent a State highway patrol, and if there are any of the chauvinists I expected, they must be hidden in the gun towers.

My only disappointments so far, are that I will not be permitted to write to my friends, and that the library here is much inferior to that of Leavenworth. But to compensate, the correspondence courses are superior.

Your loving brother,

/s/ Richard C. Franseen
Reg. No. 387

Alphonse Capone

"I'm doing very nicely here, no hardships, respect my superiors and do my work, three meals a day, plenty exercise, music and all kinds of magazines…"

—AL CAPONE in a letter to his son, Alcatraz 1938

KNOWN AS America's "Ace Enemy," Al Capone sustained as one of the paramount crime magnates of the 20th Century, and as one of the original island cast members, he remains one of the most central and historic figures linked to the history of Alcatraz Federal Penitentiary.

Capone arrived at Alcatraz on August 22, 1934 at only 35 years of age with the first group of federal inmates. He had pled guilty to federal tax evasion in 1931, and was sentenced to serve an eleven year term in federal prison. He was transferred to Alcatraz from U.S.P Atlanta where he had leveraged numerous privileges from the administration and had been rumored to govern felonious activities while inside.

In an early unpublished handwritten manuscript written while still at Alcatraz, famed inmate Roy Gardner wrote about his fellow inmate:

Al Capone looms on the horizon of public interest as the most intriguing of all criminals, and to his intimates, he is quite as mysterious and baffling as he is to the public at large.

He radiates physical energy. He's six feet of bone and muscle, tips the scales at well over 200 pounds, but contains within itself more of the force of human generosity than has ever been found in any man of his type since Robin Hood. And even in the dusk of the years with it's gathering mantel of tradition, Robin Hood appeals less to the imagination and suggests much less of mystery and power than the contemporary figure of Al Capone.

In his appearance Capone somehow suggests all the contradictory tales which pass current as factual records of his activities. His face is swarthy like that of most Italians, but from it there emulates an energy that might have made him a public benefactor instead of public enemy. The only suggestion of criminality lurks in the two livid scars which disfigure the left side of his face. Of those scars he will not speak, and on inquiry of the subject stiffens him up like a cat when a dog appears.

That he is generous by nature is evidenced by his sympathetic brown eyes. With these he looks his interlocutor direct in the eyes with a wealth of human interest and understanding. He is interested in good in all men. This is proven by his many charities, and amplified by the fact that while he was in Atlanta (U.S.P.) he spent his money lavishly; and no one appeals to him in vain. He even helped a couple of prison guards who found themselves in financial difficulties (or thought they were). This of course brought him a legion of sycophantic followers who fawned and praised until it is doubtful if Capone possessed any means of taking a proper measure of himself.

At Alcatraz his money is useless for there is no way that in which he can spend it on anyone, not even on himself. The result is that the energy of the fawners and moochers goes into reverse and expresses itself in petty jealously and hatred. The big shots who formerly respected and courted him because of their fear of the power he wielded or from their desire to share that power now have him severely alone, but keep their distance because they fear his physical strength. Capone has proven himself to be a dangerous antagonist in hand to hand combat, because he is a vicious slugger and he always fights to win. There is none of the compromiser in his makeup, and for his enemy he has neither compassion nor respect. In 1936 a man by the name of Lucas stabbed Capone in the back with a pair of barber scissors. Capone had a banjo in his hands at the time, and what a weapon it proved to be. In less than ten seconds both Lucas and the banjo were total wrecks. From that on, Capone had no more trouble with Lucas because he made it his business to stay out of reach of the Chicago gangster.

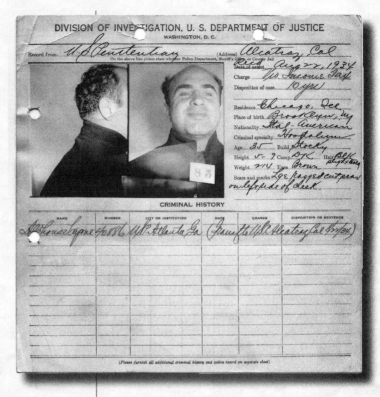

Although convicted of income-tax evasion, Capone is in fact serving time for murder. Scandal-mania and police records credit him with having had at least thirty men put "on the spot," and if that be true, it is no mean accomplishment from the standpoint of human adaptability. For as fiendish as the record seems to be, it is also true that men who commit murders for pay are not easy individuals to handle. They are everything that is repulsive to a normal man, weak sniveling cowards in human form, and the most difficult of all human rates to handle or deal with. Consider then the staggering amount of ability that be necessary to hold in line a dozen or more depraved killers who were living in the shadow of the gallows on account of carrying out the orders of their chief.

Capone denies any and all knowledge of the murders, or the reasons for the commission, but since those deaths all came at a time and under conditions that would serve the cause of his wide spread operations in liquor and gambling, and further because of he is such a commanding figure, it is difficult to regard his protestations of ignorance of the manner and reason for the deaths as justified. But to a man who knows criminals of a type who could be hired to commit murder; it is quite as difficult to conceive of any man possessing sufficient authority to hold mad dogs of that kind in check. Accordingly, whether the murders were committed upon the orders of Capone or not, he is revealed as a master of men. History has recorded the criminal accomplishments of such few men.

One of the funniest things I ever saw was when Capone assumed a condescending attitude toward Warden Johnston. At first, the warden registered amazement, and then developed into a "slow burn" like Edgar Kennedy in moving pictures. Ordinarily, the warden's voice is soft and pleasant, but when he tried to answer Capone his voice sounded like cackle from a parched throat... Capone's vanity and arrogance is the principle reason why he is the most hated man on Alcatraz, and his enemies spend much time and thought on planning a "no rap" way to kill him.

Alcatraz completely isolated Capone from public view. Despite some of the depictions made by Roy Gardner, he was generally considered a model inmate. Capone was said to quickly acclimate to the rules of the Rock, and for a short period even played the tenor banjo in a prison ensemble. His prison cell (# 181 - later renumbered to B-206) was located along the stretch of cells known as Michigan Avenue, and was considered a prime stretch of real estate on Alcatraz as it boasted clear northern views of the San Francisco Bay.

As mentioned in Gardner's writings, the most significant incident with Capone occurred in 1936 when he became the victim of a brutal stabbing attempt by fellow Alcatraz inmate James Lucas. Capone escaped with only minor wounds, but it would spark a series of petitions by his family to have Capone transferred from Alcatraz.

It was on Alcatraz that Capone started to exhibit unusual behaviors indicative of a serious neurological condition. Capone was soon diagnosed as suffering from paresis which had been derived from syphilis. He had deteriorated significantly during his confinement on Alcatraz and was finally transferred to Terminal Island in January of 1939, a federal institution in Long Beach, California to provide definitive medical care for Capone.

Capone was released from prison on November 16, 1939, after having served seven years, six months and fifteen days, and having paid all fines and back taxes. Upon his release he entered a Baltimore hospital for neurological treatment, and then went on to his Florida home, an estate on Palm Island, one of a string of islands in Biscayne Bay which he had purchased in 1928.

Following his release, he had become mentally incapable of returning to gangland politics. In 1946, his physician and a Baltimore psychiatrist, after examination, both concluded Al Capone then had the mentality of a 12-year-old child. Capone resided on Palm Island with his wife and immediate family, in a secluded atmosphere at his estate, until his death due to a stroke and pneumonia on January 25, 1947, at 48 years of age.

Several letters in this collection were

written during his time served at the federal prison in Atlanta just prior to his transfer to Alcatraz. Also included is correspondence by his brother Ralph to Warden Johnston, one of many petitions to have Capone transferred to a lower security institution.

December 24, 1932

Mrs. Theresa Capone
7244 Prairie Ave.
Chicago, Ill.

Dear Mother,

Well Ma how are you and the family. Am wishing all of you at home a Merry Christmas. Also Joe, Ralphie and Delores and Mafalda a real nice big Christmas kiss for me. Am in hope of seeing you real soon and will give you your's. Don't worry try and be merry and may God Bless all of you. Love and kisses to you the sweetest little mother in the world.

Alphonse Capone
Number 40886

Al Capone died only eight years following his release from Alcatraz on January 25, 1947. He would spend his final days in a secluded atmosphere at his Florida estate, surrounded by family members. His death ultimately resulted from a slow cerebral hemorrhage and pneumonia on January 25, 1947, both secondary to chronic syphilis. Capone was just 48-years old at the time of his death.

Letters from Alcatraz

Alcatraz

May 13, 1933

Mrs. Theresa Capone
7244 Prairie Ave.
Chicago, Ill.

Dear Mother,

It's just a simple little word. But it seems the world to me. For it means the best and noblest word that anyone can be. I know that God made that little word to stand for all that's true. I know he called mother because he named after you. All that I am, all that I hope to be, I owe all to you.

Dear Mother with the passing of years the realization of my debt of gratitude grows more profound and my love ever deeper and stronger. May God Bless you and love to all.

Your Dear Son,
Al

W. U. Postal Night Letter
Message Blank
WRITE PLAINLY

To Mrs Theresa Capone — Atlanta, Ga. May 13 1933
Address 7244 Prairie Ave
Chicago Ill.

Dear Mother
Its just a simple little word
But it seems the world to me
For it means the best and noblest word
that anyone can be.
I know that God made that little word to stand for all thats true,
I know he called mother because he named it after you,
All that I am, All that I hope to be, I owe all to you
Dear Mother with the passing of years the realization of my debt of gratitude grows more profound and my love ever deeper and stronger.
May God Bless you and love to all
Your Dear Son
Al

Name Alphonse Capone
Number 40886

To Mrs May Capone — Atlanta, Ga. May 13 1933
Address 7244 Prairie Ave
Chicago

Dear Wife
We have set apart a Mothers day from all the days in the year
And I want to bring my tribute to somebody precious and dear.
I want to wish all gladness and happiness to the sweetest woman - my wife.
For you are part of Mother's day,
And the greatest part of my life,
All that I am, All that I hope to be
I owe to you, dear wife,
With passing years the realization of my debt of gratitude grows more profound, and my love ever deeper and stronger for you,
And May God Bless you and love to all
Your dear husband
Al

Name Alphonse Capone
Number 40886

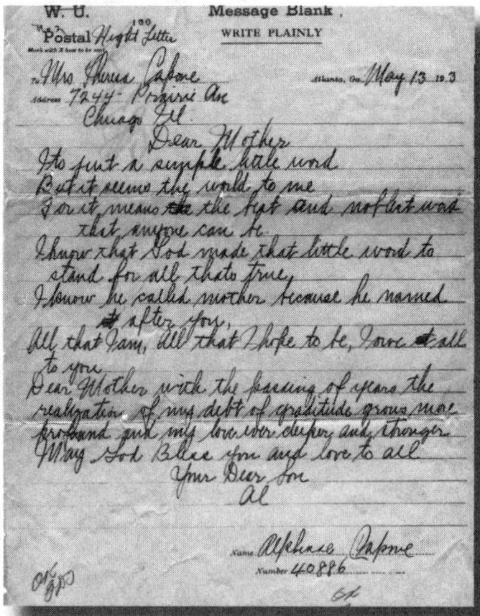

Mrs. May Capone
Atlanta, GA May 13, 1933
Address 7244 Prairie Ave.
Chicago

Dear Wife

We have set apart a Mothers day from all the days in the year. And I want to bring my tribute to somebody precious and dear. I want to wish all gladness and happiness to the sweetest woman - my wife.

For you are part of Mother's day. And the greatest part of my life. All that I am, all that I hope to be I owe to you dear wife. With passing years the realization of my debt of gratitude grows more profound, and my love ever deeper and stronger for you, and may God Bless you and love to all.

Your dear husband
Al

Alphonse Capone
Number 40886

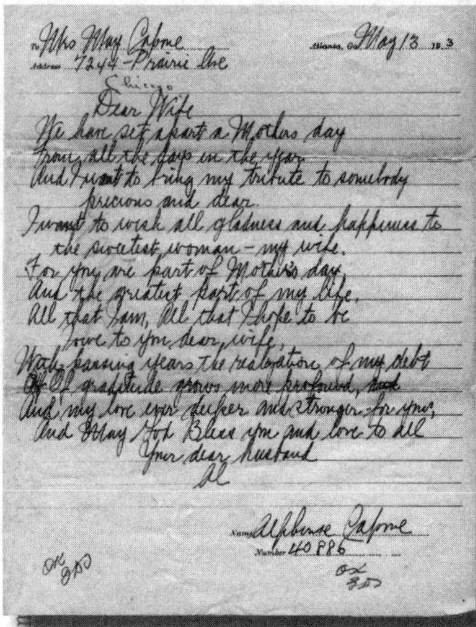

Atlanta, Georgia.

Dear Sir:

I respectfully appeal to you for a construction of "Bulletin No. 24" as it will apply to me, or rather to the visit's of my Mother, Wife, Son, and the rest of my family. Since my incarceration here it has been the custom of my family to visit me each month, and until this new rule has been applied, I have had the pleasure of having three visits a month, to run consecutively for three days, at one hour each day. Such visit's has been the privilege I have valued highest of all, for I know such visit's short as they may have been, always have been a world full of joy and happiness for my family and myself.

But if I correctly interpret the import of Bulletin 24, starting this month our visit's are to be shortened to one visit a month, and for one, and one day, regardless how far the visitor must travel to visit the prisoner relative, that kind Sir, is the point I am appealing to you for information upon. In order to visit me my family must travel approximately two thousand miles, that is the trip both way's, will that distance Sir, entitle them to at least see two days in a row, for one hour each day, Mr. Warden if you can see your way clear to allow me that privilege. I am sure that you will be doing something that will be more than appreciated, and I know it will sure make my family and myself happy and contented.

Now Sir, if you cant possibly allow me this privilege, than maybe you will possibly consider this other favor for me, will you allow me, that is if you cant do the above for us, allow me to have my same three visit's on the 24, 25, 26th of this month, to run consecutively, and at the same time as always, that is one hour each day, and than I will arrange with my family not to come down until after three months are over, now Sir, the reason I ask this favor, is the fact of the long trip, it is rather expensive, and if you will kindly give me the power of it being done this way, I am sure that we will more than appreciate it, sure hope you will consider this condition, for the sake of my family, as it sure mean's plenty to able to see them for a few hour's a month, thanking you in advance, and sure hope and pray that you will consider this favorably.

Mr. Warden, I am sorry to take so much of your time, but I would like to again have the pleasure, of again reminding you, if you can possibly give me a chance or some other detail, as I know have been here over two year's, and I am sure that my work has been satisfactory, and intend to keep it so as long as I am here, I request Sir, if you will consider me, for work either at the Baker Shop or at the Tennis court as a helper, as I am familiar with both details, and the main reason Sir, is the fact that they are both too good details where I can get plenty of exercise, and sunshine and fresh air, as I have a terrible case of nose trouble, and have been operated on twice, and Dr. Ossenfort, can also varify my condition, and as long as I can get some air and sun, and exercise, I will sure be grateful to you, and sure will do my utmost to prove the privilege will be respected.

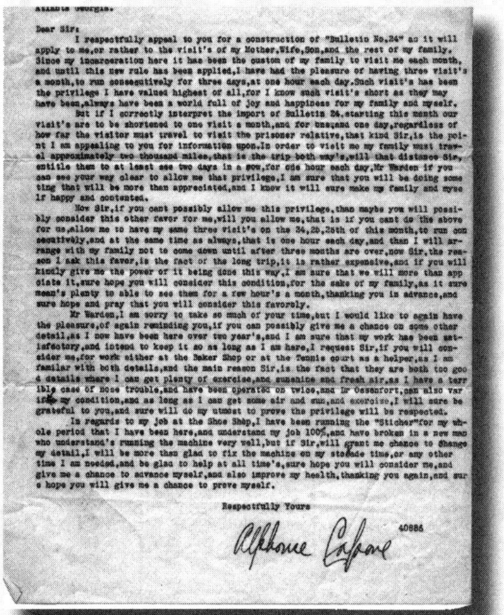

Atlanta Georgia.

Dear Sir:

[handwritten letter reproduction, largely illegible]

Respectfully Yours

Alphonse Capone 40886

In regards to my job at the Shoe Shop, I have been running the "Sticher" for my whole period that I have been here, and understand my job 100 , and have broken in a new man who understands running the machine very well, but if Sir, will grant me chance to change my detail, I will be more than glad to fix the machine on my stopade time, or any other time I am needed, and be glad to help at all time's, sure hope you will consider me, and give me a chance to advance myself, and also improve my health, thanking you again, and sure hope you will give me a chance to prove myself.

Respectfully yours,
/s/ Alphonse Capone 40886

7244 Prairie Avenue
Chicago, Illinois

December 3, 1934

Hon. Homer Cummings
Attorney-General United States
Washington, D.C.

Honorable Sir:

During all of the time my son, Alphonse Capone, was incarcerated in the Federal Prison at Atlanta, his wife and myself were permitted to visit him in compliance with the rules of that prison.

We desire to visit him at the prison at which he is now confined, namely, the Alcatraz, located in the Pacific Ocean. We understand the rules of that prison in respect to visitors are such to make it impossible to meet under the same conditions which existed at Atlanta, Ga.

We respectfully request you exert your influence to enable us to visit this prisoner as formerly, and to be accorded the same privileges as existed at that time. We trust that we are not, in this request, seeking a special and forbidden privilege, and relay upon your sense of fairness and humanity to enable us to secure this privilege.

I remain,
Respectfully yours,
Theresa Capone

March 6, 1935
Mr. Sanford Bates
Director
Bureau of Prisons
Washington, D.C.

Dear Mr. Bates:

Enclosed is a copy of a letter that Capone, Number 85-AZ, has written to his wife.

My reason for sending you a copy of that it refers to the death of his dear pal, Frank. The newspapers recently had a story about the death of one Frank Rio, Chicago. In the article referring to the funeral there was a statement that among the fl oral offering was a huge piece from Al Capone. If there was such a fl oral piece, it was arranged for by some other member of the Capone family.

If the money that Capone is going to have his wife pay to the widow merely represents charity, it is one thing, but if the deceased was one of a gang or mob, it may be looked at differently. In other words, I want to be careful that I do not allow Capone to transact any gang business from this institution but on the contrary want to do everything possible to disrupt such associations. Perhaps the division of Investigation will know some-thing about the dead man and connections.

Sincerely yours,
J.A. Johnston
Warden

Warden Johnston's suspicions were well planted relating to the subsequent letter. "Slippery" Frank Rio was alleged to be one of Capone's most loyal bodyguards, and also had served time with Capone in the cell adjacent to his at Philadelphia's Eastern State Penitentiary in 1929. Rio died on February 23, 1935, of a coronary occlusion.

Letters from Alcatraz

March 3, 1935

PENCIL DRAWING
of
AL CAPONE
85 ALCATRAZ
ISLAND

DREW BY AN
convict of ALCATRAZ
ISLAND

Capone, Mrs.

To my dear Wife:

Hello Ma, how are you, and how is our dear Son? Sure hope and pray that you both are well, after all this sad news about my dear Pal Frank. Gee, Ma, I sure felt terrible about it, to think him above all, and just at a time when he was about to get somewheres, with his dear wife and two kids. God, honey, it was awful, and I sure felt awful about it, but honey, I guess it was the will of God, and all we can do is take care of his family and pray for him. So please tell Ralph that from now on and until I die I want him to arrange with the office at home to see that Blanch gets fifty dollars $50.00 every week, and fifty more for each of his children, and the money for the kids to be put in a trust fund and not to be touched until the kids are twenty one years of age. And honey, I want you at times to keep in touch with her, and do all you can, also ask Ralph how sure he is that it was heart trouble as Honey, you know Frank was at all times real healthy and strong and really I can't understand it and for Ralph to find out and let me know. Honey, you also did right by leaving home, and doing what you did with Blanch and also about the flowers, now then honey, all I can say is I will always say a prayer for him, as he sure was a real pal to me. Also, tell Ralph to do all he can, and what he thinks is best in regards to things in general at home. Also thank him for his lovely letters, also Val's and glad they are well, and happy and hope they will be that way forever. Also, tell him I still have not heard from Ahearn, and to do all he can, and to find out about that time I did at the County Jail, if I am entitled to it as Mr. Ahearn says I was, if so them it will be time for me to go to a parole, in the meantime I won't do a thing until I hear from Ralph or you about that time I did in the County Jail, also glad that you all still feel confident that my friends still feel the same, also glad that Papie and Dennie and the Old Man feel the way they do, did you or Ralph talk to Max Baer about him seeing his friend out here. I hope you did as he is sure the right man, and can do it without any trouble at all.

Now dearest, let us forget business and unpleasant happenings and let me tell you dear, that I love, and adore you more now than ever, and my love is increasing more and more each day and as I said before, when your dear dad gets lucky and comes home again into your wonderful arms it will be a new daddy, and yours alone, so please believe me dear, as I sure will prove it to you later.

I got all of you wonderful letters up until the 25th, and honey they sure were wonderful and some of them were pips, and I sure got a wonderful kick out of them, gee, honey, how I wish I could do all I would like to and then I know honey we would all be happy. Of yet, I have not heard about Mimi and Albert coming here. When they do let them get in touch with the Warden and do what you did, about Mother, I don't want to see her until later, got two letters from Sonny glad he liked my letter, and glad he done so good at school. Also Bibo's few lines, give him my love and tell him to keep up the good work and write me every week. Also glad the weather there is getting better, and that you get plenty of sun, and honey get out and play golf every day, also glad you are feeling better, and hope you will get well soon, about you coming here for Easter, it is OK, and will be glad to see you honey get this magazine called The Reader's Digest of February, it has a story the name is A Woman Over Forty, it is OK and it will show that we can sure have plenty of good times for a long time after 40 so see dear, don't worry and all will be OK. Ha ha. Kiss Joanie and Sonnie for me. Love to Val, Ralph, Mimi, Abe, Rose, and Elsie, and Dear, I love you alone, and have forgotten all about the other party.

Love,
Alphonse Capone

May 18, 1936

Dear Ralph:

This is pertaining to your brother Al now in Alcatraz, Calif. Enclosed you will find the true statements in regards to the conditions that exist there at present. Upon arriving at the Island Al your brother was approached by the Touhy Bunch and others of his clicks to advance $5,000 to be used as an escape plan to hire a gun-boat and for people on the outside on threat of his life, which thye have attempted time and time again for him refusing to advance same. A year or so ago this same bunch planted a table knife under his seat in dining room which would have caused him going to the hole and maybe lose his good time, which the Deputy Warden knew at the time that Al could not have done it; a party by the name of Whaley working in the kitchen at the time of the last strike, with the Touhy bunch tried and are trying their utmost to poison Al with food and contraband candy. Al in turn would not touch same it being that he was told what they were trying to do to him, at the present time until I left there last month.

There are two other workers in the kitchen by the name of Sparky prison #200 and Bob Sheridan #199 which are pretending and making Al feel that they are his friend, waiting for an opportunity to knife or poison him. To be frank with you and you full realize the meaning and danger fir your brother AL is that he must by all means get out of there be sent to another prison. The have marked him for his life and it is only a matter of time you will hear the saddest news of your life, knowing beyond a doubt that his life is at stake. Being that I was the orchestra leader and due out May 6th, 1936, a party by the name of Chas. Berta and McDonald #115 approached me and said unless Al gave me the O.K. to get them $,5000 for an escape plan and forward it to the following address:

Mrs. Myrtle Bloxham,
1717 - 4th St.,
South Bellingham, Washington,

and -

Mrs. G. Berta,
1298 Filmore St.,
San Francisco, Calif.

that they would get AL and that he would never leave there alive. I was to get in contact with the following people and have arrangements made for an escape with said money to be turned over to these people.

Thomas Cros, and ex-convict out of McNeil Isl. following locations to find the above for me to get or write to the Chaplin of the Christian Science Church at McNeil Island to receive the address of the mother on false pretense to be a friend and to get in personal contact with Thomas Cross, and for me to give him the outlay of the prison ground and also the secret signals which will be as follows:

A fast motor boat with a row boat behind to go around the island two days in succession after Berta had a visit from his wife which she in turn would set the date and time; I was to see lawyer of San Francisco by name of Nat Coughlin, he is in turn would get me in touch with Berta's wife and for me to give her plans for escape and for me to write to a convict now in Leavenworth, Kansas, by name of Dooley Chas., who is due out soon and know all the plans, he in turn is a friend of Thos. Cross and also to the ones in Alcatraz Prison. Said prisoner received plans and information through a fellow that was transferred back to Leavenworth, Kansas, about six months ago by name of Mike. The previous day of my release from Alcatraz I was interviewed by the Deputy warden , called and brought before him in the show room in regards to these escape plans which he in turn happens to know all about it. He agrees with me that Al's life is in danger and would like to see him transferred out of there.

I don't believe you know the dangers as Al cannot go out in the yard; it is now going on for the past year and that he is in real danger with his life. This information is known by all the guard and officials of the Island. It seems that with all this Al is afraid to eat the food and his health is failing him. These facts are the Almighty and God's truth and all because Al refuses to be a party to these escape plans and upon it all trying to be a model prisoner. He has made more enemies by not being in with these plans and strikes. It seems and I know and fear things will get worse when some of these same men get out of solitary confinement; there are numerous other things such as burning his clothes week after week from the laundry. It seems that most of these men threaten Al's life for not sending money to different people, such as this man Jack Baker who works in the blacksmith shop, and said unless he receives $500 he will knife or poison Al or get even some dirty way. He wants $500 sent to Mrs. Grant Morrison, 127 North Edgement, Los Angeles, Calif.

These facts I happen to know as I was the music teacher for Al for 1-1/2 yrs. and knew every move and attempts that have failed towards his life and constant tortures that he is going through daily. After spending half my life in various prisons there is none so corrupt as Alcatraz. I am sure and feel that Atty. General would not stand to see Al killed in cold blood when he has proven himself a model prisoner and helped to better himself in music. I know and take solemn oath to the above facts to be truthful, and it is more serious than I can explain in writing.

(Signed) Chas. Mangiere #97

Chicago, Illinois,
7244 Prairie Avenue,

June 25, 1936

Hon. Sanford Bates,
Director,
Bureau of Prisons,
Washington, D.C.

Dear Mr. Bates:

Referring to our conference this morning relative to our appeal for the transfer of my brother Al from Alcatraz, and confirming my verbal statement to you, I respectfully state that on behalf of myself, Al's wife, and our mother, that we will gladly assume all responsibility for his safety and welfare if you transfer him to one of our other prisons.

Further, in the event of Al being transferred to some other institution, I will personally assume all responsibility and guilt for any bribes of offi cials or guards, also other prisoners, seeking any special privileges, favors, etc., and, in fact, anything of any nature whatsoever in violation of your prison rules, all of which, I repeat, I will assume full responsibility and the guilt thereof.

The family feels that an immediate transfer is vitally necessary, not only because his life is in danger, but his health is impaired due to his lack of fresh air, exercise, extreme nervous condition, mental worries, because of existing conditions and he cannot enjoy the yard privileges, being at times fearful of criminal attack.

Thanking you for kind consideration and trusting that you will transfer him at the earliest possible moment, I beg to remain

Respectfully yours,
Ralph Capone

Feb.

Mrs. Mae Capone
93 Palm Island
Miami Beach
Florida

To My Dear Wife,

Well Sweet, here I am with a few lines to you, the dearest in all the world to me. And have prayed these last few days of my sickness to our dear God above to make me so well, which she has, and I sure thanked her for making me well and sure am in perfect health again, as you and Mafalada will see on your visiting days this month. I also received all of your letters Sweet, and more than happy that you and our dear Son, are in perfect health, I also heard from my dear Sister and also brother Ralph, please give them my love, and also tell Ralph not to worry about me, as I am in good health, and intend to be home, when my time is up unless I have to go to the County Jail in Cook County, Sweet I received this month two letters dated Feb. 3r - 5th, and sure enjoyed them and happy that you and Sonny and all the rest of our dear families are in good health, give them all of my love and kisses to the kids and please don't worry about me, as you will see for yourself how I look when you get here on visit with Mafalda, so keep that lovely chin, up and remember Sweet, it isn't much longer before I will be home, and into your loving arms forever, so Sweet don't worry about me as am O.K. and will be on routine working in the yard A.M. and Music afternoon in no less than two more days.

So you see Sweet, nothing to keep you worried, as when you visit me, you will see yourself Sweet, that your dear Dad is in good health. Give my love to Mother and glad in Mafalda's letter she told me Mother is in perfect health and also the rest of our families are the same, I thank God and pray night and mornings to keep up her good work. In the meantime tell Ralph not to worry about me, as all is going to be in perfect shape, in regards to my doing the rest of time, and come in perfect health and don't intend to make any moves of any kind, outside of obeying my officers and respecting them, and doing my work, so you see my dearest, there is nothing for any of you to worry, smile and keep that smile until your dear dad comes home, and then Sweet, watch me strut my stuff, and all my love and I mean Sweet for you alone, and with heart and soul, and forever and ever.

Mae and Sonny Capone

Sweet here is my word to you, from a couple of days from now, I will be in perfect health and intend to be in perfect health when I come home which in time is getting shorter and shorter, until I see you and my dear sister, please do not worry, then you will be satisfied that I'm not in bad shape, as what you have heard. So chin up Sweet, and remember, we are going to have plenty happiness ahead for us and our future, and the rest of our lives, and Sweet remember this promise, nothing in this world is ever going to interfere with our future happiness, Sweet I mean this, and all I can add to this promise is for you and dear Son and families all keep in perfect health, and not to worry about your dear dad, as nothing is going to get your dear dad down, in the meantime tell Sonny to up the way he is doing at College and (write) me as often as he can, and kiss as often as you can for me and God Bless all of you.

Your dear dad,
Alphonse Capone #85

December 18th

To My Dear Wife:

Well dear of mine, here is your dear husband, who loves you, with all of my heart and soul. First thanks to all of your lovely letters this month. Sure glad to read the good news that you and our dear love, are in perfect health. I just came back from church, Father Clark had another priest here, who just came back from Italy, and he gave us a good sermon all about Italy and Germany. In the mean time dear heart of mine please do worry about me, as I am improving every day. I get two treatments a week and they do not hurt me at all. I work out in the recreation yard five days a week, and Saturday and Sunday. I catch up on my music and read a number a Monthly and Weekly Magazines, and a hot bath every day, and three good meals each day. I hope to see you and Sonny again before I leave here next January the 18th. I have quite a number of songs written for him to sing to them to you, and I will play them on the piano or Mandola.

Yes dear I had a nice letter from Sonny dated Dec. 3rd, and he told me that the 20th of this month he will be 20 years old. Yes Sweet, he is sure a son to be proud of, and from the day I come home, he, you, and I will sure go to town in regards to our happiness. I intend to spent the rest of my life, right there in Palm Island, and you and Son and I will get plenty of happiness in our future. We seen a lovely picture on Thanksgiving day, and we will have another one next Christmas. Yes Dear, next Saturday I go to Confession and the following day we will get Communion, and my prayers will be all for you two. In the meantime thank all of my family for all their lovely letters and give them all of my love. Get in touch with my dear brother Ralph, and for him to arrange to pay

Al with wife Mae and her sister Muriel in Florida, 1945.

Letters from Alcatraz

that $37,000 fi ne and costs I have to pay here, And then I go to the County Jail I will have to pay another fi ne there of $10,000. But when I come there I can see you, and hon, all of our dear family every week and I'm through with that Sentence, never again, will I do anything that will keep me away from you, and Son, tell him to continue his golf playing, as I intend to play with him every day and nights, the three of us will either see a Movie or a show or go to one of our own night clubs and dance all of our trou- bles away. I now weigh 204, and fell fi ne and dandy, and when you come here on the next visit, bring me a picture of Sonny, you, and his Sweetheart. Tell Ralph not to worry about me, as I'm satisfi ed with everything here and hope to see him as soon as I come to Chicago. Love and Kisses to you and Sonny,

Year Dear Husband Alphonse Capone #85

Alcatraz, California

February 17, 1938
Mr. A. Capone, Jr.
Notre Dame College
Norte Dame, Indiana

To my dear son:

Well, Junior, here is your dear Dad, with your monthly letter, and all of my hearts wishes, that it will fi nd you in the best of good health, and getting along so won- derful with your studies. Yes Son, I sure am proud of you, and pray night and day and mornings that our God above will always take good care of you, and lead you on to your future, to be a healthy and happy and successful one. Yes my dear Son, you sure are leading on the road, that will make your future a happy one and success- ful and with the fact how your dear Mother and I feel about you and our prayers and the fact that it won't be long before I'm home, and into your arms and your dear Mother's arms, who has been so good to you and me, and sure taking it on her chin with a smile and acting the part of both Mother and Wife, in an honest and respectful way. God keep her and you in the best of good health and without a doubt in my mind Son from the day I come home, we three will be the happiest in all God's creation and with a doubt, so Son of mine, keep healthy and keep up all of your good work in regards to your studies and making friends and respecting your teachers and superiors, and any time you've got something on your mind that you want to keep between you us two, not to hurt your dearest mother, as she will understand and not hurt at all. Son, I don't mean there is unpleasant as I love you both with all my heart and soul, and that means forever and ever. What I'm trying to get at is this, maybe you've got something on your mind about your future. Son all I want you to do is not hold it back as your Mother and your dear dad will go to the limit for your health and future. In the meantime, Sonny, just go along on your law course and I'll give you my word, if you still want to be a doctor just wait until I come home, so you, your dear Mother and your dear dad will get together and talk everything about your future. I'm sure when I get through, you and "Maggie" dear and I, will be happy, because it will be all of our desire's, cause at times we three will always be together, So Son, keep on going as you are in regards to Law, and about that Doctor course, we will talk it over when I come home. So chin up Junior, keep up the good work and please write me as often as you can, as it sure improves my heart and soul, when I read how wonderful you are improving, rest assured, Son, from the first day I come home, there never again will be any grief or sorrows or hardships, because conditions will be so, that the three of us will be together forever.

Now Junior, chip up, and don't let nothing get you down, as it won't be long before I'll be home. In the meantime, I'm sure in good health and intend

A contemporary view of Al Capone's Alcatraz cell. Al's cell was located on the second tier of B-Block along the stretch of corridor between A and B Blocks in cell B-181.

to continue, so we will have some good time very shortly.

I'm doing very nicely here, no hardships, respect my superiors and do my work, three meals a day, plenty exercise, music and all kinds of magazines, under the 200 in regards to my weight, I sure hope before I come home you can arrange a visit for you and your Mother as I sure am anxious to see you. From your Mother I received several letters this month and enjoyed all of them, also from Grandma and Mafalda, Matty, Annette, your dear Uncle Ralphie, and glad you and him are good pals and be that way always. Give your dear Mother a million kisses for me. Love and kisses to all families. Your dear Dad.

Alphonse Capone #85

Al's son, Albert Francis "Sonny" Capone had lived his life as an upstanding citizen and later changed his surname to avoid any so-called crime associations synonymous with the Capone name. Described as "a super nice guy who didn't have a mean bone in his body and would talk to prince or pauper on an equal level," Sonny would shy away from discussing his father and family past. He was married three times with four daughters from his first wife. Sonny Capone passed away of natural causes on July 8, 2004, in El Dorado, California.

Sonny Capone posing with his father at their Palm Island estate

George "Machine Gun" Kelly

GEORGE "MACHINE GUN" KELLY was one of the most famous inmates to ever reside on Alcatraz and one of the most iconic gangsters from the Prohibition Era. In July of 1933, Kelly and his wife Katheryn plotted a scheme to kidnap wealthy oil tycoon and businessman Charles Urschel. Kelly, carrying his trademark Tommy Gun, and two other men carrying pistols entered the Urschel's mansion in Oklahoma City. The Urschels were playing a game of Bridge with friends when Kelly stormed in and took Urschel as hostage. Urschel was taken into hiding on a rural ranch in Texas and the Kelly Gang made demands for $200,000.

The Urschel's family friend E.E. Kirkpatrick made drop arrangements and delivered the ransom in denominations of $20 bills. The money was delivered near the LaSalle Hotel in Kansas City on July 30th, with Urschel being released the following day near Norman, Oklahoma, ending a lengthy eight-day ordeal.

After splitting the ransom money with their accomplices, Kathryn and "Machine Gun" started state hopping trying to stay two steps ahead of law officials. From the several clues that Urschel was able to provide, the FBI raided the ranch where he had been held captive, and made an arrest of one of the other conspirators. The bills that had been used for payment in the ransom, had traceable serial records and the Center Bureau of Investigation (now the FBI) started a nationwide search for whom they now suspected was George R. Kelly.

Kelly and his wife were finally captured on the

George "Machine Gun" Kelly on October 15, 1933. He is shown being led to Leavenworth Federal Penitentiary following his sentencing to life in prison for kidnapping.

morning of September 26, 1933, and ultimately received a life sentence for their act. Kelly was transferred to Leavenworth in Kansas, and Kathryn was transferred to a federal prison in Cincinnati. Kelly was arrogant towards prison officials and bragged to the press that he would escape, break out his wife and they would spend Christmas together. It was decided that these threats should be taken seriously and in August of 1934, Kelly along with his accomplices Albert Bates and Harvey Bailey, were transferred from

Leavenworth by train to Alcatraz. Arriving on September 4, 1934, they would be among the first groups of prisoners. Kelly became AZ #117.

He was incarcerated at Alcatraz from 1934 until 1951, totaling seventeen years served on "the Rock." Kelly would spend the remainder of his life in prison and ultimately died of a heart attack on July 18, 1954 at Leavenworth Federal Penitentiary. Ironically, it was his fifty-ninth birthday.

Feb. 3rd - 1936
Mr. Homer Cummings;
Attorney General;

Dear Sir:-

I am writing you regarding a plan I have had in mind for several months. I realize it is unusual and that no precedent has ever been set for such issue but I understand that as Attorney General it is within your power to designate the place a Federal prisoner must serve his sentence.

As you know I am serving a life sentence for kidnapping, without any possible chance of ever being paroled.

The United States Government has uninhabited Islands in the Pacific, smaller than Wake or Midway. There is Admiral Byrd's abandoned camp at the South Pole, also extremely isolated outposts in Alaska. I feel certain there is at least one of these or some other place where the Government would like the atmospheric conditions studied over a long period of time. I know with the proper instruments and books I could make a meteorology survey of such place that would be of benefit to science and the government.

My idea is, that such a place that has never been thoroughly studied, would be too lonesome and desolate for any free man to care to stay there longer than a few months, even if he had company.

I could be taken from here secretly, placed on a boat in the Bay and transported with what supplies I would need. This could be managed in such a way that the crew need never know who I was or even that I was a prisoner from Alcatraz. Some kind of arrangements could be made for a boat to stop say every year or two, leave supplies and take back what data I had accumulated.

By this method I would be doing some useful work, serving my sentence and I believe by the time I was eligible for parole I would be shown some consideration.

With the rapid strides that aviation is making, wind conditions and air currents will have to be studied all over the world. Two years ago the Islands the China Clipper is using on its flights to Manila were practically useless, but today they are the stepping stones to the Orient, and Meteorology conditions must be known at such places, and lots of time and money would be saved by knowing these conditions in advance.

This may seem like a hair brained proposition to you, but I think it altogether feasible.

Hoping something can be done along these lines. I remain yours truly,

Geo. R. Kelly - #117

This letter was written to Charles Urschel (his kidnapping victim) on April 11, 1940. It was later reprinted by the Bureau of Prisons and is considered as one of the most profound observations ever written about time served on Alcatraz.

Mr. Urschel,

I feel at times you wonder how I'm standing up under my penal servitude, and what is my attitude of mind. It is natural that you should be infinitely curious. Incidentally, let me say that you have missed something in not having had the experience for yourself. No letters, no amount of talk, and still more, no literary description in second-rate books, and books on crime cannot but be second-rate - could ever give you the faintest idea of the reality.

No one can know what it's like to suffer from the sort of intellectual atrophy, the pernicious mental scurvy, that come of long privation of all the things that make life real; because even the analogy of thirst can't possibly give you an inkling of what it's like to be tortured by the absence of everything that makes life worth living.

Maybe you have asked yourself, "How can a man of even ordinary intelligence put up with this kind of life, day in, day out, week after week, month after month, year after year." To put it more mildly still, what is this life of mine like, you might wonder, and whence do I draw sufficient courage to endure it.

To begin with, these five words seem written in fire on the walls of my cell: "Nothing can be worth this." This - kind of life I'm leading. That is the final word of wisdom so far as crime is concerned. Everything else is mere fine writing...

Very truly yours,
Geo. R. Kelly,
#117.

Very Truly Yours,
Geo. R. Kelly #117

September 11, 1940
From: Mrs. George R. Kelly
PMB F85 Terminal Is. Calif.
To: George R. Kelly PMB 117 Alcatraz, Calif.

Mr. Dearest, Bear:

I have thought in vain, of how to work a reply to you that would express exactly how I feel about "us". And I find that it is most difficult to do. Your letter touched my heart. In fact I cried when I read it, as I expected quite a different wording: I shrink, from hurting you. That is the farthest desire of my heart. Naturally I did not think that you would be very hurt, as long as you had cancelled your correspondence to me. I suppose the best thing I can do is to simply speak plainly and exactly how I feel. First, please understand that I'm not "cracking up", neither is prison getting me down, and in dismissing the love angle, which I admit is hard to do I feel like this: that to help you in any manner I would gladly give my life, but I can't feel that I have added to you, in any manner by consistently try-ing to encourage you, by writing you the long cheerful letters that I have, these years. I tried my level best to help you in doing your time; but it seems I failed miserably. Don't think that I even considered you less strong than myself. I haven't--but I always feel that if either of us needed encour-agement, I should attempt to give it to you, because my surroundings have no doubt been more pleasing than yours.

I longed for you to avoid trouble, to stand on your own feet for what you know is right and minutely be the man you really are. Well it seems you fell down on the job. I know you have acted up in some manner, so I feel that if maintaining your position as a prison politician--big shot-- or something comes first in your thoughts then why should I hang on to a dream that could never come true. Unless you have changed a lot darling, even if we two were free tomorrow we should be forced to say goodbye. WHY? Well, because I'm happy to say that I know I shall never place myself nor permit myself to be placed in a position to ever re-enter prison. I shall be just a "little fish" so speaking if I am fortunate enough to get that one chance and like it. No more "big dough" for me in any place. In other words I find that I am completely cured of any craving for un-legitimate luxu-ries and my sincere hopes and plans for the future are of a sane, balanced mode in living. I'll never change on that viewpoint. I have gone through hell and still am plainly speaking, seeing mother as a daily reminder of my own mistake. The mistake was in my love, and marriage to you.

Not that I censure you, I don't. I blame myself. However, I've "woke up". I hoped you would but I'm not sure of what goes on in your mind. As you know I like to finish things immediately and I feel if our goodbye is to come, why not now. The hurt will at least be dimmed in the years of incarcera-tion yet ahead of both of us. I've never told you that I did not love you and I never shall. I said that "I would be happier even in prison" and I would. For I do worry about you and wonder. Love isn't everything in life. A content, peaceful existence, free from worry is most essential and I can dismiss love from my heart when my brain informs me it's best. The reason you gave for canceling your correspondence was a small rebellious boys reason. Rules are rules in an inst. and necessary. And I know that no mail censor would select your letters to heavily censor. You are just another number, the same as I, and the quicker you grasp that fact the better off you'll be. Personally, in general I have been utterly surprised at the considerate kindness I have known from the officials these seven years. I expected far different treatment.

I know you thoroughly honey, so don't think I'm harsh. What you need to do is to forget "Machine Gun" Kelly and what he stood for and interest yourself in being plain, kind George, who is just another "con" like myself. I have shared all of the lead with you. I intend to. We are not kids, we're quite aged and if its impossible for you to make yourself into a man who "thinks straight"--who will go straight when the opportunity presents itself, then I don't want you for a companion. "They all leave prison eventually" we shall too. I will be ready for a new life, fashioned on a far different scale. I don't know about you.

So that's why I asked you for a divorce. I haven't heard from Mr. Bennett yet. When I do I'll let you know. And I wouldn't dream of demanding my pictures from you, so forget that. You may certainly keep them with all of my good wishes and much love. Mother doesn't have any inkling of this. She did not know of me writing you, of my request from Mr. Bennett, nor of your reply to me, so don't think I am being advised or "ribbed". You know me far better than that. I worried a lot, when you had the food riot there and I'm fed up with worries, and God knows I have plenty of my own, so I do think I'd be perhaps a little happier, in placing you in the background and coasting along with just my own problems. You don't pay any attention or me or my

Kathryn Kelly being led from court by United States Marshals in 1933.

advice anyway. You don't seem to consider that any "acting up" you feel obliged to do re fl ects on me too, as for some reason we are more or less judged equally by the Dept. YOU'LL no doubt be angry at this letter, and if I have been wrongfully steered in somethings, I will eventually know. Take care of yourself and think a few things over, and tell me, whether you are nourishing any hair brained schemes, in that brain of yours to further spoil our peaceful old age together, or not? You should have found your true honest self by now, you were never bad, we both simply "thought wrong" and if this doesn't give you any idea of WHY I asked you to release me, then I can't explain. I will write you on the 1st, so keep smiling, and try to see our problem as I see it, and don't feel badly--I am, Devotedly, Kathryn

Mrs. George R. Kelly F 85 Terminal Is. Calif.

P.S. Honey, I have just read a letter from your Father Clark. Will you kindly thank him, and tell him that I appreciate his advice and interest in the two of us. And if you will really be happier as things are just forget that I ever mentioned the word divorce. And behave yourself and try to be what I want you to be; and I shall endeavor to be all to you that I have been in the past, as long as you play the game square. I do want you to keep your mind strictly upon a legitimate basis for our future together. Because the time will eventually come when we shall begin a new life and I do want it to be normal, happy and honest. Now don't worry, and be sweet; and let's do this bit of time with the best of grace and cheerfully. We can you know, and if you really love me as you say, you should be able to keep smiling with me, and keep your mind free to a degree of prison non-essentials, and small annoyances, and instead look forward to at some future date, creating with me, the life together that I desire. I do love you, you know mister; so shall we forget, and will you be honest with me and tell me exactly how you feel? Whether your aim is honesty in the future, that will sometime re-unite us, or whether you might feel that "the world owed you a living" and mess our lives all up again in our old age. I am feeling fi ne. I sho' did want that early transfer to Texas though, to see the folks. But, it will come later I hope. I must say bye. Wish I could see you, I do, I do. Now, settle down and be happy. "heart of heart" and let me hear from you soon. Devotedly, your Katrinka

Mrs. George R. Kelly F-85 Terminal Island. Calif.

September 26, 1941.
Mr. Jas A. Johnston, Warden

Dear Sir:

I should like to talk to you about my being transferred to one of the other institutions. I have never broached the subject to you before because I thought that I didn't have adequate time served here; now I feel that I have. I will not say that my record here has been exemplary, but I think, on the whole, that it is far from being what one would consider bad.

The first thing I would like to call your attention to is the fact that I was not sent here for any violation of the rules in Leavenworth, but because of my record outside. On arrival, I was put in isolation and held there until Sept. 4, 1934 when the first shipment was made to Alcatraz. I might mention that previous to 1933 I served three years in Leavenworth-- one year a trusty, driving the city truck--without a single report.

As you know the discipline of Alcatraz is not rigorous but it is strict, and the facilities for recreation and diversion are practically non-existent. I have served a little more than seven years in Alcatraz and, while not meaning to be flippant, I would say that seven years in this climate could not be considered a bagatelle judged by either the Gregorian or by the Julian calendar.

I do not want you to take this letter as an attitude of complaint, far from it, I am merely trying to explain my side of the question.

To be frank, I want to be transferred for reasons almost too numerous to enumerate. I should like to be in a place where I can go on the yard in the summer afternoons and enjoy the sunshine for a few months of the year. It is true that we have our yard periods here, but I know that you are fair enough to admit that with the high winds, the lack of sunshine, and for want of space, the yard is more of an aggravation than a diversion. I should also like to be where I can earn a few dollars each month in one of the industries. I am not what is known as a work horse, but I do apply myself and am not a shirker. My wife rarely has any money for the few trifles that she needs, such as newspapers, rouge, lipstick and her occasional cigarette. That applies to her mother also. If I were able to earn enough to take care of that one item I would feel that I was being of some help to my wife and making things a little more pleasant for her. My wife and I still own a little property in Texas, but the rentals just barely pay

Letters from Alcatraz

the taxes and take care of the repairs. We are trying our best to hold on to the property so that Kathryn will not be destitute when she does get out. What cash I had at the time of my arrest has been expended in educating and taking care of my daughter during the six years that she was alone previous to her marriage. So, you can readily see why I should like to be where I could earn a little something.

I am not going to say that I care nothing about the radio because I do; I am a radio bug. And the afternoon papers would not be amiss. The weekly shows during the winter would also be quite a treat. Besides I could have a visit occasionally if I were closer to home.

Mr. Johnston, I am broad minded enough to realize that a prison of this type cannot have all these things and coddle the inmates. I am not complaining of the system--it must serve some good purpose--but why discriminate? After all, there are around 14,000 men in Federal prisons, all pretty much alike. Many of them are long timers with far worse records both inside and out than mine is. I am not a trouble maker nor am I an agitator; I can get along amicably anywhere. Why shouldn't I be given a chance elsewhere? Then if I am scatter brained enough to abuse the privilege then I should be brought back and kept here without any complaint on my part.

I should like an interview with you to talk this over; the reason that I am writing you before hand is so that the audacity of my asking for a transfer will not come as too much of a shock.

Respectfully yours,
Geo. R. Kelly, Reg. No. 117

From Geo. R. Kelly #117   November 2, 1944
Alcatraz Island, California

To Mr. Francis Biddle
Washington, D.C.

Dear Sir,

About two years ago I talked with Mr. Bennett concerning my being transferred to some other Institution. At the time he implied that, in my particular case, his hands were tied; that it was entirely up to the Attorney
General. The inference was that Attorney General Cummings had instituted
some ruling to the effect that if the question of my being transferred did
arise, the decision was wholly up to him. What I should like to know is,
does that ruling still stand, now that Mr.
Cummings has been out of office for six
years?

I am one of the original homesteaders
of Alcatraz, having been here now for
over ten years. There are only about
eight or ten of us left who came out
in the first shipments and I understand that at least five of them do
not wish to be transferred either
because they have relatives close by
who visit them each month, or because
they feel that their time is now too
short to make a change.

Last week I talked with Warden
Johnston and he was non-committal
as to whether he would recommend my
transfer but did suggest that I see
Mr. Bennett when he next came to Alcatraz. In view of the fact that Mr. Bennett told me at my last interview that
it was out of his hands, I thought it
best to get your advice.

Not that I am trying to commercial-
ize on my boys' patriotism but I have two sons in the Armed Forces. My old-
est boy is a First Lieutenant in the Air Corps and has been overseas for
thirty-three months. My other son is a Corporal in the Medical Corps and is
now stationed at Camp Hawze, Texas. My son in law has taught aeronautics
and ground-flying at the University of Arizona for over two years. I mention this merely to show you something of my background.

Regardless of what you have heard of Alcatraz it is far from being a
pleasant place to do time. The climate is murderous and I, personally, have
suffered from chronic sinus trouble for years. The recreation facilities
are practically nil. I realize that is the way the department wants it, but

Letters from Alcatraz

to me it seems like an exceptionally wide discrimination is shown between the men of Alcatraz and the men in the other Federal Institutions. I should like to be where I could read a newspaper and listen to the radio for a change after ten years here. If I were in Leavenworth or Atlanta my children could also visit me. Incidentally, both my conduct record and my work record are good here.

This letter is intended solely in the vein of one seeking advice. Shall I go further into the matter with the Warden and Mr. Bennett or is it entirely in your hands? I should appreciate your advising me as to what steps to take.

> Very truly yours,
> Geo. R. Kelly - #117

From Geo. R. Kelly #117   April 1, 1945
Alcatraz, California

To Mr. Jas. V. Bennett
Washington D.C.

Dear Sir,

Some time ago I wrote the Attorney General in order to find out how he felt about my being transferred to another Institution. In view of the fact that my letter was referred to you, his attitude must be one of indifference or else his prejudice was only a figment of my imagination that formed in my mind from inferences that were made during my interview with you. Now that your hands are no longer tied in so far as my being transferred is concerned I can get down to cases.

As you know, I am not one to wail and moan over my lot but in all fairness I think I have been kept in Alcatraz far too long considering my record both here and outside. If all Federal Prisoners were run along the same lines as Alcatraz you wouldn't hear a peep out of me. Under the circumstances I consider there has been a wide discrimination shown between the men here and

those in other Federal prisons. I know there are many long timers in Atlanta, Leavenworth, and elsewhere whose records are much worse than mine.
Why aren't they on the "Rock"? My record here is good and by no standard am
I a trouble maker. Why then can't I enjoy the few privileges that men in the
other prisons are getting?

Anyone will tell you this Island has the worst climate in the United
States. I have been suffering with sinus trouble for years. My left ear has
been running for four years and I have repeatedly tried to have it and my
nose operated on, with no success. I could at least get treatment for these
ailments elsewhere. I realize all of the men who originally opened up Alcatraz were sort of guinea-pigs. No doubt some of us were kept here to justify
the expenditure. After eleven years the place doesn't need justifying - it
is here to stay; consequently I feel the Department could spare me from the
Rock quite easily. Alcatraz would be just as much a threat over the inmates
of other prisons if I were in a Federal road camp.

There is another point. My boys in the army find it very embarrassing to
receive a letter with a big ALCATRAZ on it. I realize I should have thought
of that twelve years ago when I put Mr. Urschel in the basement but that
is neither here nor there - the fact is I am here and I believe I merit a
transfer on my record alone. If it is the policy of the Depart to make it as
humiliating on a prisoner's relatives as they can, I have nothing further
to say about that angle.

Your reply to the letter I wrote Mr. Biddle was very indefinite. I believe
Warden Johnston said, "Mr. Bennett will see you when he comes here next
year." How about transferring me and seeing me in <u>Atlanta</u> next year? While
I think of it, don't you think you could see your way clear to let me write
Kathy each week? Those semi-monthly letters are pretty far apart.

In the event you do come to Alcatraz before I am transferred I should
like to have a talk with you, maybe I can convert you to my way of thinking - naturally I mean about a transfer. I talked with Dr. Bixby a few
weeks ago; he looked better than Clark Gable in uniform. I hope to see you
soon,

Respectfully yours,
Geo. R. Kelly #117

Letters from Alcatraz

From Geo. R. Kelly #117 October 1, 1950
Alcatraz, California

Mr. Jas. V. Bennett
Washington, D.C.

Dear Sir,

I thought I would drop you a few lines as a reminder that I still want a transfer to one of the other Institutions. There is a rumor fl oating around now that there is to be a transfer in the near future and I am looking forward to being on it since it has been almost eight months since our interview. Bear in mind that I have been here over 16 years and with the two years Industrial goodtime I have earned I have served the equivalent of a 27 year sentence in Alcatraz alone. You know why I was sent to Alcatraz in the fi rst place – because it was the policy of Atty. Gen. Cummings to isolate anyone who had gotten any publicity. You have transferred other kidnappers; you have

Machine Gun Kelly and close friend Willie Radkay are seen watching fellow inmates play a game of Bridge in the Recreation Yard. Radkay shared a neighboring cell (#240) to Kelly (#238) in B-Block and worked together in the industries along with Basil "The Owl" Banghart and Harvey Bailey.

Willie Radkay (seen here at Alcatraz in 2001) was imprisoned on the Rock from 1945 to 1952. Alcatraz was a small community made up of the "Cream of the Criminal Crop" and strong bonds endured even following their release back to free society. Outside of prison Radkay maintained close friendships with inmates Dale Stamphill and Harvey Bailey. Radkay described Kelly as a deeply reflective and intelligent man who was well liked by most of the inmate population. Kelly loved to read the classics and books about the Old West. He held a reputation of boasting incessantly of his early crime escapades, which some inmates found irritating. Radkay, however, enjoyed the good company and long conversations. "He was a damn good friend to pass the time with" Radkay commented in 2004. Radkay's criminal path to Alcatraz spanned far into his youth. At only 16 years of age, Radkay climbed a fence at a local airport to get a glimpse inside Charles Lindbergh's historic Spirit of St. Louis airplane during a goodwill tour in late 1927. While the aviator was distracted doing interviews at the tail of the plane, Radkay managed to reach inside the cockpit and pull from under the seat a bag of cookies, a magazine and a stopwatch.

transferred murderers, bank robbers, rape cases etc. You transferred Bailey years ago and he was in the same case so why discriminate. On my conduct and work record alone I feel I merit a transfer. I am the only man left who originally opened up this place in 1934. In June <u>1948</u> your classification board here unanimously recommended that I be transferred. Doesn't their decision of over two years ago have any bearing on the case. You will admit that as prisons go Alcatraz is low man on the totem pole. For whatever you can do you have my sincere thanks and best wishes.

Very truly yours
Geo. R. Kelly #117

From Geo. R. Kelly #44131   June 1951
Leavenworth, Kansas

To Fr. Joseph M. Clark
San Francisco, CA

Dear Father,
    I just received a letter from Bob telling of you and Dick visiting him and going to Warner Bros. Bob seems to think Mr. Foy is going to get him in some of the pictures going into production. Did he make any kind of definite promise to you? I have seen all of the old timers from Alcatraz and the majority ask about you. I didn't like this place at first but I am getting used to it and if I can get a single cell I think I will feel like I am outside. When I reached here the fellows sent me candy - cigarettes - pleasing outfits and I don't know what all. The yard is so big it looks like the

Letters from Alcatraz

State of Texas to me. We have had lots of rain but I've really enjoyed the few days sunshine we did have. Pauline and family are now in Okla. City with Olin's mother - she is dying from cancer - and later they are going to settle in Wichita. Lots of letters from Kay and in the one I received today she said Mr. Shannon and some friends were anxious to try something in their case but didn't want to make a move until the Parole Board had said "yes" or "no". As things now stand that may be another year. Do you think you could call Mr. Boyle and have him speed the Board's decision up a bit? Both Kay and Ora are feeling fairly good but are nervous wrecks from the waiting and uncertainty. I'm sure a word from you to Boyle or Leslie might turn the trick. In my opinion, I think they are going to grant the parole but are putting it off as they as they did in Murphy's case. I started to work in Industries today in the Brush Factory and am in line for a splendid job that will be open in early October. You know Father, I didn't realize anyone could wise a person as I have you. I am so used to our Sat. and Sun. chats that I actually wake up expecting you on those days. Maybe in a few years Kay and I will be visiting you in San Francisco and I mean for a week or two. I haven't been able to get you on my correspondence list but am writing you a special purpose letter. If you will attach a short note to the warden or to Mr. Miller, the Parole Officer, in the letter you write me telling them you wish to correspond with me they will place you on my list and I can write you whenever I like. Many thanks for taking care of bob and to repeat myself you are the swellest person in the world in my estimation. Give Fr. Hasting my jumbo size hello and take good care of yourself. With kindest regards and best wishes I am as ever, Geo.

Geo. R. Kelly #44131

From Geo. R. Kelly 44131 Jan. 1, 1952
Leavenworth, Kansas

To Mrs. Kathryn Kelly
Anderson W. VA. Box A

Darling, You have known me so long that you are practically able to read my mind. Although you hadn't received my two letters yet, you already knew just about what my advice would be. In view of the soft soap the P.B. gave you in the denial it would be quite a gamble to antagonize

George Kelly following transfer back to U.S.P. Leavenworth in June of 1951.

them I guess. They may be on the verge of doing something but I doubt it as I can't see where a few months would change their minds or attitude. (There was a fellow here who had been on the Rock for a few years who made parole on a 30 year sentence yesterday.) He had been denied many times and his partner was paroled to Ward in Minneapolis about three years ago; so you can't ever tell what the board intends doing. Father Clark burns me up also. Not only over not keeping the appointment with Helen but the many things he did contrary to what I told him even in Word. He won't take any particular stand and stick with it. (The new men came in from Alcatraz and there wasn't a single one in the shipment who was a friend of mine. There were at least a half dozen of real old times who I expected to make this shipment but missed the boat.) I am still in the Hospital and feel fairly good I guess. I got up for about five minutes today but I was a lot weaker than I thought so I had to crawl back in bed. I think in another week I'll be able to go back to work. This is quite a hospital here. It is new and has about six or seven wards I guess. The nurses are all inmates and treat me just about as well as could be expected anywhere. I didn't know Pearl had the Post Office there. As soon as I am back in my cell I am going to write a letter to Mr. Freeman and I think from what I have to say it will go to him instead of one of the Bureaus. I'll get a copy of the Jan. Red Book as soon as I am out of here. Now that I am in the hospital they are ready to install the bridge, which is impossible as long as I am in bed. Like you said, Angel, after this is over we will be immune to anything and nothing can hurt us. A letter came from Bob and I think you will hear from him in a day or so, if you haven't already received a letter from him. Excuse the poor notes lately, sugar, because your husband isn't up to doing a very good job of writing just now. I'll do better next week. I'll write as usual Sunday and in the mean time, I'll be thinking of you and loving you with all my heart. My love to your Mother and lots of kisses to my adorable wife. Your from Geo.

Geo. R. Kelly #44131

Letters from Alcatraz

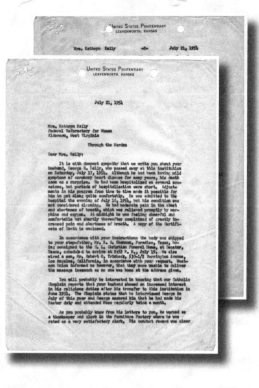

Mrs. Kathryn Kelly
Federal Reformatory for Women
Alderson, West Virginia

Through the Warden

Dear Mrs. Kelly:

It is with deepest sympathy that we write you abut your husband, George R. Kelly, who passed away at this institution on Saturday, July 17, 1954. Although he had been having mild symptoms of coronary heart disease for many years, his death came as a surprise. He had been hospitalized on several occasions, but periods of hospitalization were short. Adjustments in his program form time to time made it possible for him to get along quite comfortably. He was admitted to the hospital the evening of July 16, 1954, but his condition was not considered alarming. He had moderate pain in the chest and shortness of breath, which was relieved promptly by morphine and oxygen. At midnight he was feeling cheerful and comfortable but shortly thereafter complained of greatly increased pain and shortness of breath. A copy of the Certifi cate of Death is enclosed.

In accordance with your instructions the body was shipped to your stepfather, Mr. R.G. Shannon, Paradise, Texas, being consigned to the C.L. Christian Funeral Home, at Decatur, Texas, Scheduled to arrive at 2:52 P.M., July 19. We also wired a son, Mr. Robert O. Trimback, 538-½ Barrington Avenue, Los Angeles, California, in accordance with your request. Western Union informed us however, that they were unable to deliver the message in as much as no one was home at the address given.

You will probably be interested in knowing that our Catholic Chaplain reports that your husband showed an increased interest in his religious duties after his transfer to this institution in June 1951.

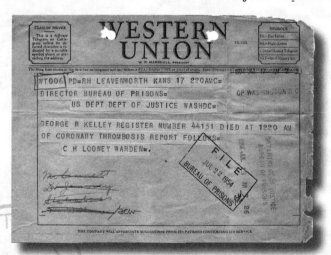

The Chaplin states that he interviewed George in July of this year and George assured him that he had made his Easter duty and attended Mass regularly twice a month.

As you probably know from his letters to you he worked as a timekeeper and clerk in the Furniture Factory where he was rated as a very satisfactory clerk.

Since 1940 he got along with others. I enclosed a copy of a letter sent to your step-father, at his request, the information to be used in arranging for funeral services.

I appreciate your letter of July 18. In regard to a keepsake, we are forwarding to your step-father at Paradise, Texas, the following personal items which your husband had in his locker:

1 each Webster's Collegiate Dictionary
2 pairs Eyeglasses
1 pair Sunglasses
2 each Daily Missals
1 each Rosary
1 each Pocket Watch
2 each Fountain Pens
1 each Mechanical pencil
1 each Padlock
1 each Nail Clipper
15 pkgs Cigarettes, Philip Morris
2 each Hair brushes
1 tube Colgate dental cream
2 cakes Woodbury soap
1 lot Letters
1 lot Photographs
1 lot Papers regarding case
1 Transcript of Record- Kathryn Thorne Kelly vs. United States of America

There is $104.56 in George's commissary account and there will be an additional credit when the July patrol is posted on August 15. When the exact amount is determined, we will advise you and forward claim forms to be completed by you.

My I on behalf of our entire staff, express our heart felt sympathy to you and other members of the family in this hour of bereavement.

Very truly yours,
C.H. Looney
Warden

July 18, 1954

Warden, Looney
Leavenworth, Kansas

Dear Sir:

   May I extend my appreciation to you,
to the institution, the medical staff, and
the inmates and friends of my husband
there, for your kindness and care of
him. I was comforted after talking with
you yesterday. I telephoned Mr. Shannon
and all arrangements with the Decatur
Texas funeral home had been completed. I
thought you might be able to mail a few
little keepsakes of his personal property
home for me. I know he had a fountain pen,
he loved, which he wrote me with, that I
would like to have just any small thing
you may be able to give me. Anything of
that sort if possible please mail to:

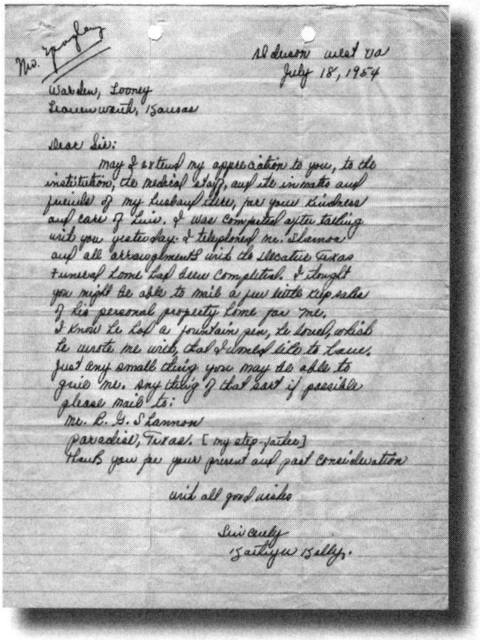

   MR.R.G. Shannon
   Paradise, Texas. [my step-father]

Thank you for your present and past consideration

With all good wishes,
Sincerely,
Kathryn Kelly

Albert Bates was a co-conspirator of Kelly in the Urschel kidnapping case. He was sent to Alcatraz due to his profile status and special custody needs. This letter was sent directly to Urschel relating to his ransom.

A. L. Bates - 137

TO: Mr. C. F. Urschel
U.S. Penitentiary
F. O. Box 1146
Alcatraz, California

Oklahoma City, Okla.October 1, 1942

Dear Sir:

Your letter of September 10th was forwarded to me by Mr. James V. Bennett, Director, Bureau of Prisons, and though there is little that I can divulge about the case that isn't known, I can answer your query in reference to the division of the ransom money.

After Kelly and I received the money from Mr. Kirkpatrick in Kansas City we returned directly to the Shannon Ranch, arriving there about 2 p.m., on Monday, July 31, 1933. We retired to the front room of the house and divided the money in privacy. Kelly had a "nut" (as we refer to an expense account in connection with any job), of $11,500.00. I did not inquire what it was for simply because it was customary for each individual of outfits like ours to keep a record of his expenses on our various enterprises. I do know that we abandoned a new Buick of his on the night of July 29th about 2 or 3 miles northeast of Luther, Oklahoma, alongside the "Katy" tracks. (There was a humorous side to that incident, but I do not wish to infringe upon Mr. Kirkpatrick as a story teller. I read "Crime's Paradise" and also tried to purchase his anthology of poems, "Dim Trails," but was informed that it was privately printed).

I received the sum of $94,250.00 for my "end", and when I left the room to clean up a bit on the back porch I saw Bailey was still there, although he had told me four days previous that his friends would call for him not later than Saturday. I had warned him that the place was "hot" on account of our past activities in Texas and our connections with detective friends, Messrs. Weatherford and Sweeny of Ft. Worth. I was in a hurry to get the job over with so I did not converse much with anyone. I gave Bailey $500.00 out of my pocket and Kelly did likewise. I left the farm with $93,750.00.

When we released you at Norman, Kelly and I separated. I drove via Chickasha to Amarillo, thence to Denver. My wife was in Portland, Oregon, where I communicated with her, advising her to return to Denver immediately. I put

Harvey Bailey and Willie Radkay at the "Outlaw," a private club in Kansas City in 1973. Both remained good friends outside of prison. Bailey was a co-conspirator of Kelly and Bates in the Urschel kidnapping case and sent to Alcatraz along with Kelly in 1934. Bailey would spend 12-years on the Rock. He died in Joplin, Missouri at 91-years of age.

$50,000.00 in a bag with surplus clothes, locked it, and left it with friends to keep until my wife called for it. I left instructions in a letter addressed to her in my post office box for her to rent an apartment upon arrival and to leave the address in that box. I had been under a tremendous strain for a week, on the go night and day, so I decided I'd have a little pleasure in Denver. I don't believe I spent over $1,000.00 during the three days I stayed there. I then went by plane to Minneapolis where I rejoined the Kellys as prearranged. I arrived there on August 5th. The following day the three of us drove to Mills Lake, a resort. Kelly told me he was leaving early the next day for Cleveland and in the event anything of importance occurred to wire him. I told him I brought $42,000.00 with me. The next day, at the Boulevards of Paris, a roadhouse, Jack Phifer, (now deceased) got word via the grapevine that the "O" were concentrating in the Twin Cities. He learned that four of his crew had been arrested and held incommunicado. I warned Kelly by wire and left that night for Omaha and Denver.

When I was alone in the apartment my wife had rented I put $41,000.00 in the same bag with the $50,000.00. I probably spent about $2,000.00 all told and had $700.00 on me when I was arrested three days after returning to Denver. I told my wife when I left the apartment on the date of my arrest that there was over $90,000.00 in a locked bag in the clothes closet.

Roy Gardner

"The talking pictures are wonderful. You will be surprised when you hear the melodrama voice of the famous Will Rogers. He sure makes you laugh when he opens up that nice looking mouth of his."

—Letter to Roy Gardner, 1932

MUCH OF Alcatraz's early reputation had been congealed by early inmate accounts printed across the nation in newspapers and magazines which ranged from true crime to trendy lifestyle themed publications. The cold veil of secrecy made stories of life inside the prison popular reading for the public at large, and Roy Gardner helped sustain that intrigue by writing prolifically about his experiences at Alcatraz in various news and media venues. Roy Gardner served at Alcatraz from 1934 until 1936, and was a well-known publicly as one of the last notorious train robbers from the old western era.

Gardner spent two years incarcerated on Alcatraz, and after his ultimate release in 1938, he peddled a small in-formational book at the Golden Gate Pan Pacific Exposition on Treasure Island, and narrated boat tours for San Francisco tourists. Gardner was known to the public as a brilliant escape artist, and he was famous for his Houdini-like jailbreaks, including a magnificent escape from a Mexican jail, when just three days

before his scheduled execution before a firing squad, he amazingly overpowered his sentry and fled back across the border to Arizona. He was later captured in San Francisco for robbery and finally found himself imprisoned at U.S.P. Leavenworth.

Surprisingly, Gardner volunteered to be transferred to Alcatraz. He claimed that he wanted to go straight, and felt that this would bring him closer to friends and family. Gardner was destined to do hard time during his twenty-five month imprisonment at Alcatraz. Warden Johnston had assigned him to work in the Mat Factory, and he would later comment that Leavenworth and Atlanta were summer resorts compared to the Rock. He wrote:

> The hopeless despair on the Rock is reflected in the faces and actions of almost all of the inmates. They seem to march about the island in a sort of hopelessness, helpless daze, and you can watch them progressively sinking down and down... On "the Rock" there are upwards of three hundred men. One hundred fifty will die there. Sometime—in ten, fifteen, twenty-five years—the others come out into the world. These, too, are dead; the walking dead. The men confined there, to all intents and purposes, are buried alive. In reality they are little more than animated cadavers—dead men who are still able to walk and talk. Watching those men from day to day slowly giving up hopes is truly a pitiful sight, even if you are one of them.

Gardner was transferred back to Leavenworth in 1936, and was finally released from prison in 1938. His wife had left him and remarried, and he drifted back to San Francisco to re-establish his life.

In March of 1939, he set up an exhibition booth at the Golden Gate Pan Pacific Exposition on Treasure Island. Gardner recounted to patrons his law-breaking stories of violence and torture, and autographed his self published memoir entitled *Hellcatraz*. Gardner's show, entitled *Crime Doesn't Pay*, failed to draw large crowds, and eventually closed. He would later spend a brief period working as a narrator on a San Francisco tour boat, before finally hitting rock bottom and taking on employment as a baker in San Francisco. His days of fame and dreamed fortunes had now passed...

Distraught, aged and without friends, he finally committed suicide at the Hotel Governor, in San Francisco on January 10, 1940. Using cyanide, sulfuric acid, and a bath towel, he draped the bathroom sink and covered his head, creating a makeshift gas chamber. On the door was a note warning the maid: "Do Not Open Door—Poison Gas—Call Police." Gardner had also left the maid a small cash tip for cleaning out his belongings. His suitcase stood neatly in a corner of his room, and the shower curtain was neatly folded across the floor to prevent any mess. Additionally, he had already made burial arrangements with the Halsted and Company, a local funeral home, leaving their phonebook advertisement neatly clipped to his belongings, and parting with no unfinished details.

The *San Francisco Examiner* provided some thought provoking perspective on the last years of Gardener's troubled life in this excerpt from a January 12, 1940 article:

> Gardner was ill in body and in mind. There was the heart condition he spoke about in the undertaking par-

lor. Six months to live–what was the use? He had written prison exposes of the "crime doesn't pay" variety, sold a script to a Hollywood producer, lectured in dingy little theaters—ended up exhausted, mentally bankrupt.

But Gardner had friends. The cops on the beat liked him. The newsboy who sold him a paper at 2:30 Thursday afternoon at the corner of Turk and Jones Streets, and thereby fixed the time of his death almost to the hour—thought he was a fine fellow.

The druggist at the same corner liked to chat with the soft-spoken ex-convict; the waiter in the café around the corner was glad to serve him, be-

cause he always left a tip and had a cheery thing or two to say.

Even the wife who divorced him two years ago - Mrs. Will Parker of Napa - expressed great sorrow, said that "Roy just hadn't been able to adjust himself to the world."

Gardner was no angel–inside of prison or out. He liked to gamble at cards and to play the races. He was too free with the money he made, too generous, and he became an easy mark, whom chance acquaintances found profitable to cultivate.

Thus did Roy Gardner live and die.

To Dr. Yoke

From: Roy Gardner #110

Dr. Yoke I am taking this method to protest against unnecessary cruelty. The food that is constantly setting here under my nose is not tempting in anyway to me. Instead it is nauseating.

Under those circumstances I feel justified in asking you to discontinue having food placed in my cell. Of course I could display my ill nature by knocking it off the fl oor, but I don't want to do that, in fact, I am not going to do it, because I do not wish to offend the attendants who are instructed to place the food in here. It is not their fault.

Won't you discontinue that practice please?

Respectfully submitted,
Roy Gardner

Leavenworth, Kansas 1924

To: Hon. H.H. Votaw
Supt. of Federal Prisons

Sir: My wife is now in Washington endeavoring to obtain from Attorney General Stone permission to have an operation performed on me for the purpose of relieving the pressure on my brain.

I understand that she bears recommendations from federal offi cials at Phoenix, Arizona, also letters from well-known surgeons setting forth their opinions in detail. The x-ray pictures that my wife carries show very plainly the portion of my skull that is pressing on my brain, not withstanding Dr. Yokis' opinion to the contrary. Whether this pressure has any connection with the criminal tendencies I have displayed since the accident causing the pressure, is problematical. I am well aware of the dangerous character of this operation but the possibilities of success which would return make me at some future date to return to society with all thoughts of crime obliterated from my mind, and make it possible for me to resume the life of a law abiding citizen, causes the danger of the operation resulting fatally to appear inconsequential. If I survive my present term of confi nement and return to society with my mind intend on further crimes, what have I profi ted and in what manner has society gained by my long confi nement? I state to you in all sincerity that my thoughts everyday dwell on criminal activities even as they did before my incarceration.

This statement may prove to be detrimental any opportunity I might have now for release in future years, but I do not desire to evade the issue. It would be unfair both to myself and society, if I should be released in my present state of mine, the cure of which I believe, lies in this operation that my wife is endeavoring to obtain through the approval of Attorney General Stone.

Down in my heart I know and realize to the fullest extent, the futility of crime. If I possessed the ability to defeat or evade the man-made laws of achieving the perpetration of the so-called "perfect crime" my ultimate defeat by the law of compensation, which is infallible in its operation would be inevitable. Although I am capable of seeing these things in the proper light, and know in my own mind that crime cannot be successful, I state to you frankly, that if I were released tomorrow, I sincerely believe a sack of registered mail would be too great a temptation for me to resist.

What else, other than a disorder of the brain would cause me to do things that I know I cannot be successful in, things that I do not want to do and which I know can only result in suffering for my family and myself. It is in the realization of the hopelessness of the situation in my present condition that I send this letter to you with the earnest appeal that my application might receive careful consideration before this one ray of hope, uncertain and fraught with danger as it is. I believe the Attorney General's action on my application will depend too on a great extent upon your recommendation, and I place my appeal in your hands with full confidence that you will accord it every consideration for which I will be truly grateful.

Respectfully submitted,
ROY GARDNER
#17060

P.S. I would appreciate a private interview with you if you can find it convenient to grant me a few minutes of your time.

Roy Gardner

Leavenworth, Kansas
May 7, 1923
To: Mr. H.H. Votaw
Supt. of Federal Prisons

Dear Sir:

This is to protest against the treatment now being accorded my wife by W.J. Biddle.

Some two months ago, I was indiscreet enough to produce a one-dollar bill that I had secured before being confined in isolation, and Mr. Biddle immediately seized it as a protest and, after subjecting my wife to a verbal grilling in his office, he continued his unwarranted persecution by suspending her visiting privileges. Seeing me for one hour every two weeks is the only pleasure the girl gets and to have that pleasure denied her on the unsupported and unwarranted suspicion of Mr. J. Biddle is, to put it mildly, unjust and ungentlemanly. If he wants to punish me for being in possession of the dollar, I am ready

Letters from Alcatraz

to stand but I am not now and never will be reconciled to having my wife punished for something that she knew absolutely nothing about. I appeal to you as Supt. of Federal Prisons Mr. Votaw, to instruct the Warden to cease his unwarranted persecution of my wife.

If he can provide one iota of evidence against her, outside of his perverted suspicion, then I will gladly withdraw his complaint.

Respectfully submitted,
ROY GARDNER
OFFICE OF THE WARDEN
September 21, 1929

TO A.H. McCormick
Assistant Superintendent of Prisons
Department of Justice
Washington, D.C.

Dear Sir:

I am in receipt of your letter of September 18th with further reference to Roy Gardner, Reg. No. 20580. As suggested by you, I have arranged with Dr. J. Calvin Weaver, former Prison Physician, to call today for a conference with Dr. Cross regarding the advisability of feeding him by force. This is his twelfth day of fasting and, from his outward appearances, he shows no signs of weakening. From the beginning of his fast, it has been my intention to resort to these measures, and I have informed him, in no uncertain terms, that unless he will willingly submit to being fed or to voluntarily break the strike, playing the manly part himself, it is our intention to forcibly feed him. He tells us that he will resist any such efforts, even to the extent of losing his life. Just how much of this attitude on his part if bluff, I am not in a position to say, but judging the future by the past, we anticipate some trouble with him as he succeeded in getting his re leased from isolation on two occasions by using these same tactics. Until after the conference of the physicians, I shall not determine just when the forcible feeding will be started, but I am inclined to think that such a move will be unwise until he has lost some of his physical strength. He is a physical giant and will put up a desperate fi ght for the time being, at least.

Gardner has been confi ned in Isolation Quarters since his attempted escape

July 18, 1928 (one year and two month). Since the completion of the stockade wall, about August 12, he has had thirty minutes exercise in the morning and thirty minutes in the afternoon of each day. Three times daily he is furnished regular meals, served to him in his cell, of the same quality as that which is furnished other prisoners in the dining room. He receives the daily papers and is given books from the library by the Chaplain. He is confined in a single cell, which is 20 ft, 5 in. long, 8 ft wide, and 12 ft high, facing the south side of the building, with a window 3 ft 8 in wide and 6 ft 8 in high. His cell is equipped with running water. Because of his depressed attitude, it has been decided to forego his exercise for a few days, least he should attempt suicide by jumping from the second story where he is quartered.

I shall keep you informed, from time to time, as to the status of the case.

Respectfully yours,
A.C. Aderhold
Warden

September 23, 1929
Mr. A.C.A.
Re: 20850, Gardner

I also want to call your attention to a similar case in this institution some several years ago. The procedure followed for this man was to force his feedings. This was done but the amount of trauma, irritation, together with the amount of energy used by the prisoner in his struggles trying to prevent such feedings made the officials very doubtful as to whether or not very much good was gained by such procedure. However, the man was kept alive for a period of 62 days, but finally died.

In looking over the reports on Roy Gardner from the Leavenworth Penitentiary, I find a report of a similar action by him while incarcerated in that institution. At this time, October 10, 1925, Major Edgar King, consultant analyst to the Leavenworth Penitentiary, was asked to examine him. The summary of his report was: First, that Gardner was of a constitutional psychopathic, very unstable and paranoid, suffering at the time from a marked paranoid reaction motivated by the situation in which he now finds himself. Second, that transfer to Saint Elizabeth's Hospital, Washington, D.C. was not recommended, but that a transfer to the Atlanta Penitentiary was recommended, the reason being that the present episode, or mental disorder, would possibly pass away as a result of a change in environment. It was also stated that it was possible that he may not have a further episode of similar nature, but that it was not very probable, and that if he did have a recurrence of the above mental disorder, a transfer to Saint Elizabeth's should be recommended.

Dr. J. Galvin Weaver, a former physician to the United States Penitentiary here, was asked to see Gardner in consultation, because the case outlined above in which forced feedings were attempted was handled during his time as Prison Physician. It was deemed advisable to have Dr. Weaver see this man and perhaps receive his opinion on the advisability of forced feedings. His advice and impressions will not be given in this letter, but will be submitted in a separate report from him.

Respectfully yours,
J.B. Cross
Assistant Physician

November 12, 1929

To: Friend - Louie

Hello Friend of Mine:

Yours of Oct. 1st received on Wednesday. It went to Alcatraz first and then came here.

That five spot surely came in handy because my system craved sugar and I am spending it for candy and chocolate.

Many thanks my friend. As soon as I fatten up I will be sitting pretty, because the food here is excellent, and the doctors in charge of the hospital are the most considerate men I ever met. We are not treated like convicts. In fact we are treated just the same as other patients who are not criminals.

Here is an example of how we are treated. The other day Dr. Gilbert took me to his office for a mental examination and he addressed me as Mr. Gardner. Can you imagine a penitentiary official doing that? And what is more I smoked his cigarettes during the examination. If I held my hand on my hip until a prison official gave me cigarettes I surely would die a cripple. Dr. Gilbert is a highly educated man and a splendid fellow also.

I wish Louie you would send Dr. Gilbert a transcript of the trial in Phoenix if you have a copy of it. If not, then write up the facts in a letter and send it to him. It will help him in making up his records of me. Tell him especially about Dr. Ferguson's testimony when he said I was insane until the pressure on my brain was removed. Dr. Lind and Dr. Gilbert are not interested in physical or legal troubles. They are brain specialists and interested in brain troubles only.

I am glad you wired Mr. Hoover because it sure got results. They suddenly got busy in Atlanta and took me out of there on the 4th of this month. The warden got a wire from Washington at 2:00 P.M. and I left two hours later that's what I call action. What did you say to Mr. Hoover to get that much speed?

Now Louie don't worry about me getting away from here. I am coming out of here a free man in less than two years, and I'm not "goofy" enough yet to spoil a chance like that by trying to get away.

You know Louie, I am quite a poker player, and I know the value of an ace in the hole and I am sure going to play the hand to win. The opportunity I now have to come out legally has knocked the get-away question into a "cocked hat". So don't worry any more about that.

Now about those five spots you have been sending me. When you send a check it has to go through the clearinghouse before I can spend it and that takes about 10 days. But if you put a bill in the letter I can spend it the same day I get it. Of course Louie, I appreciate those checks and if it wasn't for you I never would get any smokes but I would rather have the cash.

You can tell me anything you want to tell me in your letters because our mail is not censored here and nobody will read your letters but me. If you have a couple of flannel shirts and some underwear that you don't need I wish you would send them to me. You and I wear about the same size shirts, 16 and a half or 17. We wear civilian clothes here and I have only got what I have on my back now.

Write soon.

Always your friend,
Roy - Roy Gardner
St Elizabeth's Hospital 3/7/33

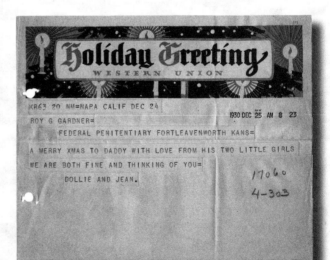

September 23, 1929

May 9, 1930
Phoenix, Arizona

From: L.S. Sonney - 15 East Washington Street, Phoenix, Arizona

To: Chairman and Honorable Board of Parole
C/o Federal Penitentiary - Leavenworth, Kansas

Dear Sir and Gentlemen:

Pardon the liberty I take in addressing myself to you in behalf of Roy Gardner who is confined in the Federal Penitentiary. I am appealing to you to kindly use your consideration and give the poor man another chance, and grant him his parole and allow him return to his little loyal wife and child, who I am sorry to say are without any means of support. The wife has a slight touch of tuberculosis, and finds it almost impossible to support her little girl, but nevertheless she is making out a small pittance by working in the hospital. There is no doubt in my mind that Roy Gardner pulled many stunts, which has brought him in the shadow of the law. And it is also true that he has on other occasions made escapes from custody at the risk of life and limb. But it is also a fact that in all of his escapades, he hurt no one or did any person bodily harm, as he has been proved on every occasion that he came within notice of the law. He invariably had an empty gun.

I am the officer who arrested him in Centralia, Washington, June 1st 1921. While wearing a disguise on his face, when I walked in on him at his motel and got him under control, I myself saw that his gun was empty. Compare such a man with Jesse James who always wore two guns loaded to the brim. Roy Gardner perhaps would have been able to better prove his case were he at the time of his arrest, able to get good counsel, who could lay his case before a jury and show that he was at the time suffering from a slight ma___ caused by an accident in a mine some years previous, and which the learned psychiatrist at Washington D.C. claimed was responsible for his actions.

Please Gentlemen, have a little consideration for the poor man, give him another chance to prove that he can be a good honest American and I know gentlemen that you will be doing a real humane act.

In my experience and travels, I have found many thousands of people who would be glad to sign a petition on behalf of this poor man Roy Gardner. If it is necessary, I can start this petition to your kindness, and I know that I can get thousands of business men, and men with whom Roy Gardner has come in contact with while enjoying honest freedom to beg of you to please give him another chance.

Please Gentlemen, Please.

When Roy Gardner's name is brought up before you for parole, use the power for good that is within you and give Roy Gardner another chance and I know that the Good Lord above will remember you for this one great act of clemency. Thank you gentlemen in advance for your attention to this, my petition in behalf of Roy Gardner.

Truly yours,
L.S. Sonney

L.S. Sonney. The man that arrested him at Centralia, Washington June 1st 1921.

June 23, 1932

To: A.H. MacCormick
Assistant Director Federal Prisons
Washington, D.C.

To: My Dear Mr. MacCormick

I talked with Mr. Bates yesterday and he told me of your efforts in my behalf. Please accept my sincere thanks Mr. MacCormick, and be assured you will never have cause to regret any action you have taken or may take in my behalf. I hope you never find yourself in a position where you need help, but should you find yourself in that position, I surely hope to be the man chosen to help you.

Should I be fortunate enough to make a parole, would it be possible for me to secure a commission in the Federal Service? (No stool pigeon service Mr. MacCormick, it would have to be a bonifi de commission).

After 11 years of constant association with Federal law violators, I have learned things that could not have been learned in any other way. I am vain enough to believe that I know the secret thoughts and actions of Federal violators from mail bandits down to dope fi ends well or better than any operative now in the Federal service. I know you have some clever operatives in the service, however they have not ate and slept with and listened to the confidences of as many Federal violators as I have. Also my reputation would give me enter into most any criminal circle and I could quickly secure evidence that would otherwise almost unobtainable through the regular channels of Federal investigation.

I realize Mr. MacCormick, this is an unusual request, however the unusual is a common occurrence in my life and I have become used to it.

If in your judgment this is a proper move for me to make, and you are willing to sponsor my application, please place me in communication with the proper authorities.

Of course Mr. McCormick, this is contingent on favorable action on my parole application by the Parole Board. I also wish to assure you that I will fulfill any and all recommendations you see fit to make in my behalf, and I will render absolutely honest service on any assignment I may get if I am fortunate enough to be accepted in the Federal service.

Please communicate with me though Warden Hudspeth, thus avoiding the prison censorship. My lawbreaking days are over now Mr. MacCormick, and I will appreciate an opportunity to prove that fact to the entire world and Federal officials in particular.

Very truly yours,
ROY GARDNER

September 28, 1932
To: Roy G. Gardner # 17080
Box 50 - Leavenworth, Kansas
From: L.S. Sonney

Dear Friend Roy:

I just received your letter and was very glad to hear from you. Yes, I have been coming east for a long time but you know how it is there is all ways something else before leaving home. I'll be coming east about the 15th of next month. I have the ex. Chief of Police of Tulare, which he wants to buy one half of my wax show, and I just have to wait. You know Mr. Hudspeth your Warden didn't send me any pass in order to see you. He stated in one of his letters that relatives are only allowed to see you. Too bad we are not brother-in-laws, according to his rules and regulations. Today I am writing to the Attorney General to see why I can't be allowed to see you if that don't give me any results, I will write direct to our President Hoover like I did before. You know I sure was surprised of you sending my letter to your wife. I always thought that you was a silent type. I have been telling people that when I turned you over to Marshall Hollahan he asked you, where did you get that gun that you stuck up his two deputies with? And your answer was, Marshall you never will know. Many people got a great kick out of that saying you never was a stooly, so I wish you would explain to me the reason why you sent the letter to your wife. I sure felt fully sorry, you should never have sent the letter to her and today I am in belief that something has come up from Napa preventing my visit. About your parole, you had better lay low and try to stay out of the hole otherwise you will lose by it.

I am sending you a five spot so you can smoke some Lucky's. I hope you didn't change the brand of the cigarettes that you used to use.

The talking pictures are wonderful. You will be surprised when you hear the melodrama voice of the famous Will Rogers. He sure makes you laugh when he opens up that nice looking mouth of his. Well this will be all for now, hoping to hear from you soon.

Your friend,
L.S. SONNEY
625 Stanford Ave
Los Angeles, California

Letters from Alcatraz

February 31, 1933

To: Roy G. Gardner #17080
Ft. Leavenworth, Kansas

Mr. Gardner:

In searching my letter records that I always keep, I found some of your valuable promises that you have gave me for the last 11 years. I also want you to notice especially Letter No. 8, where you asked me that question. I didn't give you the answer that time because I thought I was dealing with a square shooter, but after having spent a couple of thousand dollars and a lot of time begging a lot of in fl uential people and got you out of a lot of trouble. You changed the tune as soon as the real parole was coming up. You began to leave the friendship off. Remember that I have all the letters you have sent me and if you don't keep your promises, as you have told me for the last 11 years, I am going to make it a little hard for you.

This will be all for now, hoping to hear from you by return mail.

Sincerely yours,
Louis S. Sonney

P.S. Am sending some of the copies of letters I have received from you when you was in need, by emploring the Blessings of God.

NOTE ON BOTTOM OF LETTER

This letter is proof that Sonney will go to any extreme to injure me in the estimation of the Parole Board. If he cannot use me as a freak in his road show, he will try to block my release on parole.

ROY GARDNER - March 7, 1933

To: Warden,

Apparently this fellow is going to try to go over your head and get permission to visit me. If he shows up here with a pass to see me, tell him I am in conference and cannot be disturbed.

I don't want to see him. He got me "in bad" once before in 1924 by going over Warden Biddle's head, and I don't want a repetition of it now.

If you want additional reasons for barring him, consult Warden Zerbst. He made a gun play at Warden Zerbst at the other prison in 192 __.

Respectfully submitted.
By: ROY GARDNER

March 25, 1933

To: Warden
From: Roy Gardner

Warden if you are going to continue feeding us sausage and hot cakes for breakfast, I am going to decline a parole because I don't believe they feed like that at Boulder Dam.

I got that same identical breakfast (sausage, hot cakes, syrup, bread, butter and coffee) on a dining car in January 1930 and it cost the U.S. Marshall $1.25.

Keep the good work up Warden. The better class prisoners in here are for you 100 percent.

Sincerely yours,
ROY GARDNER

Letters from Alcatraz

February 12, 1934

From: Mrs. Dollie Gardner
Imola, Napa, California

To: Mr. Stanford Bates
Department of Justice
Washington, D.C.

Dear Sir:

I am taking the liberty of writing you concerning my husband Roy Gardner #17060, a prisoner incarcerated at present at Fort Leavenworth, Kansas.

Mr. Bates, I know that I have not much of an argument to put up in his favor as his record, especially on paper, is not a good one. Yet he will soon be gone 14 years, and I am so tired of just waiting with nothing to look forward to. So I take the liberty of writing you concerning Roy's parole. He is a man 50 years of age, and if he is ever to stage a comeback in private life, it will have to be done in the next few years. Maybe I am over confident in feeling that I can help to make Roy a good useful citizen.

I have raised our daughter, she being a baby when he went away, she is now in her 17th year and a lovely girl. I have lived a good life and I feel that I am a little more deserving than to have Roy returned to me decrepit old man to care for the rest of his days.

Mr. Bates, I realize that you have society to protect, and in face of the prevailing crime wave I ask you to consider paroling Roy and sending him back to us.

I made a visit to Washington, D.C. in Roy's behalf some years back, and recall the kind courteous treatment that I received at the Department of Justice, so it is with a friendly feeling I address you.

Sincerely,
Dollie Gardner

March 5, 1934
To: Dollie Gardner
From: Director Stanford Bates

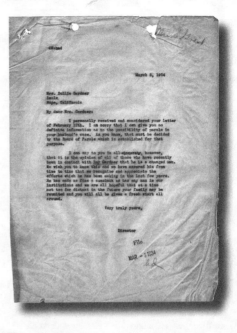

My Dear Ms. Gardner:

I personally received and considered your letter of February 12th. I am sorry that I can give you no definite information as to the possibility of parole in your husband's case. As you know that must be decided by the Board of Parole, which is established for that purpose.

I can say to you in all sincerity, however, that it is the opinion of all those who have recently been in contact with Roy Gardner that he is a changed man. We wish you to know this and we have assured him from time to time that we recognize and appreciate the efforts, which he has been making in the last few years. He has made a fine a comeback as has any man in our institutions and we are all hopeful that at a time not too far distant in the future, your family may be reunited and you will all be given a fresh start all around.

Very truly yours,
Director

Tuesday P.M.
To: Warden Johnston
Alcatraz, California

Warden my wife underwent a major operation yesterday, and considering the fact that she is in a weakened condition, her chances of recovery are bad.

It is customary in Federal prisons to permit an inmate to visit close relatives in case of serious illness or death, provided he has funds to pay the expenses of himself and the guard.

Will you permit me to go to Napa as soon as possible in order to be with her when she passes the crisis of her illness?

Respectfully submitted by,
Roy Gardner #110

POST OFFICE BOX 50

FORT LEAVENWORTH, KANSAS. *April 3rd* 193 4

Warden Hudspeth
    U.S. Federal Prison
            Warden, this is a request to be
placed on the eligible list for transfer to Alcatraz.
        I have studied this problem from every angle,
and it seems to be the logical move for me to make.
        It would enable me to again get acquainted
with my wife and daughter, whom I have not
seen for six years, and that would mean a
great deal to me. Also, I could make myself
useful to Warden Johnson, because he will
no doubt need an electrician he can trust.
        If you see fit to O.K. this transfer Warden, be
assured I will render the same loyal service
to Warden Johnson that I have rendered
to you, and if you care to make any recommendations
in my behalf those recommendations will
be fulfilled just 100 %.

                Respectfully submitted by
                        Roy Gardner #10 60.

P.S. Mr. Southcomb also thinks this is the
logical move for me to make.

                        R.G.

To Mr. Simpson

Mr. Simpson I recommend that you got a copy of Benny Leonard's book The Art of Self Defense" and read it.

Yours,
RG

P.S. You used to be able to dodge quick smatter? Have you slowed down, or just got old? During the broadcast last night, I heard Lucas say that you was a perfect sucker for a right swing, is that true?

January 23, 1936

To: Mr. Chandler

Mr. Chandler do you remember some time ago I asked you how you got that tin ear and you wouldn't tell me?

I just figured it out. You must have been winding up and the guy stepped in and "leaned" on you before you could unwind.

You was pretty lucky the other day. If that fellow hadn't reached over your shoulder while you was winding up, and tapped that con, the chances are the con would have made a total wreck of both your ears before you could unwind.

Yours in haste,
Gardner

P.S. You was luckier than Mr. Simpson at that. The con unwound him.

U. S. PENITENTIARY, ALCATRAZ, CALIFORNIA
DISCIPLINARY REPORT

Date...Jan. 24th...1936.   Time........A.M.
                                                         P.M.

Prisoner No....110.... Name...Gardner.... Cell............
has violated rule no..Disrespect, contempt & unmarnted Detail...Mat Shop....
Details -   familiarity with an Officer.

Attached is a letter I received from #110: also one received by Mr. Chandler from the same prisoner. These letters are self explanatory.

Signed J.H.Simpson   Title Jr. C. O.

February 16, 1936
To: Roy Gardner #110

Dear Daddy:

Well old bad luck kept me from coming down yesterday. Had the fl u and the old Doc wouldn't let me out. Haven't seen Jean yet, but I think she will come out to see me this p.m.

It just seems I get everything that comes along. My resistance seems so low, I guess Daddy I have gotten to the top of the hill and on the downward trail - forty you know now.

Daddy at this time I am in the hands of temptation a fi ne man wishes to make me his wife, as fi ne a man as I have met since you have been gone these 16 years. He can give me a home and care for me. What do you think of it Daddy? I am just asking you.

I read where George Austin, my good old friend is very sick, had a sudden heart attack. I would be so grieved if he should pass. There is only one G. Austin. There will never be another. He was as white a man as I ever met in the line of a government offi cial. He has just chased one mail bandit too many I think.

Hope Jean and you had a nice visit yesterday. She has rented an apartment and is spreading her wings. I hope I am able to keep her from spreading them too far. I will watch her.

Be good Daddy.
Always,

DOLLIE GARDNER

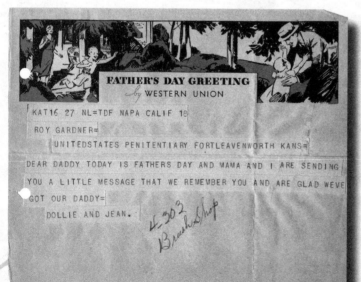

February 22, 1936

From: Roy Gardner #110
To: Dollie Gardner

Lo Girlie Dear:

Yours of the 17th received today and I was beginning to think the fl u had got you down.

Sure sorry to hear George Austin is sick. He is one man I really admired.

I can't write him so I wish you would drop him a line and tell him I am pulling for him. We saw a picture today "Ruggles of Red Gap" and I laughed my head off. It was a true portrayal of life.

I have been thinking hard about your temptation and I don't know how to advise you. It is a proposition you will have to decide for yourself because I don't know the man in question.

I am sure you made a mistake by waiting 16 years for me, however that 16 years is gone and you must look to the future instead of the past. I am going to be honest with you and tell you the truth, and then you will have to use your own judgment.

I still have about three years to go yet, and when I do come out I won't have a dollar. I don't know what I am going to do for a living, but I do know that I am not going hungry.

If you wait this other three years for me you may be glad or you may be sorry, it depends on how I fi nd conditions when I come out.

A bird in the hand is worth two in the bushes, and if you can insure your declining years by marrying that fellow, you had better take him because my future is sure uncertain.

Think it over carefully girlie, and then do as you think best.

Lovingly Daddy,
Roy Gardner

April 16, 1936

From: Dollie Gardner
To: Roy Gardner #110

Dear Daddy:

Received your letter a few days ago,
and really Daddy I did not like the little
references in it, or shall I say sarcasm. I
would not like you to take this matter in a
nasty little light.

I am doing this Daddy because I think it
is best. I am not well and I am so tired I
do not think you even realize. In 16 years,
I have never once laid the pack down, nor
have I ever had a soul I could put my hand
out to. Daddy if I could look forward to see
a light for us I could go on but today I
can not.

Well, Parker is a good man I think Daddy in principal, one of God's finest.
He neither drinks or smokes, and I would trust my child with him anywhere.
He is a Mason and an Odd Fellow. He is not very big but he has certainly
been good to Jean and I. I have known him three years.

No Daddy, I do not want you to look at this in any other than a straight
clean way, or I might not think of you as I would like to.

I will come to see you always and write as always.

My friend Roy Lockman has advised an annulment as the quickest way
without a lot of fuss and publicity. Will let you know. Please Daddy do not
get all upset. Will close now with love. Will write in a day or so.

Love,
Dollie

[Handwritten] Note:

Warden: You can prevent this marital wreck if you will just throw the
switch.
Roy G.

April 22nd 1936

To: Roy Gardner #110
From Dollie Gardner
271 San Jose Avenue
San Francisco, California

Daddy Dear:

I've gone and done it and I am so miserable. I didn't think that if I made up my mind it was for the best, that it would hit me so hard. So remember Daddy if you are miserable I am too. I took the annulment way, as it will be over and finished at one time. The newspapers can only yell once, it was better for Jean.

Please Daddy be good and don't kick over the traces. I will come to see you as soon as it is safe as the newspapers have be hounding me. I am too hysterical and cry babish now. When I think I can talk calm I will come.

I suppose after I get this I will have to write the Attorney General for a permit. I will write the Warden. Be good Daddy and remember you will always be with me.

With love,
DOLLIE

[Handwritten Note] She filed the annulment suit April 21st. If I could assure her that I would be released any day soon, I am sure she would withdraw the suit and wait for me.

Roy G.

July 12, 1936

To: Warden Johnston
From Roy Gardner #110

Warden Johnson:

Warden if my former wife asks permission to
visit me, please advise her that only relatives
are permitted. I prefer not to see her but I would
like to see my daughter.

Please do not let my wife know that I have
made this request. It would hurt her unnecessarily.

Respectfully,
Roy Gardner

Note:
July 15, 1936
Interviewed - Told him I would act in accordance with his request.
J.J. [James Johnston]

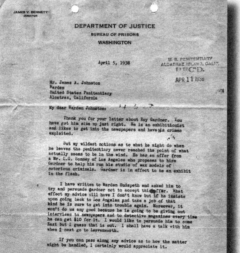

April 5, 1938

To: Mr. James A. Johnston, Warden
United States Penitentiary
Alcatraz, California

From: James V. Bennett, Director
Department of Justice
Bureau of Prisons
Washington, D.C

My Dear Warden Johnston:
    Thank you for your letter about
Roy Gardner. You have got him sized
up just right. He is an exhibitionist
and likes to get into the newspapers
and have his crimes exploited.
    But my wildest notions as to what
he might do when he leaves the penitentiary never reached the point of
what actually seems to be in the wind.
He has an offer from a Mr. L.G. Sonney

of Los Angeles who proposes to hire Gardner to help him run his studio of wax models of notorious criminals. Gardner is in effect to be an exhibit in the fl esh.

I have written to Warden Hudspeth and asked him to try and persuade Gardner not to accept this offer. What effect my advice will have I don't know but if he insists upon going back to Los Angeles and take a job of that kind he is sure to get into trouble again. Moreover, it won't do us any good because he is going to be giving out interviews to newspapers and to detective magazines every time he can get $10 for it. I would like to per-suade him to come east, but I guess that is out. I shall have a talk with him when I next go to Leavenworth.

If you can pass along any advice as to how the matter might be handled, I certainly would appreciate it.

Yours very truly,
James V. Bennett

June 7, 1938

To: J. V. Bennett
Washington, D.C.
From: Roy Gardner

Dear Sirs:

Upon the advice of Warden Hudspeth, I am submitting for your approval a rough draft of my MMS based on Alcatraz. Also a scenario book on the story. I am sorry I could not have the MMS completely typed, how-ever my typewriter connection blew up and I had to fi nish the rough draft in longhand.

When rewritten and smoothed out I feel sure the MMS will bring me in some much needed cash. Also you will see that I am not directing criticism to-ward any Federal offi cial in fact, I intend to dedicate the book to Warden Johnston. If you fi nd anything objectionable in the MMS, please blue-pencil it and it will be deleted. Also I will appreciate any constructive criticism you may offer.

On page 51 of the MMS you will find a list of the notorious characters that I intend to present to the reading public in their true light. A short two or three page biography of each of those fellows will round out the MMS to about 60,000 words, and probably double the sale. If it is not asking too much Mr. Bennett, I will appreciate it if you will arrange for me to be supplied with a picture and the case histories of those men. It would save me a lot of expensive research, which I am not able to bear at the present time. I feel sure Warden Johnston would be willing to furnish it if you would suggest it to him. Also I would be glad to submit the finished MMS to either you or Warden Johnston for censorship before I submit it to the publishers.

In closing I wish to assure you Mr. Bennett that I am going out (June 17th) without any feeling of bitterness toward any Federal official. In fact I consider a number of officials, including yourself, as personal friends and I value that friendship highly.

I realize it is going to be tough sledding for me until I become socially acclimated, and I would like very much to keep in touch with you Mr. Bennett, and to feel that I could call on you for advice if and when I need it.

Warden Hudspeth advised me that you were in touch with Singer Machine Company, regarding employment for me. That will suit me fine.

The cataract on my eye is handicapping me for precision work, however I intend to have the cataract removed as soon as I am financially able.

I am going from here to Los Angeles, and then to San Francisco about July 1st. Please address me in care of Warden Johnston until such time as I secure a permanent address.

Respect fully submitted by,
Roy Gardner
July 14, 1938

To J.V. Bennett
Director

From: Roy Gardner
Hotel Governor
Turk and & Jones
San Francisco, California

Dear Sir:

In 1931 or '32, Mr. Sonney wrote a letter to Warden Hudspeth accusing me of having immoral relations with a Mexican girl in Phoenix, Arizona in 1921. Warden Hudspeth sent the letter on to Mr. Bates and Mr. MacCormick asked me about it in 1932. I would like very much like to get that letter, or a copy of it, Mr. Bennett because I am now being threatened with legal action by Sonney. The letter is on file in your office, and if you will send it to me, I will return it within ten days.

Sincerely yours,
Roy Gardner

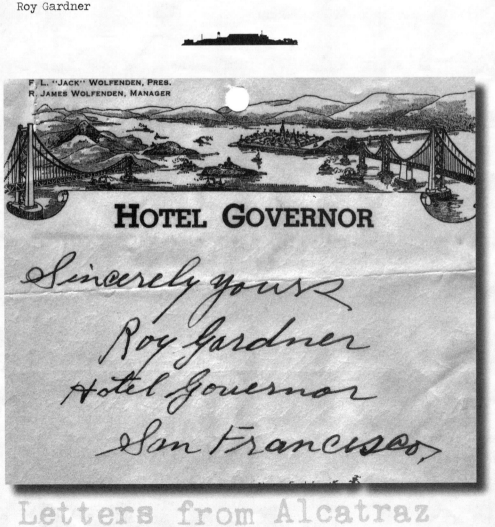

F. L. "JACK" WOLFENDEN, PRES.
R. JAMES WOLFENDEN, MANAGER

HOTEL GOVERNOR

Sincerely yours
Roy Gardner
Hotel Governor
San Francisco,

January 17, 1940

To: James A. Johnston
Warden
United States Penitentiary
Alcatraz, California

From: James V. Bennett
Director

My Dear Warden Johnston:

I read in the newspapers with some dismay of the suicide of Roy Gardner. He chose the same spectacular manner of taking himself out of the world, as he had followed all his life.

I would like to see the text of the final note he left. If you could get a copy of it for me, I would very much appreciate it.

Sincerely yours,
James V. Bennett

Roy Gardner playing cards with a fellow inmate at a county jail just prior to being transferred to U.S.P. Atlanta, circa 1925.

copies of notes left by Roy Gardner when he
committed suicide date —————— *Jan 26 1940 taken from originals*
~~filed~~ in his own hand writing which are filed in
~~coroners~~ office San Francisco, Calif

To Whom it may Concern

Please deliver my body to Halsted & Co. 1123 Sutter St. they know
what to do with it.
  Call R. P. Nelson, Trinidad 5377, Oakland, and tell him there is a
letter of instructions here for him. He is my brother-in-law, and he
will make the necessary arrangements with Halsted & Co.

To the newspapers

Please,(the last request from me) do not mention my daughters married
name in connection with this. Her in-laws do not know she is my
daughter, and it would probably wreck her happiness if they found it
out..
        Thanks boys.
          Roy Gardner.

To the newspaper reporters.

Please let me down as light as possible boys. I have played ball with
you all the way, and now you should pitch me a slow one and let me hit it.
  I am checking out simply because I am old and tired, and don't care
to continue the struggle.
  There are no love affairs or disappointments of any kind connected with
this in any way, just tired thats all.
  I hold no malice toward any human being, and I hope those whom I have
wronged will forgive me for it.
  If I had realized what the future held for me, I would have "checked out"
in 1920 and saved my loved ones the disgrace and shame that they have
had to endure these many years. Also I would have dodged plenty of grief
that I endured unnecessarily.
  All men who have to serve more than 5 years in prison are doomed, but they
don't realize it! They kid themselves into the belief that they can
"come back", but they can't there is a barrier between the ex-convict
and society that cannot be leveled.
  Every man on Alcatraz today would be better off if they would jump in
the bay and start swimming to China. If you think I am wrong, just watch
Mooney or Beesemeyer and see how they wind up.
  I did not decide to check out on the spur of the moment. In fact I bought
the cyanide 2 months ago for this very purpose. I got it at a drug store on
the north side of Market st. near Kearney. I don't remember what name I
signed, but my address was given 1404 Post St.
  Good bye and good luck boys, and please grant my last request. Thanks.
              Sincerely yours
                Roy Gardner.

Do Not open this door. Poison gas. Call police.
  (Above was written on the back of Hotel Governor stationery.)

      Do not disturb.
  (Above was also written on the back of Hotel Governor stationery.)

Edward Wutke

ANOTHER ALLEGED casualty of the silent system was thirty-six year old inmate Edward Wutke. Prior to his imprisonment at Alcatraz, Wutke was an able seaman employed on the steamship Yale. When a friendly drunken scuffle with a close friend turned into a serious fight, Wutke drew a small pocketknife and stabbed his friend in the groin area, fatally severing his femoral artery. The wounded man would bleed to death before the ship made it into port at San Diego. Wutke became panic-stricken upon realizing the gravity of his act and had to be shackled to a fixed object. Following his conviction for murder on the high seas, Wutke became withdrawn, and was sent to Alcatraz because of what officials described as a "desperate disposition."

On December 27, 1934 Wutke refused to report to his work assignment, and was sent to the lower solitary unit below A Block, better known as the "dungeon." He would remain in the damp, dark dungeon for eight days. Wutke made his first suicide attempt in January of 1936. He complained that he was unable to do his time "under the present conditions," and indicated that the silence and harsh rules had finally become unbearable. Using a small contraband blade, he sliced a prominent vein near the elbow, and bled profusely before a guard was able to intervene. The resident physician sutured the inmate's wound and then admitted him to the hospital for an examination by the prison psychiatrist.

Wutke's unsuccessful suicide attempt would only intensify his hatred of the Alcatraz regimen. He remained incorrigible, and found himself locked in solitary on at least three later occasions.

Deputy Warden E.J. Miller and Dr. Beacher were called to Wutke's cell on November 13, 1937, after the prisoner was found dead by one of the officers. Following his suicide, numerous stories were leaked to the press alleging harsh confinement practices at Alcatraz. Countless inmates believed that the unrelenting torture of strict confinement had contributed to several inmates "going crazy."

Edward Wutke was buried on Novem-ber 17, 1937, at the Cypress Lawn Cemetery in Colma, California, with only a small marker with the plot number #66 engraved. Fellow inmates had felt that Wutke's suicide was a serious injustice and they viewed him as somebody who "was not prison material." He was described as being too easy going and found death more favorable than spending the majority of his life behind bars on Alcatraz. Though no letters directly from Wutke were ever known to be preserved, a singular letter in his file from a family member represents a tragic finale to a life gone cold at Alcatraz.

```
Warden of U.S. Pen.
Alcatraz
California


Dear Sir
    Having heard that Edward
Wutke is a prisoner at Alca-
traz his parents would like
to know on what charge he
has been sentenced. The file
number is 12020-26644.


    Yours truly,
    Henry Wutke
    1843 Trumbull St.
    Bay City
    Michigan
```

[Handwritten Note] Interviewed Wutke #47 says writer is his brother (half brother). That he has not written to him as he did not want to on account of his imprisonment but inasmuch as his relatives appear interested he will write –

JAJ 10/7/36

Letters from Alcatraz

Henry Wutke
1843 Trumbull St.
Bay City, Mich.

Dear brother Edward,

We received your letter and were very sorry to hear that you are in prison. We know that you always try to do right and avoid trouble so we believe it could not have been your fault.

The first news we had of your whereabouts was when a man from the Dept. of Labor came down from Flint, Mich. and inquired if you where an alien. Mother and Dad gave him all the information they could and he seemed satisfied and went away.

We are sending you a little money 5$ in Money Order and if there is anything we

can do for you we would be glad to help.

I know you would like to hear some news of the family so here goes.

We are all well and Dad and I are working every day. Mary is married to Cecil MacDonald who teaches at the local high school. Julia is living in Flint and has seven children 6 girls and one boy. One of her girls married about 2 months ago.

I forgot to say that Mary has a 4 month old baby boy it's named James Henry. That is all can think to write at this time. Please write soon.

Your brother and family

Henry

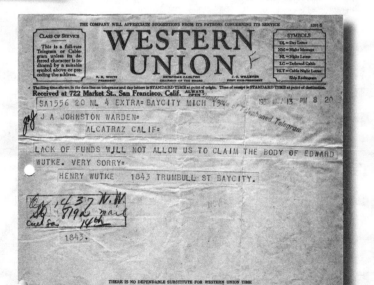

WESTERN UNION

LACK OF FUNDS WILL NOT ALLOW US TO CLAIM THE BODY OF EDWARD WUTKE. VERY SORRY=

HENRY WUTKE   1843 TRUMBULL ST BAYCITY.

Robert Stroud
"The Birdman of Alcatraz"

ROBERT Franklin Stroud, the infamous "Birdman of Alcatraz", emerged as an iconic figure in America's 20th century history. He was seen by many as a martyr of America's penal system, becoming a self-educated and self-proclaimed ornithologist while serving over 54-years in prison; 42 of those spent in solitary confinement. Stroud's image and the circumstances of his murder convictions were softened by a gentle portrayal in a best-selling biography written by Thomas Gaddis, later made into a major Hollywood motion picture.

Stroud was never permitted to have birds at Alcatraz, leaving left behind a thriving breeding business at Leavenworth Federal Penitentiary up until his transfer in 1942. In 1909, Stroud was convicted of murder in Juneau, Alaska, of a 33-year old bartender who worked at the Montana Saloon, one of Stroud's frequent haunts. Stroud had come to Alaska in 1907 and was allegedly known by many as the "Peanut Kid" for selling peanuts on the streets and working odd jobs in the red light district in the now abandoned small town of Katella. It was here he had met Cordova prostitute and cabaret dancer Kitty O'Brien. One article derived from early Alaska oral histories described O'Brien as a "faded, wrinkled, blonde who was a wild-living drug addict, alcoholic and whore." The *Daily Record* in January of 1909 wrote "Her face is badly marred with sores at

Biographer Thomas Gaddis (right) on the set of Birdman of Alcatraz with Hollywood actor Burt Lancaster in November of 1960. Lancaster's softened portrayal inspired thousands worldwide to lobby for the release of convicted murderer Robert Stroud. While their efforts proved unsuccessful, the actor's depiction won the public's sympathy and cast Stroud into history as a martyr of the American penal system. Gaddis's biography became a literary classic, and also helped shape the public image of conditions at Alcatraz, even decades after its closure.

edly murdered the bartender using a .38 Colt revolver for failing to pay O'Brien for sex, for whom he was pimping in Alaska. After the murder, Stroud took the man's wallet to ensure that he and the prostitute would receive compensation for her services. In 1911, Stroud was convicted of manslaughter and sent to serve out his sentence at McNeil Island, a Federal penitentiary in Washington State. During his trial, the *Daily Record* reported that Stroud "appeared to glory in the notoriety that he obtained by the killing."

His inmate case file indicates that he was a violent and difficult prisoner to manage. While serving his sentence at McNeil Island, he viciously attacked another inmate. This resulted in his transfer to U.S.P. Leavenworth, Kansas. In 1916, he murdered a Leavenworth guard, was convicted of first-degree murder and received a death sentence. His mother pleaded for his life, and in 1920, President Woodrow Wilson commuted the death sentence to life imprisonment.

It was Stroud's violent behavior that earned him time in segregation. Over the course of Stroud's thirty years of imprisonment at Leavenworth, he developed a keen interest in canaries, after finding an injured bird in the recreation yard. Stroud was initially allowed to breed birds and maintain a lab inside two adjoining seg-

the present." She was known by locals for robbing drunks and disorderly conduct, but she had somehow developed a close bond with Stroud. The Record wrote, "They were both degenerates and criminally inclined."

Although the details of the incident remain vague and unclear, Stroud alleg-

Robert Stroud, circa 1909, McNeil Island.

(Top) Philip Bergen visited Stroud's prison cell at Leavenworth (depicted here in the motion picture Birdman of Alcatraz) prior to his transfer to the Rock. He stated that his two adjoining cells looked very similar to those replicated in the classic motion picture. Stroud often had his birds perform circus style tricks and his cell was a favored stop for visitors touring U.S.P. Leavenworth. Bergen indicated that there were "absolutely no accurate parallels" between Stroud and the character depicted by Burt Lancaster.

(Middle) Burt Lancaster received an Academy Award® nomination for his portrayal of Robert Stroud, the infamous Birdman of Alcatraz. Lancaster had never met Stroud before or during film production, but developed an idealistic and humane characterization of his subject. Many of the officers who guarded Stroud depicted him as a genius whose personality was "composed, manipulative, and calculated with vicious, predatory, and murderous ideals."

(Bottom) Despite his designation as the Birdman of Alcatraz, Stroud was never permitted to have any birds while imprisoned on the Rock, but had been allowed to complete one of his avian books and for a limited period continued public correspondence relating to bird care. Philip Bergen, Captain of the Guards, indicated that once Edwin Swope was appointed as the new Alcatraz Warden in 1948, he stripped Stroud of all remaining privileges that were not in compliance with the standard set of rules and regulations. Swope banned all outside correspondence and fully isolated him from all avian forums and communities.

Letters from Alcatraz

Stroud at the Federal Penitentiary in Leavenworth, Kansas, circa 1912.

Stroud's informal research, prison officials discovered that some of the equipment he had requested was actually being used to construct a still to make an alcoholic brew.

Stroud was transferred to Alcatraz in 1942, where he spent the next 17 years (6 years in segregation in "D Block" and 11 years in the prison hospital). In 1959 he was transferred to the Medical Center for

regation cells, since it was felt that this activity would provide for productive use of his time. As a result of this privilege, Stroud was able to author two books on canaries and their diseases, having raised nearly 300 birds in his cells, carefully studying their habits and physiology, and he even developed and marketed remedies for various bird ailments. Although it is widely debated whether the remedies he developed were effective, Stroud was able to make scientific observations that would later benefit research on the canary species. However, after several years of

Federal Prisoners in Springfield, Missouri, and there on November 21, 1963, he was found dead from natural causes by convicted spy, close friend and former Alcatraz inmate Morton Sobell. Stroud had never been allowed to read the biography of his life story, and was also never been permitted to see the movie in which Burt Lancaster portrayed him as a mild-mannered and humane individual. *Birdman of Alcatraz* later earned Lancaster an Academy Award nomination for best actor. During the televised broadcast of the ceremonies in April of 1963, Stroud was able to view a short movie clip of Lancaster's portrayal as an aging Stroud. In one account, it was stated that when Lancaster the lost the Oscar to Gregory Peck for his role in *To Kill a Mock-*

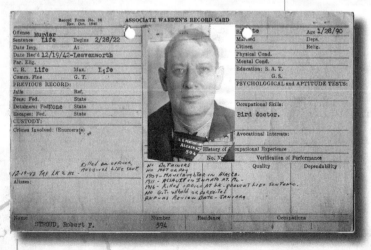

Robert Stroud, at U.S.P. Alcatraz in December of 1942. Stroud spent the entire duration of his imprisonment on Alcatraz in isolation. He was never permitted to integrate into the general population.

Letters from Alcatraz

An Appeal For Justice For One Who Has Given Years of Valuable Service to the Canary Hobby

By DELLA JONES

You all know Robert Stroud. For years you have seen his advertising, you have bought his birds, you have told him your troubles, you have had him examine your seed; and when contagion struck in your flock, you have wired for his *specific*. And in every case you have received prompt and valuable service. You may have addressed your letters to E. J. Stroud, but the long helpful letters of advice that came back were always signed by Robert Stroud. Often these letters were hard to read, but they gave you a new insight into the causes of your trouble, and explicit instructions that were not hard to follow.

You have expressed the desire to meet this extraordinary man. Maybe you have invited him to call at your plant when in your neighborhood, maybe you have expressed the hope that you would be able to see him at one of the Kansas City shows, and maybe you have gone to the trouble of calling at his Kansas City address. But in every case you have been disappointed. When you called, the little white haired woman who identified herself as E. J. Stroud always informed you that her son was not at home.

Recently you have had the pleasure of reading many fine articles from the pen of Robert Stroud. The Roller Canary Journal has been glad to secure the exclusive rights to these articles, for they have treated the more serious diseases of canaries in a scientific, yet understandable manner, made possible only by Mr. Stroud's many years of original research.

Surely, you all know Robert Stroud, but you have not known that this service came to you from a solitary cell; that the man who labored into the dead of night, every night, that you who enjoy freedom might be saved from worry and the loss of your birds, has never in his entire adult life been free.

Robert Stroud was born at Seattle, Washington, January 28, 1890. Due to a ruptured home he was thrown out upon his own resources at the age of 13. He became a wanderer and eventually found himself in Alaska. In Juneau, Alaska, January 18, 1909, he killed a man who had abused a woman with whom he was friendly.

Robert Stroud

The woman, old enough to be his mother and of questionable character, was arrested with him. Stroud claimed that he had acted in self-defense, but in order to free the woman, he took all blame and accepted a plea of guilty to manslaughter and a sentence of 12 years in prison. He had been in prison 7 years when a brutal guard tried to club him. The guard was killed. The many witnesses testified that Stroud had acted purely in self-defense, he was sentenced to death. He was saved from death by the late President Wilson. He has been confined in solitary at the United States Penitentiary at Leavenworth, Kansas, since March 26, 1916.

Facing a life sentence in solitary confinement, Stroud set out to find some method of earning money. His mother had reduced herself to poverty and debt to save his life, and he hoped that he might find some way whereby he could at least partially repay this debt, which of course, he could never hope to fully repay. He had always been interested in pets but had never tried breeding them. No pet birds were permitted in the prison; no prisoner was permitted to sell anything of his own production, and he was the last who could hope to obtain special favor.

Undismayed by these handicaps, Stroud set out to establish himself in the bird business. He caught a pair of sparrow chicks, raised them on bits from his own food, and taught them to do tricks. He finally got permission to get bird seed for them. It took one year to get his first canary, and it took another year to get a mate for her. It took a year to get a box from which he could build his first cage, and he had to build it with a safety razor blade and a nail for tools. But all this time Stroud was reading birds, observing birds, thinking birds. He had to move with extreme caution, but he did move, and it was ever forward toward his goal.

Living with birds as few have, he studies them as none have. The limitations of his environment made it difficult for him always to get the things that they needed, and misfortune after misfortune overtook his small flock. Rickets and iodide deficiency took his young. He studied until he had found the cause and the cure. Septic fever decimated his flock and he cured it and thus discovered his well known *specific* for Avian Septicaemias. With a persistency that refused to be defeated he rose above each failure and disappointment; and each time came out fortified with new knowledge.

Slowly, surely, with unlimited patience, this man has plodded on and on, day after day, year after year, he has built up his birds and his knowledge of them. That lonely solitary cell has been converted into one of the best appointed bird rooms to be found anywhere—$500 worth of new equipment, a thousand dollars worth of fine birds that represent years of skilful breeding. He has put thousands of dollars into the development of his treatment, and with its aid he has saved hundreds of breeders from serious losses. He has educated and equipped himself to study the diseases of birds, scientifically, and by this study he has added immeasurably to human knowledge. The results of these researches this Journal has been glad to pass along to you. In his treatment he has discovered a hitherto unknown chemical reaction that permits him to kill the germs of a septicaemic disease in the blood stream without harming the patient. He has made the ignorant, uneducated boy who entered prison 22½ years ago

---

ingbird, Stroud remained stoic and simply got up and headed off to bed. At the time of his death, he had served the longest term in solitary confinement than any other federal inmate in American history.

This collection is primarily comprised of correspondence during his incarceration while segregated at U.S.P. Leavenworth.

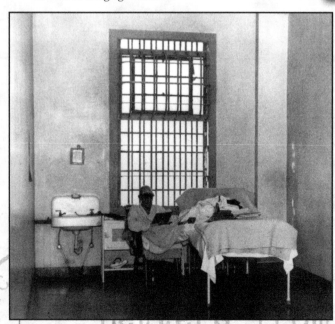

(Above) Stroud, circa 1951.

(Above) Stroud was confined in D-Block from 1942 to 1948, residing in D-4 along the flats and cell-41, second to last cell on right of the upper tier. Stroud remained in this location during the Battle of Alcatraz in 1946, surviving heavy gun and mortar fire while barricaded behind wet mattresses for cover.

(Below) Robert Stroud was transferred from Alcatraz to the Federal Medical Prison at Springfield Missouri in 1959 and subsequently released from isolation status. By the time of transfer, he had already served more than forty-two years in isolation.

(Bottom right) A contemporary photo of Stroud's cell. It remains reminiscent of the period when he was secluded here. This area of the prison remains isolated with only limited public access to the hospital ward.

(Bottom left) Robert Stroud seen reading a book in his Alcatraz Hospital Ward Cell. Stroud would remain isolated in this cell from 1948 until 1959. Initially Stroud was forced to use a bedpan to relieve himself until a toilet was installed in July of 1956. Stroud spent eleven years locked down in this cell with only one visit to the recreation yard per week, usually by himself. He would spend a total of seventeen years on Alcatraz, with all of his time in a segregated status.

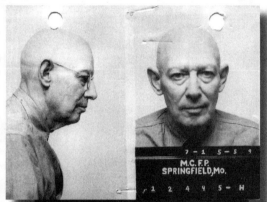

JANUARY 30TH 1915

Mr. Fred G. Zerbst,
Deputy Warden U. S. P.

Sir:-

Stroud Reg. No. 8154, is af fl icted with chronic nephritis (Bright's Disease) of a mild type, but suffi ciently severe to necessitate his remaining in the hospital most of the winter months and during periods of inclement weather.

On account of the man's disposition to be meddlesome and his inability to comply with the hospital rules in small matters, his presence is demoralizing, and I suggest that you give him quarters in the isolation building, at least temporarily, where he will be equally well housed and can be served his milk and medicine without detriment to his physical condition.

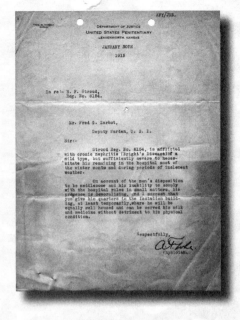

        Respectfully,
        A.F.W.
        Physician.

ADDRESS REPLY TO
"THE ATTORNEY GENERAL"
AND REFER TO INITIALS AND NUMBER

DEPARTMENT OF JUSTICE,
WASHINGTON, D.C.
T.H.D.

July 8, 1916.
Mr. Thomas W. Morgan
Warden, United States Penitentiary,
Leavenworth, Kansas.

Sir:

For your information there is enclosed herewith a copy of a letter this day addressed to the United States Marshal at Topeka, Kansas, relative to the execution of prisoner Robert Stroud.

The Department thinks that a suitable place can be found for the execution within the prison inclosure and entirely out of sight of the prisoners. If the execution is fixed to take place early in the morning, say between midnight and 6 a.m., it would not disturb the daily routine of the institution and it would save locking up the prisoners, which would have to be done if the execution took place during the day.

Respectfully,
For the Attorney General,
Assistant Attorney General.

December 12, 1928

The Honorable E Lewis
U.S. Circuit Court
St. Louis, MO

Hon. Sir:

This is an appeal to you for a recommendation of executive clemency written by Robert F. Stroud whom it was your disagreeable duty once to sentence to death.

This appeal is not predicated upon your sentence of any kind, there is no desire to play upon your sympathies so all facts that would tend in that direction will be passed over lightly; though of necessity some must be touched upon, there are other facts that you will no doubt find more interesting; those will be treated in some detail.

When I found myself facing a sentence of life in solitary confinement, upon the commutation of my death sentence in 1920, I was somewhat downcast. To sneer at death is easy, but it is not easy to sneer at four blank walls of a cell, or at the face of men over you who are bitter because they have failed to bring about your destruction. It was under such circumstances that I faced the most difficult problem of such circumstances that I faced the most difficult problem of my life, the re-organization of my whole system of life and thought. I had contended at my trial that my act was justified I did not, or have I now, abandoned that contention, but I had from the very first realized that just or unjust it had been foolish and expensive. A lot of innocent persons have been made to suffer - no one had benefited. I left deeply upon this subject, for I believe that every man is fully responsible for the results of every act. He may not be able to discharge that responsibility, but he is morally obliged to make an effort to do so.

In this case the possibilities of doing anything in that direction looked absolutely hopeless. There was just one point which I was determined, and that was to incur no new obligations, and to do this even involved finding a way to earn money, for I had developed an intestinal

trouble which made fruit and green food a necessity in my diet. This could
be bought but I had no taste for them if the funds were to be supplied by
my mother, who had reduced herself to the status of a factory hand to save
money to save my unworthy life. By all these laws of right and justice
it was my duty to try to make it the other way around. It was with these
thoughts that I searched my environments for a means of converting my
modest ability into an income. I don't cite these refl ections because they
are to my credit; they are not. It is to my discredit that they did not put
in an appearance much earlier in my life, before such mess had been made
of things. They are only mentioned because they furnished the motivating
impulse for my actions that followed.

My fi rst efforts were of an artist nature. From a fellow prisoner I got
a box of water color paint and a few pieces of bristle board. From these
fancy greeting cards which were sent out to friends who disposed of them
for me. These sales were disguised as gifts for at this time no prisoner
was permitted to sell any object of his creation (It took some years of
painstaking effort to change this rule). With the funds thus obtained better tools and materials were acquired just as fast the permission to have
them could be obtained. This was not always easy for two factors had to be
constantly considered. First; the animosity created by my four years battle
for life had to be overcome, and second; it was necessary to avoid exciting
the envy of jealousy of more indolent prisoners. You can be sure that I had
to walk softly. The development of perfect self control was an absolute necessity.

Despite discouragement I made progress. With no great ability, I learned
to draw and color, I progressed from water colors to oil and I managed to
create salable pictures in both. My process of doing so was extremely laborious, however with what was lacking in the native skill had to be made up
by patient work. This tolled upon the eyes and after six years of work had
to be given up. It was given up without deep regret. It had served its purpose by fi nancing my other effort.

When still under a sentence of death a book on canaries came into my
hand. It was read with care. The possibilities of these delightful little
creatures as a means of revenue greatly appealed to me. I could picture the
long walls of my cell covered with the cages full of birds with many sales
at good profi t. This dream was confi ded to but few and those that did not
it pronounced it a plan of madness. "How are you, whom they won't even let
have a pen point, going to get permission for all these things, how could
you sell the birds if you had them?" I confess I did not know... I was logi-
cally hopeless, but refused to give up.

One of my fi rst acts after commutation was to catch a pair if young
sparrows; they were nesting and had fallen into the little court where at
this time I was permitted thirty minutes per day for exercise. They were
taken to my cell and there fed by hand upon bits of my own food as they
grew up they became very friendly and were taught a number of tricks. They
were well educated before anyone's attention was called to the fact that I

had them; they were then shown to the deputy warden and made to do their tricks. He being a great pet lover was very much interested in them. During the discussion the idea was put over that they could not thrive for long without bird seed. The result was that I was granted permission to but bird seed-something I could not have a chance to get had I been chumpy enough to ask for it. That was the first step.

It took one year to get my first canary, another year to get my first cage which was made from a packing box with the aid of a razor blade and a nail for tools. These like the sparrows were acquired as opportunity presented or could be created, for I had to step carefully, believe me. This first permission I asked regarding the canaries was when I had the birds of my own breeding sent out.

My first birds were common chopper canaries. The money derived from these was used to stock fancy rollers. The first cage grew to a row, to two rows, until my whole cell was covered with cages until much of my dream had come true. Until I had created a profitable bird business from the four blank walls of my solitary cell.

I now stocked from forty to eighty high class rollers, have a new strain of my own creation well on the road to perfection and will raise and sell from three hundred to five hundred dollars worth per year. And as I live with birds I study they - probably more closely than any free person with a multitude of interests could do. This study has been very interesting and the happiest hours of my life have been spent right here with my birds. Their exacting needs, the fact that I am responsible for their health and happiness has much to do with the regulating of my own habits. Their value represents a property right; the building up of that value and its enjoyments has given me a broader view of property right than I ever had before. If a dealer ships me unfit seed or sick birds I demand correction. If it is not forthcoming I return the goods at his expense or send a wire that will eat up any profit that he had made by his dishonesty or carelessness. I know how I feel in such cases, and knowing that I don't want people to feel so towards me is the best incentive in the world for avoiding such practice. The result is that I have not a single dissatisfied customer. But while the effort of this business upon my character and outlook has been great, these have been even greater results in other directions.

The condition under which I keep my birds, are unique and to meet the needs of the birds decrease labor, and make the most of my available room. I have designed each item of my equipment along lines intended to make it give me the greatest service, and the greatest return on my investment and labor. This has led to a number of original features; some of which are undoubtedly patentable and of commercial value. These have been passed on for the benefit of other breeders.

I have carried on extensive experiments in foods which have added new knowledge. Some of this knowledge has been on to the fancy: some of it of greater commercial value has been retained. One discovery relating to the relation of certain minerals to the reproduction is now being commercialized by the Miracus Bird Food Company of Clifton Hill, MO., a concentration organized for that purpose; a creation of my imagination.

The facts merely show that I have been competent along the line to which my efforts have been devoted. They are not greatly to my credit or otherwise. Another so situated might do the same thing, but this competency is exactly of that kind that leads to the success in any field, under any circumstances. It is for that reason and also because it forms a background of what is to follow that I have gone into such details. I must now digress for a moment.

There is a disease which is known by such various names as septic fever, cholera, canary nervosas, canary typhoid, septicemia, shipping fever and others. This disease is due to the action of two germs, one of which attacks the internal organs (those of digestion), and one of which attacks the lungs, throat, mouth, head and other parts of the body. This disease is highly contagious, and heretofore was practically always fatal. The germs have a period of from fourteen to twenty-one days of incubation. The birds infected can spread the disease from an entire juiary or bird room before they can be detected. Thus it causes great loss; frequently running into thousands of dollars and wiping out entire flocks.

The desire is an interrupted fever on the one hand and is closely related to Diphtheria and is the same as in a human being. Croup in poultry is not identical with them; it is also more or less closely related to Erysipelas. Scarlet Fever and other diseases of this nature and has many curious points of resemblance to hoof and mouth disease among cattle. And it may here be noted that it originated in the same part of central Europe as did human Diphtheria (I wonder if the hoof and mouth disease also came from that locality, as much of our cattle did).

On the other hand microscopic examination of the exterior shows the presence of large numbers of the germs of avian cholera of a very malignant variety. This aspect of infection shows a close relationship to such infection as cholera in both hogs and human beings as well to other contagious of the intestinal tract.

This disease was introduced into my flock last spring with some imported birds that I had bought. It ran through my stock like wild fire. It took fifty birds and cost me at least five hundred dollars, but it was subjected to much closer study from a sympathetic angle than ever before published. Many new facts were discovered concerning its nature and diagnosis. The existence of germ carriers had long been suspected. This was definitely established and described; but still my birds were being lost at the rate of three per day. Fully expecting to lose my entire stock, I was determined to get all knowledge possible from the experience. With this end in view, I undertook a series of experiments and based upon the theory that most doctors would call absurd. That was that there must be some substance that would kill the germs inside the birds but that would not harm the birds. I began adding germicide to their food. Frankly this was done without hope. I tried things that no sane person would try, and observed results. Driven by desperation, I found what I sought; a non-poisonous germicide, with a germ killing power comparing favorably with carbolic acid and potassium permanganate. I cured birds at the point of death in a matter of a few hours. I established the fact that this substance kills all of the germs in the digestive tract at the first administration and that it greatly reduced the number in the blood stream. Eruptive processes on the various parts of the body healed without local treatment, though as a matter of fact they healed quicker when local treatment was given.

This is important from the bird keepers point of view. It is easily understood, but it is not at all, the substance used is not a selective germicide like salvarsan, but a general germicide. It kills all microorganisms both avian and mammalian. It is not poisonous to mammals as to birds. These facts have been placed before a competent bacteriologist and I am informed that such properties had not been hitherto known.

The formula has been prepared and put on the market for the use of bird breeders and dealers; as soon as the necessary experiments cane be made it will be put on the market for the poultry breeder, in forms adopted for the treatment of Roup and White Diarrhea; but this does not exhaust the possibilities of the discovery. There is no one of the diseases mentioned above but what could undoubtedly be more effectively treated with this substance than is now the case if necessary techniques were worked out. That, however, is beyond my resources and the limitation of my environment. The only tests I have been able to make have been with common coal. In this case a single treatment proved effective. There are many germicides that can be applied to the mucus membranes which will effect the same results. There are not many that can be used internally.

Now, Sir, you have heard many appeals for clemency and in each you made your question at issue as always been "What is the probability that the party in question of himself, a useful citizen if restored to society?" That question does not exist in this case. I have developed in limited environment to the full extent of its possibilities. Isn't it logical to suppose that now at an age when all men are set in these habits that I would continue as I have for the last nine years? There are persons, some of them high in the present administration, in D.C. and who will be higher in the next administration, who think that the answer to hat question should be yes. It is they who are sponsoring this move. Whether it will prove successful or not, I do not know. I do know that it is far from being the forlorn hope that some of my other efforts have seen, only to work out successful. Be that as it may:

It has been argued that you would prove the greatest obstacle to success. Some have been so convinced of this that they have argued that it would be a foolish waste of effort to address any appeal to you whatever, that the logical thing to do was to set you down for an adverse report and try to offset same else where.

I have not been able to subscribe to that view: despite the fact that our only contract was under circumstances which could hardly be to advantage

of either of us in the eyes of the other. I have always felt that you were
a broad open minded man bent on discharging your duties with as high a
degree of justice and fairness as is humanly possible. I can not believe
that you would prejudice any man or fail to alter an opinion of the past
if facts presented convinced you that justice demanded it. It is this belief
that has given me tetemerrity to address this appeal to you.

I have above mentioned the success of my undertaking. I have successful to a large extent, but I have failed also. The habits of my environment
have been reached. I have established myself an earning power but the extent of that earning power is limited by the room at my disposal to a figure
that prevents me from discharging any but the minor of my obligations
in life. My mother who is now crowding the three score and ten mark still
has to earn her living as a factory hand. If the duties I owe her are not
discharged, soon it will be too late. My food business and that of my fever
treatment may earn money enough, but it is doubtful if they can ever earn
what they should while deprived of my personal management.

This I would be able to discharge these obligations if free is beyond
doubt, for I have already been pledged sufficient financial backing to establish a bird plant for 10,000 capacity plant- and a few people realize to
profits to be made in this business by large scale production. It cost about
$2.60 to raise a male bird in a cage and he is worth about ten dollars. It
cost about 60 cents to raise him aviary and he is worth five dollars.

Should you desire confirmation of any statement made herein I shall be
more than glad to furnish it.

In conclusion I wish to state that no attempt to obtain an unconditional
release is contemplated. All I want all I ask, is a chance to continue to develop myself along the lines indicated above. There is no reject, so long as
the opportunity sought is provided. And I may ad that in this respect the
officials here have reasonable possible, but the too are limited with the
responsibility for the management of over three thousand prisoners resting upon their shoulders. They have done well to permit me to go as far as
I have. Something I shall always deeply appreciate.

Confident that you will give the above your careful consideration and
act in such a manner as you sincerely believe to be in the best intent of
all of the society you are sworn to serve;

I am with every element of respect

Yours,
Robert Stroud /s/

Leavenworth, Kansas Aug. 13th 1918

Dear Bessie,

I received both of your letters, and I must hand you some compliments. "The bird of paradise" made a hit and I will have to plead guilty, and promise to pull no more "tail feathers."

I have reason to know that the Dr's. view of that clipping is erroneous. Yes Mrs. T. sure made some "bonehead" plays, and when she appointed herself my spiritual advisor I was not present. I guess you know that I am egotist enough to consider myself well off to take care of my own spiritual well being. I appreciate your attitude on prayer more than anything I have read in many a day. To me, to wail to my creator over what is not his fault would be disgusting and lower me in my own self esteem and if you think I would trade your wholesome comradeship for a bunch of that "sob-Sister religion" you just try me and see how quick I will jump on your neck. No if a man has not got the nerve to stand on his feet he deserves to go down. My case was fought this last time on that theory by my instructions and I have the satisfaction to know that my defense made a better impression this time than ever before.

Our views of death are much the same, only I want it to be night, outdoors and in the snow, and if I could pick the method it would be from loss of blood or freezing. I want to be alone and on my back so I can see the stars. That is all due to my esthetic taste. I saw a man in that position once and the cruelest act that I ever witnessed was some would be friends taking him to a Dr.

The only answer I can give to your question of "reward" is, that the same thing makes them do that, as makes them think of a nice friendly pick in a corner when they sing of "the streets of gold." In fact I think the golden streets were put there to suggest the pick.

Your prediction was correct. I spent a most enjoyable afternoon over those criticisms and had many a good laugh - To think that I considered your fi rst choice as being to rotten to even pick to pieces. I'm very glad you sent them for they showed me how poor some of my expressions look after they get cold. I will make a bet though and that is that either the house on Chester Street or the little maverick comes out fi rst.

I hope that you don't find your studies disappointing. So much of that correspondence stuff is useless on the faculty of self teaching and then they really don't need it only to keep the honest with themselves. That gives them always a good check on what they are doing.

I sympathize with the cucumbers and don't blame them for bucking against such a combination as heat, bugs, and worst of all "bug juices." It would discourage most any self respecting plant. Better luck next time though.

When I got your letter telling of your lovely swim it was 112° in the shade outside and believe me Bessie, there isn't as much air in a cell as there is outside. I have swam in the rain and know just how nice it can be. It was some satisfaction to know you thought of me, for you couldn't have thought of me in connection with anything I would have enjoyed more.

I don't blame you for not have heart enough to exercise this weather - it takes all the never I have to stay with it. I take it as soon as I wake up. That be yes little

Well Bessie there is no news as yet about the care. I am getting on as well as can be expected. It is too hot to study much, but I have been spending a little time writing Guitar accompaniments for some of the music I have. Another fellow down here has a Guitar and we play them together (or try to). Most of the time we are really a long ways apart, but even at that it helps some.

Say let me know how Johnson comes out as I haven't been able to see anything of his case in the paper. Mrs. Leasures letter is amusing. I received dozens like it the first time I was sentenced. One woman wrote me twice and insisted I tell her anything that would add to my comfort. She understood anything. I told her; Bull Durham and brown papers - she didn't answer my letter. I would have liked to have seen her horrified look as she read it.

You need not mind about "Patsy" for I am getting the proper news. I have been greatly interested in "Fill," and her constant qualification that he is "pretty good for a boy." Her egotism is delightful and she always seems to justify it.

So long Bessie,
As ever Robert.

4--18--20

Warden Anderson

Esteemed Sir:

Perhaps you will think strange that I did not write to U S P before in order to save a life but I wrote to the Dept which was the proper thing I believe.

I was the direct cause of Stroud killing Turner altho innocent of any part in the actual crime.

The whole thing started in the barber shop the day before the killing. Turner told me to get in a "pig scraper's" chair and, as I held an important clerical position I defied him and waited for my own barber.

Turner then angry, afraid to put me in for fear of my superior took his anger out on Stroud who sat near waiting and silent. There was very little said and Turner did all the talking, (abusive it was). It was what he was afraid to say to me but meant for me to hear to show his fearlessness.

I'm sorry, I never harmed a person in my life, but if you will ask Stroud about this he will tell you it is the truth. I started the whole thing and I cannot bear to have that poor devil suffer so much on account of my refusal to obey Turner.

Very Sincerely L W K

March 13, 1920.

Mr. A. V. Anderson,
Warden,

Sir:

Since you have placed a death watch upon me, I have been deprived of pen and ink for writing; I have spoken to Mr. Fletcher about it and it appears that the only valid objection he makes, is that you have ordered that I be so deprived. And at Mr. Fletcher's suggestion I am writing you this note - he has promised to speak to you again about the matter.

Now, Sir, it seems that your only object in depriving me of this privilege, is a fear that I contemplate self-destruction, and a desire to be on the safe side in case anything of that nature should happen. And I will be frank enough to say that I don't relish the idea of being the principle actor in the show contemplated but let that be as it may. Your fear in regard to the pens is groundless. For I will give you my word - and keep it - that, should anything of that kind come off, I will not take advantage of this privilege to bring it about.

On the other hand: I have a great deal of writing to do, that I would like to get finished, and, perchance, only a short time to do it in. Naturally I would like to make my work as neat as possible. Therefore, I beg that you reconsider this matter; and as time is short, let me know your decision at your earliest convenience.

Respectfully,
Robert F. Stroud

3-20-20

[Handwritten Note] Under the existing circumstances and on accounting certain things found in your possession I cannot see my way clear to grant you this request.

Warden

Leavenworth, Kansas Sept. 14, 1928

Mr. T. B. White
Warden

Sir:

I am sorry that I was not in my cell the other day when you made your inspection. You were quoted to me as saying: "Tell Stroud that if I ever find his bed again as it is now I shall take away his birds. I wanted to speak of it when Mrs. Willebrandt was here but did not." Is that a correct quotation, Warden? If it is, I beg you to peruse the following carefully,

The day of Mrs. Willebrandt's visit I was expecting her and had that morning straightened up my whole cell. I was glad when you came in for I surely thought that my efforts to have the place looking neat would please you. I wanted to do that;

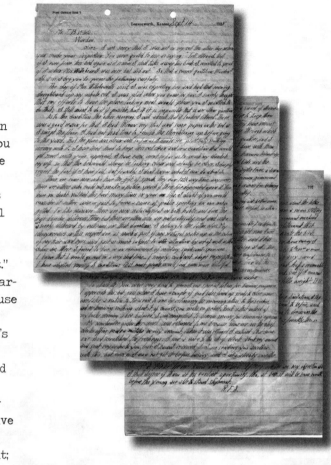

I still want to do it if possible, but if it is impossible that is another question.

As to the condition the other morning, I will admit that it looked littered. There was a good reason for that. I had thrown my stool and some papers on the bed as I swept the floor. I had not had time to finish the straightening up before going to the yard. But the place was clean and so far as I could see, practically nothing wrong with it. I have tried hard to keep this cell clean and in a condition that would meet with your approval; I have even went so far as to wash my blankets myself so that the bed would always be looking clean and actually be clean. I deeply regret the fact, if I have fail, but, frankly, I don't know what I can do about it.

There are some men who have the gift of speech. They can talk anytime, anywhere; there are others who could not make a public speech if their life depended upon it. You have no doubt noticed this fact many times in your life. I doubt if you would consider it either wise or just to force a career in public speaking on one not so gifted. In like manner there are men naturally neat in both habits and dress. The least disorder distressed them; but there are others who are not naturally neat and who are sorely distressed by extremes in that direction. I belong to the latter class. My idiosyncrasies in this respect are as much a part of my natural make up as the colors of my hair and eyes, and just as much subject to alteration by act of will as the colors are. Were I forced to live in an environment of military spick-and-span-ness I know that I would go made in a very short time—I simply could not adapt myself to this. I have adapted myself to conditions that most people would find even more distressful which would balance things up to some extent.

As to my birds, if you have any intention of using them as a sword of armor, I will be pleased to know it now. I certainly have no desire to keep them under those circumstances. They have given me much pleasure. They have meant hope, ambition, decency and self respect. They have provided an avenue through which I could exercise my best faculties and bring out my best qualities, and I believe that I have a just right to be proud of what I have done with them.

I have not made much of a financial success but I have added to human knowledge. I have learned the cause and cure for congenital baldness in line bred birds and the principle cause of unhatchable eggs, and I've discovered a specific for septic fever, a disease that has baffled bird keepers for two hundred years and which the German government has spent large sums trying to control. This is important for there are good reasons for believing that the same treatment would wipe out roop and white diarrhea in poultry.

You once said that you considered your task here as one of turning out better men. Do you think that the birds have helped make me better and more useful, or otherwise?

When Manuel figured that conditions and circumstances made it impossible for him to continue to keep his birds, I thought him too easily discouraged; but right now I am pretty well disgusted myself. You have been extremely kind in this matter and it has only been your innumerable favors that have enabled me to keep going at all—this and my faith in your fairness and open mindedness, which has given me confidence to surmount difficulties that would have otherwise made the conditions hopeless. For all this I am and shall always be deeply grateful. Conditions and circumstances now, however, continue to shape up in such a manner as to make further effort seem useless.

To illustrate: You were very kind to permit me special letters for business purposes. I appreciate this; but just when I have a couple of good sales lined up ready to close some one take a notion to tie a rock to me by returning the incoming letters to the senders, and me knowing nothing about it, of course, can make no protest. Result is that instead of my books showing a nice balance, I am compelled to borrow money for running expenses.

My merchandise order this week was returned to me because someone in the chief clerks office made a mistake in my account. When it was returned I noticed that someone had scratched the fresh eggs. I sent a note to the chief clerk about my account and sent my order to you, but I haven't received it. I am sending you another with this, but even though I can not get it before Tuesday, and I already owe the man in the guards mess five eggs.

These are little things; they are disheartening, though. The one about the letters is not so little either. I just this moment received a letter from a man stating that an order for $143.00 worth of birds with check for that amount enclosed in a registered letter was returned to him unopened with a statement that I am in prison and not permitted to receive it. And he still wants the birds. This with others losses that I have been able to trace - God know how many I have no knowledge of - of a similar nature amounts easily to $300.00 or more.

Can you now understand why I don't feel like accepting any sword of democulese status for the birds. If I can keep them with just half a reasonable show to care for and handle them, I will be deeply grateful, but if I cannot do so, it is sure the threat of taking them from me will have little weight. It is no loss to lose something that has already been destroyed.

I fully realize that you are only human, and like myself, have limitations. I try to keep this in mind, for I firmly believe that you sincerely want to be fair, and I know that the responsibilities of you position often force you to decisions the full affect of which it is impossible to forecast. I have written you thus frankly, though, so that you could see my point of view with equal clearness.

    Always Gratefully Yours,
    Robert F. Stroud
    114B1
    Isolation.

P.S. Please let me know about the birds. If they are in an way objection then I shall dispose of them at the earliest opportunity, though, at best it will be some months before the young are able to stand shipment.
    R.F.S.

May 13, 1929

Mr. T. B. White,
Warden.

Sir:-

Concerning this green food problem, which confronts me every breeding season there is a very simple solution if you would dare to permit it.

A great deal of soil is washed down into the lower end of our yard. If I could retain this in a space about 10 x 20 it would grow all the green food my birds could eat during the growing season and it would always be available when needed. The only things necessary would be the placing of two 2" x 6" boards to form the plot and a little soil for a starter. I have talked to Mr. Edmonds, the guard in isolation (who by the way is one of the most efficient, conscientious and thoroughly reliable men it has been my pleasure to meet. Absolutely impersonal in his dealing with us - a quality that in the past has often been conspicuous by its absence) and the only difficulty in arranging this matter is a possible objection from you.

If you have no objection, your approval on this note is all that will be necessary for me to accomplish what I wish in this respect.

And while addressing you, I wish to express my thanks and appreciation of your kind thoughtfulness in permitting us to attend the entertainment in chapel a week ago Sunday. That this was granted of your own volition shows a disposition on your part that is highly commendable and which I have and shall continue to try to merit by my conduct. For this as well as your other innumerable kindnesses, I most sincerely thank you.

Very Respectfully Yours,
Robert Stroud
17431 - Isolation.

Box 7, Leavenworth, Kansas,
October 6, 1931

Miss Enona Watson,
Watson Sanitarium,
Paola, Kansas.

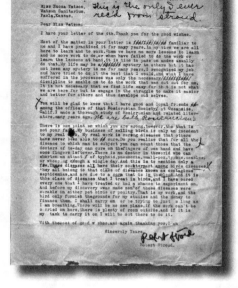

This is the only I ever rec'd from Stroud.

Dear Miss Watson:

I have your letter of the 4th. Thank you
for the good wishes.

Most of the matter in your letter is familiar to me and I have practiced it for
many years. In my view we are all here to
learn and to work. When we have no more
lessons to learn and no more work to do, or
when have failed to do the work or learn
the lessons at hand, it is time to pass on
and we usually do that. My life may be a mystery to others but it has not
been any mystery to me for many years. I recognized my job and have tried
to do it the best that I could, and what I have suffered in the processes
was only the necessary discipline to enable me to do the work that was cut
out for me. It is not necessary that we find life easy for that is not what
we are here for but to engage in the struggle to make it easier and better
for others and thus develop our selves.

You will be glad to know that I have good and loyal friends among the
officers of that Rosicrucian Society at Oceanside, Calif. I made a thorough
study of Rosicrucian and related literature, many years ago. We are both
Rosicrucian's

There is one point on which you are wrong, however, though that is
not your fault. My business of selling birds is only an incident to my
real work. My real work is curing diseases that others have never been
able to cure. Do you realize that for all the disease to which man is
subject you can count those that the doctors of to-day can cure on the
fingers of one hand and have some fingers leftover. There is no doctor
in the world who can shorten an attack of typhoid, pneumonia, small-pox,
typhus, measles, or whooping cough a single day. And this in to mention
only a few. These diseases all have their counterpart among birds diseases. They all belong to that class of diseases known as contagious
septicemias, and are due to a germ that is in the blood. And it is this
class of diseases that I treat in birds, and I have cured every one that
I have treated or had a chance to experiment on. And before my discovery was made none of these diseases were curable in either pet birds or
poultry. That is my work, and the bird only furnish the grounds for my
studies and the money to finance them. I shall carry on or be trying to

just as long as I am breathing. There will be no new plans. If the work can't be carried on here, there is plenty of room outside, and if it is my task to carry it on I will be out there to do it.

With the best of good wishes, and again thanking you, I am

Sincerely yours,
Robert Stroud.

Pittsburg, Kansas
October 5, 1931

Warden T.B. White
Leavenworth Federal Prison

Dear Sir:

I bought a Kansas City Star yesterday. I saw about Robert Stroud and his canary birds. There is a lot of publicity about it. All you can hear all over this town is "Did you read that about Robert Stroud," "Isn't it a low down dirty shame they way they are doing him, by taking his birds away from him?" The only way he has of supporting his old gray headed mother. The only thing he has in the world is his birds and his mother.

He is like any other son, he doesn't want his mother to go to the poor farm. I know some men that wouldn't care. I helped one man that was in solitary confinement for 2-years and 3-months. He would have been there the rest of his life. He was in a certain penitentiary in the U.S.A. Robert Stroud is not a bit worse than this fellow I am telling about. Further more this fellow is up for parole now.

Why is it any worse for Mr. Stroud to have his canary birds, and to sell them to take care of his aged mother? When Clarence Fisher were there he made pocket books and the prison sold them. My sister-in-law has one she bought. They have prison made garments in these stores for the citizens of the U.S.A. to buy and wear. I don't think it is any more than right that he can't have his birds to sell. His mother is old and can't get a job to at now. What if you were in his place and had an old gray headed mother to take care of. You would want to do the same thing. You wouldn't want your own mother to go to the poor house?

He did all his crimes in self-defense. I would do the same thing if a man started to kill me. You or any other man would be a damn fool to stand and let someone kill you, and not try to fight back. A man would be a fool to swear against another to get his parole and freedom.

Mr. Stroud's picture doesn't look half as bad as some of your noble guards. If you care to answer this you can. But do not write a hard letter like you did to Mr. Stroud's mother. Listen White, this is man-to-man. You are not writing to a woman now. This Indian is not scared of any man White. If

you have any questions about this letter I will be glad to answer. I may
come up in the near future to see Mr. Stroud. I will have my attorney to
look up and see if I can't see him a few minutes. Also solitary confinement.

Yours truly,
K. Basley

December 31, 1931.

Miss Mary B. Minor,
12 Minor St.,
Sturgeon Bay, Wis.

Dear Miss Minor:-

I am glad that you got the bird o.k. and
that your sister likes him. I thought that
she would. I told you that I would choose a
nice one.

Now about the bathing. The reason that
he will not bath is because he does not
understand that kind of bath that you are
using. I use outside bath houses and let my
birds bath out doors. Every noon when I go
out into the yard for exercise I take the
birds out. I run about a dozen of them into
a breeding cage. I have bath houses three
sides of which are closed in with caging and the other open. These hang
over the door and the birds bathe and dry them selves in the sunshine. You
can get an outside bird bath at any bird store. If the weather is real raw I
would suggest that the bird be placed on the fl oor or table in the sun to
bath, not in the window. There is always a draft in a window not matter how
tight it is, due to the different temperatures on the inside and out side
of the glass. If you have an open cage cover three sides of it with a towel
before you take the bird out doors in it. Never leave him in the sun till he
pants. Never leave him out on cold days till he chills.

I hope that you have your seed by now. Mail has been pretty slow the
last couple of weeks.

When your friends express their liking for that bird you can tell them
that there are always a lot of good ones where he came from.

With sincere good wishes for the New Year, I am

Very Truly Yours,
Robert Stroud.

Box 7, Leavenworth, Kansas
December 31, 1931.

Dear Hilda:-

I was glad to get your note and to know that you got my card o.k. I will tell the world that you have not been forgotten. I have thought of you often and wondered why you did not write and many times Dell has asked me about you and if I had heard from you. Many times I would have written to find out what was the matter but I have been very busy, Honey, and when I say that you do not realize the half of it.

I am sure sorry that you did not have a nice Christmas, Honey and I do hope that the new year brings you nothing but happiness, all the happiness that you have always craved, Darling. And you do not have to stop your letters because you might tell me things. You know that what ever interests or affects you is always interesting to me. Tell me what that article said, Honey, There have been a lot of them going all over the country and some are good some other not so good and I am wondering which it was. I wish you had sent it to Dell. I do not know what the New Year is going to bring for me. One thing sure it cannot bring much more in the way of work and this one that will be gone in a few moments now. But even if it has brought me lots of work and a lot to worry about this year just leaving has not been so bad for me, for it has brought me thousands of friends, too. It has failed to bring me the things that I want most but then the new year may do that.

The whistles are blowing now, Honey, and 1931 is over and I will make a wish for you and call it a day. I sure hope that this finds everything going well with you.

Love and KISSES, Honey,

Bob.

JOHN EDGAR HOOVER
DIRECTOR

U. S. Department of Justice
Bureau of Investigation
Washington, D. C.

PERSONAL AND CONFIDENTIAL

February 1, 1932.

Mr. T. B. White,
Warden,
United States Penitentiary,
Leavenworth, Kansas.

Dear Tom:

    With further reference to your inquiry concerning one
DELLA JONES, who has been in contact with Robert Stroud, a
prisoner in isolation in the Leavenworth Penitentiary, I am
enclosing, for your information, copy of a report submitted
by Special Agent L. J. Grout, dated at Kansas City, Missouri,
January 23, 1932. I am forwarding the report in view of the
detailed information set out therein concerning the interview
with Mrs. E. J. Stroud, the mother of the prisoner.

    Should you desire any further information concerning
this subject, I shall be very glad to have such further inquiry made as you may suggest.

    With best personal wishes, I am

        Sincerely yours,

        J. Edgar Hoover
        Director.

Encl. #726878

Box 7,Leavenworth,Kansas,

January 1,1932.

Miss Marie Gerard,
750 W.Market St.,
Genevieve,Mo.

Dear Miss Gerard:

I amsorry that I did forget to tell you how tosex the birds.
When I come tothat question in your letter I passed it put because it was necessary to make drawings and I thought I would
make them at the end of the let er and then forget it in the
press of other work.I have now made them on another peice of
paper.They are not much in the way of drawings but they
will tell you the things to look for.

In the drawings of thevents of the young birds note most the
angle of the vent.In the hen the angle with the tail is less
than in the male,I can often tell birds this way when they
leave the nest,tho,one can not always be sure at that age.
Next turn the paper over and notice the positions of the birds
at rest and theline of the feathers on the abdomen.The hen is
concave in the upper part of the line and convex in thelower.
Thin in thechest and full in the abdomen.The male sits lowere
over his perch with his head more forword.The line over his
chest is convex and that over the abdomen concave so that
his feather taper off smoothly into the line of the tail.
The line of his body while at rest will always be nearer the
horizontal than that of the hen.When the cock sings the head
is thrust forward and held there;whena hen sings her head is
thrust forward the same as the cocks,tho not so much,but between
each burst of song she retracts her head.The cock does not do
this.The birds stand differently at different times and sometimes the vent does not tell well so that you can not be sure
about anyone of these things,but when one takes them all into
consideration one can't make a mistake very easily.A sick cock
may stand like a hen.And unmated hen in breeding condition
may stand like a cock and make a fair pretense of singing but
you can always tell by some of these things.N w stufy these
indications in your old birds that you know the sex of and then
go look at them in the young.You will find that you can sex
most of them at a glance.Those that are duobtfull should be
put in a seperate flight and watched.You will soon have them
all spotted.

NO there is no need to send another male right now.I think
I will take the rest that you have left within a few days
and I would like to know how many there are.We will adjust it
when we pay you for the ballance.

No I do not think that it will hurt those hens to wait a couple
of months to be mated if you do not feed them too much egg
food and bring them into lay.Most of my hen have been ready
to go for a month.I will not start until April,However.

With the best of good wishes for the New Year,I am

        Sincerely,   Robert Stroud

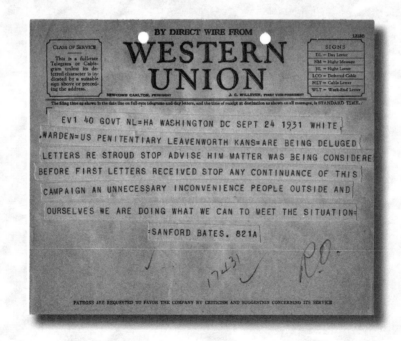

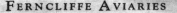

FERNCLIFFE AVIARIES
Home of winning
YORKSHIRES, AND OTHER EXHIBITION BIRDS
Proprietors

ARMISTEAD CARTER	N. E. R. CARTER
Judge of type canaries,	Letter head designs
British and Foreign birds	Bird and Animal designs

KALAMA, WASH. ......March 1st 1934......193....

Inventor of Perfection Breeding Cages.

❧❧❧

The perfect mite control cage with running water.

❧❧❧

As far ahead as radio is over letter writing

❧❧❧

They cost no more than the other kind.

❧❧❧

Seed Specialist Mixtures that are specially mixed for Linnets, Goldfinches and Bulfinches a different mixture for each one

❧❧❧

Fanciers write "My birds like your seeds better. There is a reason!

❧❧❧

Best seeds at wholesale prices to fanciers.

❧❧❧

A Letter head design of your own like this, will bring business.

❧❧❧

N. E. R. Carter's bird designs are in a class by themselves.

Dear Bob:-

Your letter to hand, I am glad the birds suit you. It takes a lot of work to breed birds up, but in frills it is easier than in any other breed, as we want roughness. Always remember that size comes from the cock, so that in crossing use a big cock. Double buffing will increase size of your cocks. Whilst this would be taboo for breeding Yorkshires for show, it will do no harm to breed some rough Yorkshire to help breed up the frills. The Lancashire and Scotch fancy have the size as well, and the Scotch fancy is always inclined to frill, of course he has the hump, but if you have a good market for freaks, you could probably dispose of the birds you did not want to propogate your frills.

I see Fogg is making another attempt for the limelight, with a scheme for federation, with Fogg as chief at $250.00 per month. He claims he has turned down a contract of 5% commission on all the birds he can buy, as it would tarnish his honor and principle. I am glad to learn he has some. Yet in his propaganda, he finishes with the words that Sears sells 60,00 birds a year, but they want them graded therefore it would be up to the Federation to grade them properly. What a poor crook he is. He evidently lacks education, or he would see how he convicts himself with his own writing. He evidently is in Sears Roebuck employ, though he claims not, but he wishes to get $250.00 per month out of the federation, and then get 5% from Sears, for buying the birds for them. He would evidently double cross his own mother. Nick turned him down. He has sent on the scheme for me to criticise.

I have applied for the position of manager of the Pet shop department for Miers & franks, as I heard the Scotchman they had was going to quit. I also heard that they were willing to put up $1000.00 to have a real bird show put on in their store. I have got a reply from them that seems favorable, in the event that Holmes their present man wuits. I may get the job anyway, as they are investigating my qualifications, and I doubt if there is a man better qualified to give them what they want. Show experience is not common in America, and men that know all branches of the bird business are not so frequently met with. If I get the job, I shall be importing lots of type birds and shall be able to give you good prices on any birds that you may want. I shall have at least ample capital to work with.

I believe if you went about it right, you could get another edition of your book printed that would cost you nothing, by selling advertising space, then you would have the whole thing for your self, and leave Powell high and dry with his edition. Make a new and improved edition. My wife could make the cuts you need, and take the pay in copies of the finished book to sell. I would like to see you make something out of that book, but if you would take a little advice from me, you would always translate the Latin terms you use into plain everyday English. I get so many letters from people that say I like your articles best for the reason they dont shoot over our heads. They often mention your articles as being unintelligible to them. Most bird keepers are not scientific persons.

I am enclosing a check for $1.00 to square the overpayment in express. On second thoughts you said I should send the cheque to your wife, so I will do so.

If you want any help in putting out your book in the way of cuts let me know. I feel sure you could get away with the proposition better than I could, and I not enough to pay all the expenses of publication with the exception of $5.00.

There is a steady dribble of these Yorkshire books going out. Nick has sold a lot of them in fact he has sold twice as many as I have. I let him have them at 70 cents each.

A dollar book is a popular price. Write when you feel like it

Sincerely yours

Armistead Carter

Minneapolis, Minn.
Feb. 9, 1932

[Handwritten] Copy to Stroud

Dear Sir:-

Have you an inmate who raises
and sells birds? Would it be too much
trouble to find out, if he has any literature on the care and ailments of
Canaries. If he has some is it for sale
and for how much?

Waiting and hoping to hear from you
by return mail. Thanking you, I remain,

Yours very truly,
Mr. A. M. Amundson
3046 - 18th Ave. So.
Mpls., Minn.

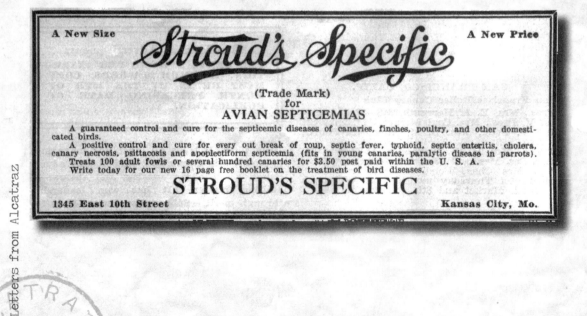

Letters from Alcatraz

1353 East 10th Street
Kansas City Missouri
October 21st 1933.

Mr. Zerbst
Warden USP
Leavenworth, Kansas

Dear Sir,

I clipped this notice an item from this mornings K.C. Times. Will you kindly inform me if such is correct?

If so will you be kind enough to tell me when and where such ceremony took place.

I was unaware that the government permitted marriage of life term prisoners.

Hoping I may hear from you soon I am very respectfully

Mrs. E. J. Stroud
(Mother of Robert Stroud)

Personals

VIOLET—Waiting home all day for your call. Phone anytime. L.

LADY will help drive to Spokane for transportation. WEstport 0049.

MERCY HOSPITAL still needs 100 baby pads. Write or telephone for directions.

THE Altman Shoppe, jewelers, 101 East 11th, now has an optical department.

NOT responsible for bills unless contracted by myself. Ralph Bowers, 834 Quindaro.

NOT responsible for Sylvia Hendrix's debts after this date. Oscar Hendrix, 1912 East 80th.

WITNESSES to street car collision with grass mower and tractor, Lexington ave., Oct. 6, call WAbash 3248.

PARTY who bought small leather trunk, Ambassador hotel sale, Oct. 5, call Mrs. Carter, Ambassador hotel. Important.

DAHLIAS are blooming; visitors welcome; come now before frost. Frank Payne. ½ mile south Shawnee, Kas., highway 50.

REWARD for address of Karl Jahnke and recovery of Ford truck motor 1043890, Kansas license 1-2678. CHestnut 6590.

KENNETH WAYNE'S Placement Exchange for beauty operators and domestic help, now located 415 Chambers Bldg. GRand 1621.

ANYONE having old diaries written by pioneers before 1880, please communicate, scribe fully. Sender, 5845 Central, Kansas City, Mo.

ROBERT STROUD of Leavenworth, Kas., and Della May Jones of 1345 E. 10th st., Kansas City, Mo., wish it known that they are man and wife.

WESTERN UNION

The filing time shown in the date line on telegrams and day letters is STANDARD TIME at point of origin. Time of receipt is STANDARD TIME at point of destination

Received at 107 South Fourth St., Leavenworth, Kansas   TELEPHONE 2760

KAH115 10 XC=METROPLIS ILL 20 1023A   1938 AUG 20 AM 11 26

ROBERT STROUD=

 P M B 17431

MOTHER DIED AT 930 LAST NIGHT FUNERAL MONDAY AT TWO=

 MAME.

Telephone No.
Telephoned To
Time D
By

1345 East 10th Street
Kansas City, Missouri.
February 2nd 1934

Miss. Eilen Turner,
2525 Lakeport Street,
Sioux City, Iowa.

Dear Miss. Turner:

You have no doubt been looking for the prices of birds I
told you my husband was sending you, since I sent you the
seed prices and samples. The
fact is Mr. Stroud wrote to you,
but because his writing privileges have been taken due to
the fl ood of letters which the
public has written him since
that article appeared in the press, it made the Warden mad and he has tak-
en all his writing privileges from him. Before this he was allowed to answer letters regarding his bird prices.

I am inclosing prices herewith, and Mr. Stroud said to tell you that he
was sure that you would be able to fi nd in this list some birds that you
like for they are all the very best of their kind to be had. He does not
have any scrub birds.

He has on hands now just one cinnamon coated bird. It is a little border fancy hen and is priced at $3.00. He has several pink eyed birds in his
Yorkshires and yorkshire cross bred birds. They are cinnamon with yellow
coats. They will throw cinnamon or cinnamon marked birds, but all of the
cinnamon birds have been sold.

There are two cinnamon greens in the Yorkshire cross bred birds. These
birds if mated to females from the same stock would throw you some fi ne big
cinnamon birds. He had planned to use them himself but would be glad to
sell you one.

Trusting that we may have the pleasure of serving you, we remain

Very truly yours,
STROUD'S SPECIFIC

Mr. Robert Stroud.

P.S. All further correspondence should be sent to the above address as
well as all orders.

March 2, 1937
Mr. Robert H. Hudspeth
Warden
Institution.

Dear Mr. Hudspeth:

That interview I spoke to you about the day you visited my cell has probably slipped your mind. And though I realize that you are a very busy man and dislike to intrude upon your time, this is the month of March, the month when I must start to breed my birds if I am going to raise any this year, and there are several problems confronting me that I cannot solve without your aid, and I cannot start breeding my birds with any hope of success until they are solved.

So, if you will be kind enough to grant me that interview at your earliest convenience, I shall be very grateful.

Very Respectfully yours,
Robert Stroud

[Handwritten note]
No interview necessary.
Advise you comply with past rules governing your privilege, keeping your rooms clean and sanitary, and keeping your number of birds down to a minimum.

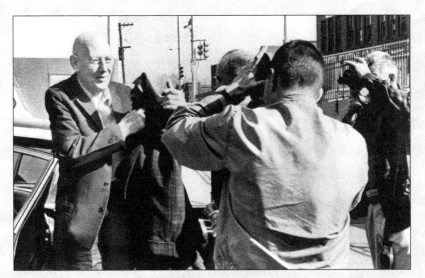

Robert Stroud is seen in this rare press photograph, entering the U.S. District Courthouse in Kansas City on March 28, 1963. This represented one of only a handful of opportunities for Stroud to view free society following his arrest for murder in 1909. He had already spent 54 years in prison, and by this time served the longest period in solitary confinement of any inmate in the United States. Stroud was protesting the Bureau of Prison's refusal to allow him to publish additional books on bird care and diseases. He would die less than a year later.

Ralph Roe

ALCATRAZ'S reputation as America's ultimate escape proof prison would be shattered in less than four years from its opening. In 1937 two accomplices would break free undetected and both disappeared into the icy waters of the turbulent San Francisco Bay. Though the fateful escape would end in the suspected deaths of both inmates, their escape was partially successful. Until the escape of Ralph Roe and Theodore Cole, the name "Alcatraz" had been synonymous with the word "escapeproof." Theodore Cole and Ralph Roe had been long-term associates at McAlester and Leavenworth prisons, both had established escape records, and each was known in their own right as a Houdini of escape. Their crafty escape plan would give them the opportunity to sneak beyond the view of a correctional officer, and then slip past the barbwire fences and into the chilly waters of the fog-laden bay, never to be seen again.

Roe and Cole maintained a close friendship at Alcatraz, both taking paying jobs and working side-by-side in the Mat Shop. The Mat Shop was a facility where prison workers transformed used car tires into rubber mats for the Navy, and it was located on the bottom floor of the Model Shop Building at the northernmost tip of the island. The area was recognizable by the piles of discarded tires that were pitched down from the industry building, littering the waterline.

The two inmates had spent several weeks in preparation for their escape, studying the habits of the correctional staff, and working to identify potential loopholes in the security system. Using a stolen hacksaw blade, they were able to saw their way through the steel sash window grill, packing the saw gaps with grease and shoe polish to avoid detection. On the morning of Thursday, December 16, 1937, dense fog forced the docking of almost all the small vessels in the area. The forceful currents leading out past the Golden Gate Bridge and toward the Pacific Ocean were fluctuating between seven to nine knots, creating what were considered death-trap conditions for anyone willing to try their fate in the perilous waters. The two inmates were likely not aware of how dangerous the currents and foggy conditions could prove to be. It was speculated that they might have seen the spell of bad weather as an opportunity to escape under cover of dense fog.

It is alleged that Roe and Cole bent out the sawed bars using a heavy wrench, punched out two panes of glass, and climbed through the window, dropping down to the ground below. They swiftly ran to a locked gate that led down to the waterline. It is also believed that in preparation for the escape, the two inmates had constructed floats from lightweight metal five-gallon fuel canisters with specially made handles, and they carried these makeshift floats with them. Using the wrench, the inmates quickly unfastened the bolts of a chain-link gate, and then laid the gate over the five rows of sharp barbwire, thus making a protected pathway down to the water's edge.

Fellow inmate, Theodore "Blackie" Audett, later recalled that he was able to watch the two inmates as they made their entry into the bay and began their swim. He noted that he saw Roe come up out of the water several yards off the island, appearing to be struggling desperately,

and attempting to stay afloat in the rough waters. Audett claimed that Roe came up and then drifted into the dense fog, never to be seen again.

The *San Francisco Chronicle* would later run several reports of various sightings of the escapees, and all leads were rigorously investigated with no fruitful results. Nonetheless, the articles kept alive the idea that such a discovery was possible, since both inmates remained unaccounted for. In an article published following the date of the escape, the closing statement read simply:

With long years of prison ahead of them, Ralph Roe, Muskogee, Okla., robber and Theodore Cole, Cushing, Okla., kidnapper, defied science, the natural hazards and the guns of guards, escaped and shattered a national byword, the legend of "escape proof" Alcatraz.

Both inmates remain officially classified as missing and presumed dead. The early writings of Roe show him as remorseful and pleading innocence. His writings in this collection precede his confinement on Alcatraz.

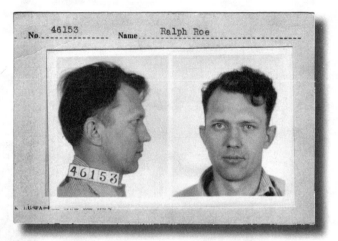

POST OFFICE BOX 7
LEAVENWORTH, KANSAS
April 30, 1935

Mr. Sanford Bates
Drctr. Fed. Prisons

Dear Sir:

Am I bothering you with this, because I do not know what dept. it should be sent too - if there is such a dept. Sincerely hope you have the time to look into this; or will refer me to the dept. to which this should go.

I have a life sentence in this place for something, I had absolutely nothing to do with. Another has signed a confession that he is the guilty man.

I will explain the case the best I can. The charge was bank robbery at Sulphur Oklahoma - Sept. 10 1934. There were two men on the job.

There were nine eye witnesses to the robbery - Six inside the bank and three outside - One man positively identified me. All nine positively identified the man who was on trail with me. Most of them said "they got a fair look at the men, that I was six to eight inches taller than the smaller robber (I am six foot)

I was in Dallas, & McKenny, Texas on the day of the robbery - But as the circumstances were I had only one man by whom I could prove this - He was a negro - My lawyer advised me not to call him - Said, "him being a negro would leave a bad impression." Two witnesses which the government had called, came to me, after the jury retired and wanted to know why they were

not put on the stand
- Said they knew I was
not one of the men."

I had no witnesses
called for the defense
only <u>two</u> were eye witnesses to the robbery. I
made every effort to find
all who saw those men.

I have no explana-
tion to offer why that
banker would positively
identify me - only this,
a woman came to me (She
saw the men before, &
after the robbery) Said,
"She went to the sheriff
of that county, After
she had looked at the
other fellow, & myself,
and told him I was not
one of the men. He (the
Sheriff) told her to just be quiet
about it - that the case would be
tried on <u>its</u> <u>merit</u>. My lawyer advised me against appeal - Or said,
it would be useless. I have since
had another lawyer look into the
case, He says the case was terribly bungled, and that an appeal
would be useless now.

Here is the other side of the
case - I realize it is much against me - Though I know I am innocent of this
crime.

I was arrested in the company of the other defendant, and a third party.
I was an exconvict at the time of arrest. I had been arrested before in the
company of notorious criminals.

All this was just before the jury - By me taking the stand. Still the
jury was deadlocked for twenty six hours before reaching a verdict. I have
learned since the trial, that the gun which this banker identified as the
one he was robbed with - Was purchased after the date of the robbery.

Mr. Bates I do not mean this as an appeal or your sympathy. Every statement I've made here can be checked by any competent investigator. I only
want to get in touch with someone who is interested in seeing justice done.
Of course if being an exconvict entitles me to a life sentence for someone
elses crime, then I have my just deserts.

Let me also state in my own behalf, that the guilty man is confined in this place. And that he fits the discription given by all eye witnesses; with the description of the one. <u>Ennis Smiddy</u> is the man who has signed the statement.

I have appealed to the social service man here. He's advised me to write you. I have no one outside who could, or would, do anything. I do hope you can see your way clear, to help me in this matter - If not will more than appreciate it if you can put me in touch with someone who may be interested in a matter of this kind - Thanking you in advance.

I remain
Respectfully yours.
Ralph Roe
#46153

POST OFFICE BOX 7
LEAVENWORTH, KANSAS Oct. 6, 1935

Mr. Stanford Bates
Washington D.C.

Dear Sir:

I wrote you several months ago about my case, & asking for your help or advice. You referred me back to the warden here. I don't want to seem sarcastic about it - But he gave me no help. He refused to let my wife visit me after she had made a trip of five hundred miles up here - Because she did not have a marriage license with her. He has kept me confined in isolation every since I've been here - I have broken no rule - He informed me several months ago, that I would probably be locked up about six months until he made a decision on my case - It is now going on nine - Surely that is plenty of time - So am hoping that if you have any say so in a matter of this kind, you will call it to his attention, & ask him to make the decision soon.

As I told you before Mr. Bates, I don't mean this as an appeal for your sympathy - But surely there must be such a thing as right, & wrong even in a place like this. I have life in here for something I had absolutely nothing to do with. Again I want to ask you; can you refer me, or my case to someone who would have authority to get something done about it, should they find in my favor, after a thorough investigation. The Warden here did inform me, "The Gov. did not furnish help to get criminals out of the penitentiary." I don't know what an investigation of that kind would cost - I can possibly raise four or five hundred dollars if it could be made for that amount - By offering to pay for the investigation: I don't mean I would expect every doubt to be turned in my favor - Only a fair deal for both, & should they decide against me (I know they won't) I will abide by their decision without a protest.

Mr. Bates does it seem reasonable to you, that out nine eye witnesses to robbery in broad daylight, only one would identify one of the men - Yet all would positively identify the other - They all swore at my trial, that the men were seen both inside, & outside of the bank, One (Gov. witness) swore I was not one of the men - Three (Gov. witnesses) swore that I was four to six inches taller than the man they saw - After being arrested I learned who did rob the bank, He is four to six inches shorter than I - He has signed a statement of guilt - Perhaps you will think - Why didn't he tell this before or at his trial - Ennis Smiddy the guilty man was arrested several months after I was: on another charge. We had the same defense attorney - On his advice, & statement that I could not be convicted on the evidence at hand, & would only hurt the other man by bringing out certain facts - I went to trial - A life sentence was the result. After the jury had returned with a conviction - Two witnesses who the government had called, but failed to put on the stand, came to my attorney, & ask why they were not used, & that they knew I was not one of the men.

I asked the judge to give me a couple of days, & I could produce the guilty man; He refused, & I was brought to the penitentiary that night. I realize my record was bad, & know that is all that convicted me.

I don't like to criticize - Also know most losers always squawk frame'up". But we were the first to be tried (in Okla) on these charges - Looking back on it I can see a thousand mistakes, & realize that a trial before Robert L. Williams of a man with a past record - A conviction was a certainty.

I don't want you to waste your time on something you may think is hopeless. But I will more than appreciate it, if you will help me in this matter.

Respectfully yours
Ralph Roe #46153

Rufe Persful

"I want you to order my cell door padlocked, leave me where I am at, leave my radio and smoking tobacco in here and shoo everyone to hell away from me."

—RUFE PERSFUL, 1943

IN THE EARLY YEARS of Alcatraz, the strict protocol of censorship and an iron fisted grip of what information was released to the public, the image of Alcatraz was molded by speculation and widespread rumors. When the prison first opened to receive federal inmates, Warden Johnston employed a silence policy that many inmates considered to be the most unbearable punishment of all. Prisoners were not permitted to talk to each other while confined to their cells, while walking in line formation through the cellhouse, or during inmate counts. They were only allowed to talk quietly in the Dining Room when seated; at their job assignments, as long as it didn't interfere with their work; and at other community events such as motion picture shows and church services. During the silence era, inmates were harshly disciplined for even the slightest violation of this rule.

There were exaggerated reports that several inmates went slowly insane on Alcatraz because of the "severe order of silence." Former gangster and kidnapper Rufe Persful, took a fire ax from the prison garage while working a garbage detail and chopped off four fingers from his left hand in order to win a transfer off the island. Rumors among

DIVISION OF INVESTIGATION, U. S. DEPARTMENT OF JUSTICE
WASHINGTON, D. C.

Institution United States Penitentiary Located at Alcatraz Island, California

Received Dec. 22, 1935
From USP. Atlanta, Georgia
Crime Kidnapping & Robbery
Sentence: 20 yrs. X mos. X days
Date of sentence Nov. 26, 1934
Sentence begins Nov. 26, 1934
Sentence expires Nov. 25, 1954
Good time sentence expires April 30, 1948
Date of birth 5-25-06 Occupation Farmer
Birthplace Ark. Nationality Amer.
Age 29 Comp. Dark
Height 69 in. Eyes Blue
Weight 160 Hair Brown
Build Slim

Scars and marks. Small scar in center of forehead. A long scar on left side of face extending from temple to corner of mouth. Small scar corner right eye. Small scar at elbow of right arm.

CRIMINAL HISTORY

NAME	NUMBER	CITY OR INSTITUTION	DATE	CHARGE	DISPOSITION OR SENTENCE
Persful	#45205	USP. Atlanta, Ga.,		Transferred Dec.22,1935 to Alcatraz #284-AZ	

(Please furnish all additional criminal history and police record on separate sheet)

the inmates indicated that Persful begged fellow inmate Homer Parker, who was assigned to the same job detail, to "finish the job" by cutting off his right hand. In later years several other inmates used similar tactics, such as slashing their Achilles' tendons to protest the alleged harsh confinement practices and mental harassment they said they suffered at Alcatraz.

Persful later alleged the incident was both an accident and a misunderstanding, but regardless of the truth, it was clear that Persful wanted to be transferred from Alcatraz.

The silent system was relaxed in the late 1930s following extensive scrutiny by public officials.

September 14, 1936
Warden Johnson,
Alcatraz institution.
Institution,

Sir:

I am writing this in order to save you the trouble of an interview. To you, this may appear fantastis and immature but, to me, it is decidedly a serious proposition. As you know, I once worked in conjunction with the Texas Rangers and the Burns Detective agency, and after entering the Arkansas State Prison, served in the capacity of a trusty guard, carrying firearms. In the course of events, occasions arose whereby it became necessary for me to execute the duties to which I had solemnly subscribed: namely, the killing and wounding of a number of prisoners attempting escape. As a result, it is only natural that many enemies were made among the criminal element.

When upon entering the U.S.P. at Atlanta, several of these enemies were found there, I right away requested a removal to this institution. In the meantime, two of the more desperate antagonists were brought here. But I could not then get canceled the requested transfer. Now it is a well-known fact that these same two men made a determined effort to poison me while in the Arkansas State Prison. It is also a known fact that they, assisted by some of their friends, are planning, and have already tried to do the same thing here. Numerous times I have found small pieces of glass in my food - even called your guard's attention to it upon one occasion. This clique, which is so solidly allied against me, has repeatedly declared that they were going "to get" me, and they are in the ideal spot to do so. There is the skeleton of the facts - cold facts; not exaggerated delusions. Therefore, I am requesting a transfer to McNeil's Island Prison.

Their School facilities will be open to me, and no one knows better than you how badly I need the benefit of instructive schooling. Because I advanced no farther than the third grade, correspondence courses are of very little value to me. I would not prefer Leavenworth, for, like Atlanta, many there also are vengefully against me. Now I do not wish to offend by trying to go over your head with the matter, therefore, am bringing it directly to you. But, if you think it necessary as desirable, I shall be glad to consult Mr. Bates, asking his co-operation in the matter. Thanking you for your kindness, I am,

Very respectfully yours,
Rufe Persful.
Register No. 284.

[Handwritten Note] Interviewed - talked over matter - reviewed it from several angles - told him how to conduct himself so as to avoid trouble - I could not see any evidence of anyone bothering him here - he will probably apply to director Roe - Hansley - Mclain served time with him in Arkansas. JAJ 9/16/36

Alcatraz Island
June 25, 1937

To: E. J. Miller, Deputy Warden
From: Horace Diesch, Junior Officer
Re: PERSFUL #284-Az

On the afternoon of this date, I took the two inmates who are on my detail (Garbage Collection) to Building #19 where they change clothes.

We were a few minutes early, the time being 3:40 P.M., as I told them to sweep the floor before they changed clothes. They did so and gathered the dirt onto a dust pan which

#334-Parker put into a trash can I had on my truck. At this moment #284-Rufe Persful walked into the garage and I started to make out my check list for the afternoon. I heard a shout and ran into the garage and saw #284-Rufe Persful walking towards me with a fire-axe in his right hand and the four fingers of his left hand cut off just below the knuckles.

I immediately put a tourniquet on his wrist and put him in the truck and had #334-Homer Parker ride on its side to help him if necessary. I drove up to the cell house and with your assistance took #284-Rufe Persful to the hospital.

Horace Diesch
Junior Officer

Alcatraz, California
Nov. 19, 1937
Deputy Warden
Hor: E. J. Miller

Sir

A letter in behalf of my case. Since June, 25th, at 3:45 p.m. o'clock.

On that date, down at the old garage their were an accident happened.

And in that accident I - Rufe Persful, No. 284, a prisoner, of Alcatraz, Island, did accidentally lose my left hand.

But the circumstances would not let me tell the truth to you. Therefore I got the blame for cutting my own hand off, which was, an were right, but not on purpose, it happened in the queerest of accidents, which if I had at the time or any time it would have sounded impossible.

That is the reason why I did not tell, and why that I wont tell. But Sir I would not have lost my hand for nothing in the world, believe it or not.

The prison guards here which that I have worked for have, not mistreated me. But what do they do? Try to bug me. Am I crazy? Why of course I am. Why? Because they said I was. That is since that I have been here in the hospital. Oh - no, not all of the guard attendants or nurses up here have misused me. Some of them have treated me very nice. But others badly mistreated me.

What the - "Department of Health" wants you to keep clean an sanitary. But they won't let me wash my hands and face, or teeth, before meal. Will you please tell me what I can do about it?

Respectfully,
284 - Rufe Persful

December 16 - 1938.
From Spring Field, Missouri.
Post Office, Box 1000.
Pocahontas, Arkansas

To Miss. Ethel Persful.

Dear Sister:

In reply to your letter of November, 26th that I just received this morning I would have got it sooner if you had not neglected to put the Post Office Box No. 1000 on it. I sure was glad to hear from you and to hear you all were well. But sure was sorrow to hear of Walter being in the Hospital. Hope that he has recovered by now. As for me, I'm well. Hope when these few lines reaches you they will find you all well. I'm sure glad to hear that you are at home to stay for the winter. Well it sure is looking like snow this morning. Maybe we will have a white Christmas. It is so cold this morning. Well tell Marthia, Decker Hello, and that I would write to her if I could, and to be a sweet little girl just for me. I received a letter from Jasper, and Reba, the other day. Pauline sent me one of her pictures, with her boy friend, it was nice. Say Sister, I wrote you the other day about coming up here. If I was you I would not come. Not that I would not like to see you. But I don't thank it best you know. But Jasper, and Drue Bower's; could come any time; of course if Drue; would not drive him up here. Maybe he could get Jackie, Schooner to drive him up here and it would not cost much. I no that you folks kneed the money, that would make the with. I'm sure either one of them would be glad to drive him up here.

Well I suppose Henry and family will come down for Christmas. Tell them Hello for me. Write and till Walter, that I hope that he is getting along fine by now.

Well I suppose that old Santa Claus will visit you this Christmas, and bring you lots of fine presents; hope so.

Well Sis I hope to hear from you soon. I must bring this letter to a close for the present time.

So Love to you all.

A Merry Christmas, and - a Happy New Year to one and all.

Respectfully Your Brother.
Rufe Persful
Reg. No. (1442)

Extrolite FIBRE LIMBS

SERVICE

MINNEAPOLIS ARTIFICIAL LIMB COMPANY

MANUFACTURING SPECIALISTS IN LIMBS AND ORTHOPEDIC APPLIANCES

QUALITY

RAY TRAUTMAN, President
JUDGE W. A. ANDERSON, Vice-President
LUCIUS TRAUTMAN, Secretary
J. E. TRAUTMAN, Treasurer
DR. OSCAR J. ENGSTRAND. Consulting Physician
950 Medical Arts Bldg.
Minneapolis, GE. 6457

TELEPHONE: Office
MAin 2339

AFTER HOURS
WAlnut 0048
WAlnut 3648

MEMBER of A.L.M. ASSOCIATION OF LIMB MANUFACTURERS AMERICA

FIBRE-LITE

Doing business as

RAY TRAUTMAN & SON

240 South Fourth Street—Dean Building
Corner Opposite Court House
MINNEAPOLIS, MINN., U. S. A.

Aug. 13, 1937

Associated Service Agency

Claim Agent,
The Alcatraz Prison,
San Francisco, Calif.

Dear Sir:-

    Do you happen to know a Mr. Rufe Persful
and can you tell me if it is true that he did have to
suffer the loss of his hand and do you know anything
about how he is now?

    Can you tell me who his doctor is and what
hospital Mr. Persful is in, or just how I can reach
him at this time?

    Thanking you kindly and hoping to hear from
you soon, I am

        Sincerely yours,

        RAY TRAUTMAN & SON

JET:J

        By _J. E. Trautman_
           J. E. Trautman.

We have special branches .... in Canada where you will receive home service.

January 19 - 1939:
From Springfield Missouri:
Post Office Box, 1000.
Pocahontas; Arkansas:

To Miss Ethel Persful:

Will take the pleasure to write you a few lines this morning; hoping that when they reach you that it will find you well. As for me I am well and in good health; although some blue. Well this morning is a warm sunny day; the snow is now melting fast; It snowed all day the 17th. about three inch snow at the end of the day. I suppose you had snow down there to? It made me think of when we were just kid's at home, when we would get a sled and go to the hills for a slay ride; Oh, that was some life; Or go a rabbit hunting in the snow: And to have snow ice cream when we came home. Oh yes that was a wonderful life for us children. But those days are no more; they are just memories to me, although sweet one's.

I wrote to Mother yesterday; I hope they are well. When you come up here write and tell me the date that you are coming please. So I can talk to the doctor about it in advance. Tell Jasper, and Family hello for me and that I sure would like to see them all.

I don't know the doctor told me that I may go back to prison before long. Sure hope that I do. I can get to work and make some good time there and could go to a picture show once a week to. Well when are you going to go back to work? Well Sis I cant think of much to write so I will close for this time. Answer when you can. Love always, Your Bro.

Respectfully yours,
Rufe Persful 1442.

March 26, 1939
From Springfield, Missouri:
Box 1000.
Gary, Indiana:

To Mr. Walter, Persful

Forgive me please, for neglecting to write to you sooner than this: Hoping that these few lines may in reaching you find all in good health and enjoying life: Sure was sorry to hear of your sickness; But was more than glad to know of your good recovery back to health: Hope - Eva, and the children are doing fine; tell them hello; Sure would like to see them: Little Emmajean, ha grown so since last that I was there that I would hardly know her are MacDivell. Oh it would be a great pleasure to see them and more. They are going to school I am sure; Tell them to be good and mind their teacher and learn all that is in their power. Be sure and send me their pictures; It would be great to set down to one of Eva's, good and delicious, dinners, once more. She sure is a wonderful cook: It seems a thousand years since last that I was there. Ethel, wrote and told me of you and Mack, visiting Father and Mother; Sure glad you did they are getting very much up in the ages; and have not much longer in this old world you know. Tell Clarence, and Marie, King; hello, also Luther Rose. I suppose that they all have good obs; Reba, Jasper's, Girl, She wrote and told me that Shorty Massey, was up there now; does he live close to you? Well it came a slow Spring rain last night and leaves everything so fresh and green this morning; It is warm and beautiful weather here. I get to get out in the sun and fresh air 30 minutes each day except on Sundays, I don't work; I have not worked any for two years; now: I have plenty of Books and Magazine's, to read to pass the time. But still it goes very slow. Of course you heard of my accident when I very unfortunate lost my left hand. The News Papers put it out that I cut it off intentional. But far from it. I had no intention of cutting it off. Say Walter, when you write to me. Always sine your full name and address at the closing of your letter and put your name and address in the left hand corner of the envelope at the top, and my corret address. Other wise it will not reach me. Well I think I will write Henry, and Amy, sometime this week are next; I have not wrote to them for three years. You know there is never very much news, here to write. Well dinner is coming, so I must hang off for this time. They serve my meals in my cell so I don't have to go no place to eat that is something. ha, ha.

Well I will be looking forwards for an early answer. So Love to you and your family.

Respectfully, your, Brother.
Rufe Persful (1442)
Box 1000
Springfield, Missouri

Sept 6, 1941.
From Rufe Persful.

Honorable, Warden:

Sir, on the eighth of October, next I shall on that date have been under your Administratorship one year, and in that time I have been deprived of my wrights as a model prisoner here in your Institution. I have not received no yard, fresh-air and sunshine in that time. Only one bath a week. Always deadlocked day in and day out.

Sir, I realize the source of my trouble as well as anyone. But I also realize that my health is in very bad condition at present and that is why that I must ask you for help in my case.

I have tried very hard since being in the Federal Institution to live by the rules, which was made by the Warden of the Institution where I was at; and in seven years I have been written up by offi cers three times for fi ghting and it was not always my fault. Out side of those three times I have had no trouble, and have caused the offi cers no trouble in that seven years.

Please don't misunderstand my meaning. I have not been mistreated since being here, only confi nement is getting me nerves and I cannot stand it much longer. That is why I am going to ask one last favor. Please, transfer me to Sand Stone, Minn, Federal prison, or back to Springfi eld, Mo.

Because I can have more sunshine and fresh air there.

Respectfully
Rufe Persful
14945

Refer to SC 9/30/41
for general review

December 4, 1942.
From Rufe Persful #14945

To Senior Warden

Sir:

In regards to my case here, I have been in this Institution going onto three years, and have been confined in Deadlocked all of that time. I have been in Deadlock most of the past six years, except the last three months that I was at Springfield, Missouri. There I was aloud to go to the yard and get sunshine and fresh air. I have been locked up so close, that I am now speedily loosing my health. I cough constantly if I do the least bit of work. I have a constant severe pain in my chest if I take a deep breath.

I have spit up blood after working at work which required me to stretch my arms above my head. My present health is not good. I shake like a leaf after a very small amount of movement around in the Cell. I feel that my health is gradually slipping away. And I feel that it will continue to slip each day I remain here. There fore I am asking you to get me transferred back to Springfield, Missouri, where I can have yard and sun Shine.

Thank you in advance.

Respectfully,
Rufe Persful 14945.

June 29th, 1943.
From Rufe Persful
To Mr. P. J. Squires, Warden
McNeil Island, Washington

Sir:

Since Oct. 8, 1940, when I came here I've caused no trouble. I don't want to cause any so I'm writing to you. In view of the thoughtful little considerations you've given me, I regret I must ask you a favor, but you will see why the best I can explain it and still not put anyone on the spot. I have 4 1/2 years left here to do in Deadlock and I can't make it. You know I wouldn't say this if it wasn't so. I don't cry. But (9) years in prison, with nearly 2 1/2 years here in the deadlock, Close Supervision, no exercise, or yard and sunshine, and the aggravating human relations has broken my health and morale to a midway point in the fag between T. B. and another trip back to Springfield. You know the rea-

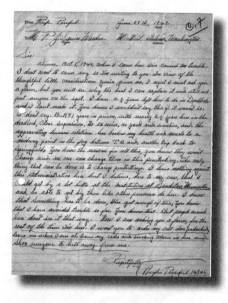

sons for all this, you know they won't change and no one can change them in this penitentiary. The only thing that can be done is to change penitentiaries. I have nothing against this administration here but I believe, due to my case, that I could get by a lot better at the Institution at Sandstone, Minnesota, and be able to get by there like other prisoners do here. I know that something has to be done, I've got enough of this, you know that I have avoided trouble so far. You know that. But people around here don't see it that way. Now I am asking you a favor, for the rest of the time I'm here. I want you to order my cell door padlocked, leave me where I am at, leave my radio and smoking tobacco in here and shoo everyone to hell away from me.

Respectfully
Rufe Persful 14945
2-A-9.

December 17th, 1943.
From Rufe Persful
To Associate Warden,
Mr. Delmore:

Sir, I don't know just why I have been deprived of my exercise. The Officer in here said it was for running around on the tiers. If he said it, it must be so, because he is an officer; and yet I have not been on no tiers, except when I put out Magazines and radio programs. I have put them out for the past 3 years, and never had any trouble with anyone.

Your officer never told me not to put them out. I ask him why did not he tell me to stay down and he said that I would have only blew up.

I would appreciate it if you would let me out like I was. That is all the privileges that I have had for six years and a half. And being locked in my cell for twenty-three and one half of an hour gets awful long. Anything you can do will be appreciated.

Respectfully,
Rufe Persful
14945.
2-A-9

P.S. I will go nuts in here!

Rufe Persful pictured following his Alcatraz release in 1938 to another federal institution.

Donnis Willis

ALCATRAZ MIRRORED the culturist biases existent in 1950's American society, and segregated African American inmates in the cellblock section known as Broadway. The tragically deep undercurrents of racial tension remained a palpable presence amongst the inmate population until the prison's closure in 1963. Former Public Enemy Number One, Alvin Karpis chronicled in his personal memoir entitled *On the Rock* the severe racial tensions occurring under Warder Swope in 1954. He wrote in part:

> Racial prejudice, in existence before, is nearing the point where racism is bubbling and boiling... There are only seven or eight white guys celling anywhere on Broadway now due to the shortage of cells since half of the inmate population is now black. I recall the early days when there weren't even enough Negroes to make up one table in the dining hall. Now it's a split mess hall with blacks on one side and whites on the other and trouble lurking somewhere in the middle. Swope forces whites to cell on Broadway beside or across from Negroes as punishment but he has never been foolish enough to precipitate another riot by placing a Negro in the outside cells which are the exclusive white suburbs of Alcatraz.

Ron Battles, one of a handful of African American officers employed at Alcatraz during its tenure as a federal prison, acknowledged the tense racial environment at Alcatraz. Racial tensions sometimes expanded beyond the inmate population and into the ranks of the officers.

Donald Willis's writings are reflective of the biases highlighted by Karpis:

> I, Donald Willis, make the following statement and claim that, on or about April 22, 1953 while serving a prison sentence and incarcerated in the Federal prison at Alcatraz, California, and in custody of Warden E. B. Swope and associate warden T. Delmare Jr.; I was confined in a segregation cell in T. U. Building, by associate warden T. Delmare Jr. for having refused to cell in the negro's quarters of the institution. I was confined in a segregation cell, starved and exposed to the cold, by the said prison authorities, in their effort to force me to move to the negro's cell block, to humiliate me before the other inmates.
>
> On the afternoon of May 1-2, 1953 and while confined in cell #6 in T. U. Building I, in protest of the discriminative treatment the officials were imposing upon me and from the infuriation of such treatment, wrapped a piece of cloth around my hand and with my fist, broke the light fixture in the cell and removed two small pieces of angle iron. I then used the pieces of angle iron together, as a tool to break the toi-

let bowl; Inmate Frank Davenport was brought to T. U. Building and placed in cell #6 with me. I explained to Davenport the cause for the cell being torn-up and impressed the hope that my action in tearing up the cell would occasion an investigation of the institution by the Attorney General of the United States, and my belief that following such an investigation the Attorney General of the United States would put an end to the discriminative punishment that was being imposed upon me, that he would grant better medical care for the inmates, better food, an inmate commissary, newspaper, radio, and other privileges that are given to prisoners in other Federal prisons.

When I had completed this exlination to Davenport, the guards brought our supper. After eating our supper we both went to sleep and sleep until about 7 o'clock when I was awakened by the other inmates making noise. I got up and made noise also by stomping on the bottom of the bunk. When the bottom of the bunk came loose from the angle iron frame I doubled it up. I then took the two small pieces of angle iron that I had taken from the light fixture and used them to knock the washbasin off the wall. I made noise by pounding on the wall with the pieces of angle iron until I tired. Davenport did not make noise saying that he was sick at the stomach.

We laid the small piece of blanket, the only piece of clothing in the besides our pants and shirts, on the floor and set talking about the other inmates who were making noise. We had been sitting on the floor and talking for about

one half hour when several guards including, Lt. Rychner, Lt. Suiverson, Lt. Stucker, officer Kirpatric, officer Runyon, came into the building dragging with them three high pressure fire hoses and turned them on the inmates. We listened as these guards went from cell to cell with the hoses. When they came to Davenport and myself, officer Rychner, acting captain of the guards and in charge of the "Strong arm squad" told the other guards that ours was the cell that they were looking for and told them to pour it on us. At that order the guards turned all three hoses on us. One or two of the guards then brought a long pole that was used for opening the windows and began jabbing us with it. We huddled in a far corner of the cell in a position so that the guards could only beat us one at a time. The guards continued to beat us in this manner for about one half hour before leaving our cell. In about one hour they returned to our cell again, ordered us to get on our feet, when we did they turned the hoses on us again. The force of the water, sand and gravel

Donnis Willis

in the lines knocked us off our feet, while we were down the guards jabbed us with the long pole. This second beating lasted for close to one hour.

The guards left us, after opening all the windows, sprawled in about four inches of water. The beating left us both sick and vomiting. Davenport hurt his back from one of the falls and was unable to stand up on his feet. The following morning several guards came to our cell, asked if we were still alive and ordered us to stand up. Davenport complained of his back hurting and asked to see the Doctor. Then two of the guards came into the cell and stripped Davenport of all his cloths and one on each arm carried him to the dungeon. Later in the day the Doctor came to my cell and treated my ear which was injured by the water hoses. I told the Doctor that their was a sick man back in the dark hole; and if he would look at him and examine him he would see that Davenport was sick, but I do not know if he examined Davenport or not.

I did not see Davenport again until on or about May 6-7, 1953 when he was brought from the dungeon and again placed in a cell #33 with me, where he remained for one night and then taken back to the dungeon. A few weeks later I was taken from segregation and tried for my goodtime for destroying the light fixture, toilet bowl, bed bottom and wash basin. Associate Warden L. Delmare Jr. was head of the committee that tried me. I pleaded not guilty to the charges but was found guilty by the committee and forfeited 245 days

goodtime and fined thirty-nine dollars ($39.50) and fifty cents cost. I did not see Davenport again to speak to him until about June 20-21, 1953 when I learned that he had also been accused of tearing up the cell fixtures and tried for his goodtime. A month or so later he informed me that he had been found guilty, had forfeited goodtime and fined thirty-nine Dollars ($39.50) fifty cents). With this information I immediately sought an interview with Warden E. B. Swope and explained the situation to him. I assured him that I tore up the cell, busted the toilet bowl, light fixtures, wash basin and tore the bottom out of the bunk, and that Davenport had absolutely nothing to do with it and was in no way responsible for my acts. The Warden E. B. Swope promised to check into the matter, but when I consulted him a second time a few months later he informed me that I had pleaded not guilty to the charges of tearing up the fixtures when I was tried for my goodtime, that the goodtime committee had acted and that their decision must stand.

The prison officials neglected their duty of determining who was responsible for the property being torn up. Warden E. B. Swope has refused to accept the facts when presented to him. This negligence of the officials is no doubt responsible for Frank Davenport being severely and cruelly beaten with the fire hoses and for the forfeiture of several hundred days of his goodtime. It is my hope that this negligence and gross injustice can, and will, be remedied.

James Boarman

"The last time I saw your boy he was swimming towards Sausalito on his way to freedom. Don't think ill of the boy he wanted to go and all your prayers would not stop him."

—R.R. BAKER, 1943

ON A FOG shrouded morning in April of 1943, James Arnold Boarman, a small time bank robber from Indianapolis, would lose his life in an ill-fated break to escape the Rock. At only twenty-four years old, Boarman along with fellow inmates; Harold Brest, Floyd Hamilton (famed getaway driver for Bonnie and Clyde), and Fred Hunter took two officers hostage while at work in the Alcatraz industries. The inmates smuggled military uniforms from the prison laundry and had stuffed them into large canisters to be used as floats. The canisters offered perfect concealment and water protection for their clothing, and were a seemingly perfect float device with which to swim gracefully across the bay.

The environmental conditions seemed ideal for the escape, with densely layered fog enveloping the island. It was later speculated that the inmates had cut through one of the steel-mesh window guards in the old Mat Shop during the previous weeks, hiding their work by using grease mixed with other agents to fill in the tiny sawed gaps. One by one, the men climbed through the window, negotiated the wire fencing, and then hurried down to the rocky shore. Boarman and Brest attempted to maneuver the float canisters through the window without success, so they were forced to leave them behind, along with the clothing they contained. Hunter had injured himself when dropping from the

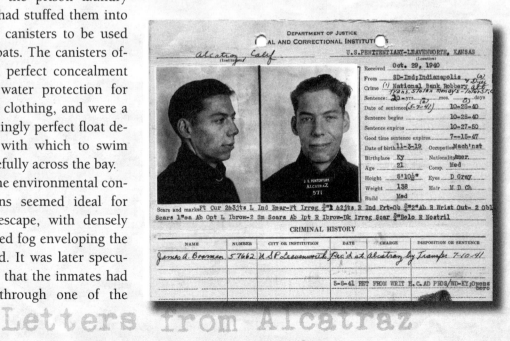

fence, and he took refuge in a small island cave that was recessed under the industry buildings. Boarman, Brest, and Hamilton each started their swim to freedom, partially obscured by the breaking fog.

Meanwhile one of the hostage officers had succeeded in loosening his gag and started yelling for help, but due to the noise of the loud machinery, his cries went unheard. At about the same time, another officer Frank L. Johnson who was assigned to the tower atop the Model Shop had already contacted Armory Officer Cliff Fish indicating that he was unable to make contact with the officers in the Mat Shop. Fish, who was just being relieved from duty, responded to the industries to investigate the problem, accompanied by officers Phil Bergen and Earl Long. Johnson stepped outside of the tower booth, and immediately spotted several figures in the water, swimming away from the island.

Lifting his rifle, Johnson strained to peer into the target site as several faint figures continued to advance away from the island in the foggy seascape. Watching the figures move in rhythm with the sea, he drew his grip tight, and squeezed the trigger until the pressure of the spring gave way to a ragging explosive shot. He repeated the process, sighting each moving figure, then firing his Springfield .30-06. Each round released a caustic smell of burnt gunpowder mixed with the misty salt air. Brest and Boarman saw the geyser-like splash patterns in the water around them, accompanied by the distant sharp cracking sound of a high-powered rifle. After each round was fired, silence would drape the water until the next blast racked the air. As Brest and Boarman swam almost side-by-side a few hundred yards from shore, the sounds of Boarman's thrashing suddenly stopped. As Brest reached out to examine the now silent form of his fellow inmate, the water surrounding them started to turn an eerie red.

Boarman's eyes were open, but glazed over by the seawater as Brest tried to maintain his grip on his accomplice's limp body. Boarman was bleeding profusely from what appeared to be a bullet wound behind his left ear. The prison launch pulled alongside the two inmates, with an officer aiming his muzzle at Brest's head. Brest struggled to hang on to Boarman's belt, but as the officers attempted to latch it with a boat hook, the belt broke, and Boarman slowly disappeared into the green murky depths. Brest was pulled into the launch and wrapped in blankets, then returned to the island. He was immediately taken to the prison hospital and examined. He had sustained only a minor bullet wound to his elbow.

Hamilton was initially presumed drowned. However, after hiding out for two days in a small shoreline cave and suffering from the severe effects of exposure and hypothermia, he made his way back up to the industries area where he was discovered by a correctional officer. Hunter had hid in the same cave, but surrendered quickly after the escape.

Boarman's death was the end of a long rudderless course that had started early in his youth and finally landed him on Alcatraz. Born on November 3, 1919 in Whalen, Kentucky, he was the sixth in a family of eight children. His father, who had supported the family as a carpenter, died of an accidental drowning when James was only seven. His mother, a homemaker, relocated the family to Indiana where they would all share residence in a small apartment. Boarman attended Catholic School in Indianapolis, and dropped out to work as a gardener at age fourteen. His mother would later state that James always had brought his earnings home, and never complained about the family's financial troubles. Despite their hardships and their dependence welfare support, reports state that his family was close, and all worked together to help and support each other.

Boarman's bouts with crime first began when he was still very young. In May of 1936 he stole his first automobile, and after being arrested and placed on probation, he stole two other cars and headed for California with two accomplices. His mother pleaded his case in court, stating that she had been hospitalized due to illness, and that he had lacked proper supervision when he needed it most. The court proved unsympathetic to her pleas,

and on January 30, 1937, Boarman was sentenced to three years in the Federal Reformatory at El Reno, Oklahoma.

Boarman and four other inmates plotted an escape from El Reno, and later recommended for transfer to a more secure prison facility at Lewisburg Federal Penitentiary in September of 1937. At Lewisburg he continued to assemble a record of conduct violations. In 1940, following another violent escape attempt, Boarman was recommended for transfer to Alcatraz.

Boarman's mother never seemed to lose faith in her son, uprooting her life and moving to San Francisco to provide her son support and companionship. Until the end, Boarman remained a difficult and challenging inmate. There are only a few letters remaining in Boarman's file, but they remain a tragic bookend to one of the hopeless dreams of escaping life at Alcatraz.

Nov. 29, 1940
Indianapolis, Ind.

Dear Sir;

My letter was returned to me stating that I am not listed as an approved correspondent of James Arnold Boarman. Arnold and I are about the same age and have always been pals. It would be awful if I could not write to him. He will be away from home a long time. Please, please, reconsider to let me write to my brother. When Arnold was in prison before I never received a letter back but once and that was because I failed to write my whole name which is Mary Louise Johnson. I omitted

Letters from Alcatraz

Letters from Alcatraz

JOHN EDGAR HOOVER
DIRECTOR

Federal Bureau of Investigation

United States Department of Justice

Washington, D. C.

July 7, 1941

went to Alcatraz last night

MEMORANDUM FOR THE DIRECTOR
BUREAU OF PRISONS

RE: JAMES ARNOLD BOARMAN,
with aliases

        In view of the various attempts of James Arnold
Boarman to escape Federal custody, one of which was a wanton
effort to wreck the automobile in which Boarman and two
guards were riding, I wanted to specifically call your attention to his activities as reflected in the parole report
of Special Agent Francis X. Jahn, dated May 13, 1941, at
Louisville, Kentucky, a copy of which is attached.

                                Very truly yours,

                                John Edgar Hoover
                                        Director

Enclosure

SEP 16 1938

ME
9-15

DEPARTMENT OF JUSTICE
DIVISION OF RECORDS

Indianapolis Ind

1938 SEP 13 PM 12:53

Sep- 11- 38.

U S Parole Board.
Gentlemen :

Will you please take my son's case, James Arnold Boarman # 5950. Now in Lewisburg Penitentiary under consideration

Please see if you can get him a release on parole. He has now served over half of his sentence.

Please help my boy.

Yours Very Sincerely,

Ella Boarman.

RECEIVED

SEP 13 1938

Office of Parole Executive

Mary and it was returned to me. Perhaps you returned my letter because I wrote a joke in it which I am very sorry for if it was.

Arnold broke my heart when he got into trouble again. I, so much wanted to see him go straight and be happy. We were in an orphanage together and I love my brother so please let me write to him.

I know how this would make my mother feel if she knew, as she always depended on me to write as much as I could to him.

Arnold was swell to me and always called me "Butch." Maybe you have someone in your heart like that you love. Please let me know by return mail as I won't tell my mother until I hear from you. Hoping that you will understand.

Yours Respectfully
Mrs. Mary Louise Johnson

2820 Campbell St.
Kansas City Mo.
Aug - 26 - 1941
Warden,

Dear Sir,

In regard to my son James A. Boarman, 571. Will you please let me know how he is getting along.

He writes me he is getting along fine. Will you please tell me what the visiting rules are?

Yours Very Truly
Mrs Ella Boarman

[Handwritten Note] Interviewed - he says his mother has raised large family (8) that he is black sheep caused her lots of trouble and she gives him lots of attention and is now talking about coming to San Francisco so as to be near him but he has attempted to advise he against moving - says he is well and getting along OK -

JAJ 9/3/41

1422 California
San Francisco, Calif.
February 9, 1942

Warden James A. Johnston
Alcatraz Island
San Francisco, Calif.

Dear Sir,

I have come to San Francisco
to live so that I might visit my
son, James Arnold Boarman #571,
as often as possible. I have obtained employment and as yet
I am not quite certain of my
working hours. I was told that I
could not visit on Sunday. Would
you please inform me as to when
I can visit him and how I should
go about it.

I would also like to know if
there is any way that I can receive mail from Alcatraz without anyone
knowing about it. As I intend to make my home here, it would be somewhat embarrassing as you can see.

Thank you very much.

Yours very truly,
Ella Boarman

1671 Bush St.
San Francisco, Calif.
March 15, 1942
Mr. James A. Johnston

Dear Sir:

May I please visit my son James A. Boarman 571. March 26th

Thank you

Yours truly,
Ella Boarman

February 11, 1942

Mrs. Ella Boarman
1422 California Street
San Francisco, California

Dear Madam:

Under the regulations an inmate may receive one visit a
month from relatives. No visits are allowed on Sundays or holidays
but visits may be arranged for on any other week day morning than
Sunday or a holiday. There is no particular day set aside for any
particular inmate or his relative as their day for visiting but each
visit is arranged for upon the request of the relative and we endeavor
to fix a day that will be the most convenient for the visitor. The
boat that you would take leaves San Francisco at 10:00 A.M. and on
the return trip leaves Alcatraz at 11:20 A.M.

Keeping in mind the above regulations we will endeavor to
accommodate you. When you would like to have a visit write me a letter
about two weeks in advance. State the day that you would like to visit
and I will do my best to arrange it and will send the necessary pass
with instructions as to how to reach the Island.

All of our letters pass through the Post Office on Alcatraz
Island and therefore bear the mark. If it is embarassing to receive
mail at your home address you can arrange with the United States
Probation Officer in San Francisco to have the letters that your son
may write addressed to you in care of the Probation Officer and then
you can call for them at the Probation Office at your convenience.
Mr. Charles H. Upton is the United States Probation Officer, Room 415
Post Office Building, Seventh and Mission Streets, San Francisco.
If you would like to make the arrangement that I have suggested call
to see Mr. Upton and show him this letter and I am sure that he will
be glad to receive the letters that your son may address to you in
his care.

Sincerely,

J. A. JOHNSTON
Warden

UNITED STATES PENITENTIARY

Alcatraz, California

Date 7/15 1941

    I, The undersigned, authorize the Warden of the United States Penitentiary, Alcatraz, California, or his authorized representative, to open all my mail matter, express and other packages, which may be directed to my address, and to sign my name as endorsement on all checks, money orders or bank drafts, for deposit to my credit in the prisoners trust fund, as long as I am a prisoner in this institution.

    Dated at the United States Penitentiary, Alcatraz, California.

This day 7/15/41

Signed: *James A. Boarman - 571*

     Name   No.

Witness: *R. Groens S.O.*

FPI INC—FLR-7.25.36—100—11364-1

[Handwritten Note] Told that he would half to work and behave if he wanted his mother to visit him.

Stated he did not think he was going to work. And wished we would just tell his mother that he was all right. I told him we would half to tell his mother the truth.

This inmate is in solitary.

March 20, 1942

Mrs. Ella Boarman
1671 Bush Street
San Francisco, California

Dear Madam:

Responsive to your note of March 15, 1942, I am sorry to say that I cannot comply with your request for you to visit your son at this time because his failure and unwillingness to comply with necessary, reasonable regulations requires a temporary suspension of privileges.

When your son indicates willingness to comply with regulations and performs his allotted tasks, his privileges will be restored and at that time I shall be only too glad to issue the requested pass for you to visit your son.

Sincerely,
J. A. JOHNSTON
Warden

2027 N. Park Ave.
Indianapolis, Ind.
May 11, 1943
Warden James A. Johnston

Dear Sir:

   Am enclosing papers which are to be filled out by the last Doctor who attended my son James Arnold. Also I must have a statement of some kind that will be proof of death.

   I will pay any expenses entailed in securing desired statement. This is necessary in order to collect on insurance.

   Also wish to say if my son's body should be recovered. Please notify me at once.

   Thanking you in advance.

   Sincerely yours,
   Ella Boarman

Mrs. Ella Boarman   (2)   5/28/43

        You may show this letter to the officials of the Insurance Company, and they may be willing to accept it in lieu of a statement from a physician which is impossible to secure.

                Sincerely,

                J. A. JOHNSTON, Warden

1 Enclosure:
     Physician's Statement –
     National Life and Accident Ins. Co.
     returned herewith.

Alcatraz, Cal.
April 14, 1943

Mrs. Ella Boarman
1707 Octavia St.
San Francisco, Cal.

Dear Madam:

I am sending your last letter to James, back to you. I am sorry that I can not make delivery. I know that you will be deeply hurt over the tragedy but please try to remember that the boy went out a man. It takes nerve, spunk, backbone, to do what he did.

Alcatraz Mail Officer Bob Baker at his desk in 1949.

The last time I saw your boy he was swimming towards Sausalito on his way to freedom. Don't think ill of the boy he wanted to go and all your prayers would not stop him.

Perhaps I am taking too much upon myself in writing this letter, but please believe me I have seen you so often and talked about the boy with you that I almost feel that a note from me might help you. After reading your mail and his mail for almost two years.

Yours truly,
R.R. Baker
Mail Officer

Harold Brest

BOARMAN'S accomplice to the 1943 escape Harold Martin Brest, inmate number AZ-380, would be one of the few select inmates to be committed to Alcatraz twice during their lifetime. Brest was sentenced in January of 1937 to serve a term of life and a concurrent 55-year sentence for kidnapping and bank robbery. He was sent to Alcatraz on March 13, 1937 for "adjustment purposes" as indicated in his inmate case file. Brest submitted a petition of habeas corpus which was granted and he was remanded to trial court. He was eventually retried; convicted and returned to Alcatraz in September of 1939 until his transfer to another federal prison in April of 1950.

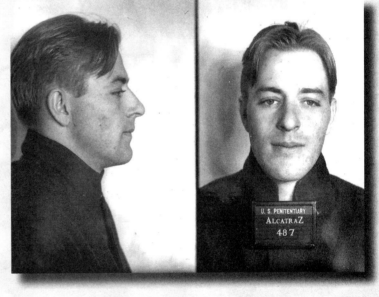

21st January 1944

Carol Rogan
East Sydney
Australia

Dear Harold,
   You won't know what to think at getting a letter from me but first I will explain. I am an Australian girl my age is just eighteen. Tonight is January the 20th 1944. On my bed next to me is my 17 year old sister. She has just finished reading "True Detective magazine." She and I just read a story about you and those other prisoners who tried to make that prison break.

We felt very miserable when we read about you and I said a prayer for you. I have never been in prison myself but I have a pretty good idea what "hell" it must be. I don't ever go out much down here. Australia is a pretty quiet place you know. There's no night clubs or like of any description. The "Yankee" soldiers see it a lot different to back home. I have 6 sisters and two brothers. My young brother is just 2 months old. He's a little ginger headed bloke. He's lovely.

My sister here and I left home a month or so back and came up north. It's about a thousand miles from home. We get awful homesick so we're going home on the 15th February and never going to wander for a long time.

Although after the war we are going to be stewardesses on a ship going from here to America so I'll probably call in and see you. That's if you're allowed to see visitors.

I am a waitress. I work in a large hotel. I wait on all kinds of people, mostly rich people. I often wish I was a little better off but I don't mind being a good hard working girl. I have 2 sisters who are machinist. They have been at their jobs 8 years but my other sister and I are the two tomboys. I suppose we've have worked in "chocolate factories" woolen mills" and all kind of places but its fun. We like a change now and then.

The large town hall clock has just struck 11 o'clock and all my workmates have just came home from the pictures and they are all talking about their romances. You know when girls are at that silly age and they won't stop talking about who they have been out

with, funny we two never bother going out much. I don't think the girls can
understand it. We are said to be attractive but that's neither here or there.

Well I really don't know what to say to you in this letter only I hope
you don't get very miserable for your not really missing much not the way
the world is today with all this war and killing and one thing and another.

I know you aren't as tough as they make out you are when I read about
how you tried to keep your dead mate a fl oat when they shot him. I knew
then you must be a pretty decent bloke.

Well Harold I suppose you're tired of my silly girlish rambling so I'll
close. But remember don't get too miserable or down hearted for there's 2
"Aussie" girls who are praying and thinking of you and they both wish you
all the luck in the world so goodbye for now Harold and keep your chin up.
I think you're a fi ne fellow.

    Lots of luck
    Carol Rogan

    P.S. Please write soon and if you ever need any little thing let me know.

CLASS OF SERVICE

This is a full-rate Telegram or Cablegram unless its deferred character is indicated by a suitable symbol above or preceding the address.

WESTERN UNION

A. N. WILLIAMS PRESIDENT — NEWCOMB CARLTON CHAIRMAN OF THE BOARD — J. C. WILLEVER FIRST VICE-PRESIDENT

SYMBOLS

DL = Day Letter
NT = Overnight Telegram
LC = Deferred Cable
NLT = Cable Night Letter
Ship Radiogram

The filing time shown in the date line on telegrams and day letters is STANDARD TIME at point of origin. Time of receipt is STANDARD TIME at point of destination.

LD 17NV 87   MAIL

Duplicate of Telephoned Telegram

SAN FRANCISCO CALIF MAY 3 1946 631A

WARDEN JAMES A JOHNSTON

U. S. PENITENTIARY
ALCATRAZ ISLAND CALIF.

ALCATRAZ CALIF

MAY 4 1946

GOD SPEED TO YOU AND YOUR VALIANT MEN WE FERVENTLY WISH AND PRAY
THAT NO MORE OF YOUR COURAGEOUS OFFICERS ARE INJURED IN THEIR
EFFORTS TO QUELL THE RIOTERS OUR HEARTFELT AND DEEPEST SYMPATHY
GOES OUT TO THOSE ALREADY WOUNDED AND THEIR FAMILIES MAY THEY
ALL RECOVER IT WAS TRAGIC THAT A HEROIC OFFICER LIKE HAROLD
STITES SHOULD BE KILLED TO YOU WARDEN WE WISH TO EXPRESS OUR
SINCERE APPRECIATION FOR YOUR EXCELLENT AND WONDERFUL COOPERATION
IN TAKING TIME DURING SUCH STRESS TO SEND US DETAILED BULLETINS

JOHN D HANLEY

INTERNATIONAL NEWS SERVICE

720A

U. S. PENITENTIARY
ALCATRAZ ISLAND, CALIF.
RECD
MAY 4 1946

THE COMPANY WILL APPRECIATE SUGGESTIONS FROM ITS PATRONS CONCERNING ITS SERVICE

Golden Gate NRA, Park Archives, Alcatraz 1946 Riot Collection, GOGA 18308

CLASS OF SERVICE

This is a full-rate Telegram or Cablegram unless its deferred character is indicated by a suitable symbol above or preceding the address.

WESTERN UNION

A. N. WILLIAMS, CHAIRMAN OF THE BOARD — JOSEPH L. EGAN, PRESIDENT

SYMBOLS

DL = Day Letter
NL = Night Letter
LC = Deferred Cable
NLT = Cable Night Letter
Ship Radiogram

The filing time shown in the date line on telegrams and day letters is STANDARD TIME at point of origin. Time of receipt is STANDARD TIME at point of destination.

Duplicate of Telephoned Telegram

LD190 NF 68   MAIL

SAN FRANCISCO CALIF MAY 2 1946

U. S. PENITENTIARY
ALCATRAZ ISLAND, CALIF.
RECD

WARDEN J A JOHNSTON

ALCATRAZ CALIF   MAY 4 1946

NEWSPAPERS AND RADIO ACROSS THE COUNTRY ARE DELUGING US WITH INQUIRIES
ON ANY FURTHER CASUALTIES IN RIOTING STOP THEY ALSO ASK CONFIRMATION
OF THE REPORT THAT A PRISONER NAMED COY STARTED WHOLE THING BY
OVERPOWERING A GUARD AND PRESSING A BUTTON THAT OPENED ALL THE CELL
DOORS AND INVITING OTHERS TO JOIN HIM STOP CAN YOU CONFIRM THIS AND
GIVE US MORE ON COY IF THIS IS TRUE PLEASE

ROGER JOHNSON UNITED PRESS

1140P

THE COMPANY WILL APPRECIATE SUGGESTIONS FROM ITS PATRONS CONCERNING ITS SERVICE

May 13, 1946,
Washington D.C.

My Dear Warden Johnston:

Mr. Bennett has just given me an account of the manner in which the courage, bravery and quick thinking of you and your staff prevented the mutiny at Alcatraz from becoming a truly serious calamity.

I would like you and every member of your staff to know of my appreciation and admiration for the outstandingly courageous and intelligent with which you and your officers coped with the revolt. All of you performed a signal service in protecting the public from the desperate criminals with whom you must deal and showed a devotion to duty which I am sure will command the admiration of every good citizen. The fine job you did under extremely difficult and seriously dangerous circumstances will add further to the excellent reputation the Federal Prison Service has earned.

Our sincerest sympathy goes forward to the familes of those officers who died shielding the lives of others and our best wishes for a speedy recovery are extended to those who performed their tasks so unselfishly.

Sincerely yours,

Tom Clark
Attorney General
United States of America

Battle of Alcatraz

ON MAY 2, 1946, six convicts embarked on one of the most violent escape attempts ever made on the Rock. Many historians rank this as the most significant event in the island's twenty-nine-year history as a Federal penitentiary, and it was appropriately labeled by the contemporary press as the *Battle of Alcatraz*. Of the thirty-nine convicts who attempted to escape over the years, Bernie Coy was the only one to successfully plot and execute a plan to secure weapons — and they were used with deadly consequences. In the wake of the conflict, two correctional officers and three inmates lay dead from bullet wounds, and several others were left seriously injured. This legendary escape attempt would remain a topic of dis-

The Battle of Alcatraz *was one of the most violent prison escape attempts ever recorded in United States history. Reinforcements were brought in from a variety of agencies to help gain back control of Alcatraz Island. They included personnel from the Bureau of Prisons, law enforcement agencies, and the military.*

Letters from Alcatraz

Spectators lined the shores of San Francisco, watching the embattled prison. The sounds of gunfire and bombing resonated throughout the city.

cussion by inmates and guards alike until the prison's closure in 1963.

Forty-six-year-old Bernard Paul Coy was a hillbilly bank robber serving out the remainder of a twenty-five-year sentence on the Rock. His escape plan had been derived from carefully studying the habits of various guards and their assignments over a several month period. On May 2, 1946, Coy, with the help of accomplice and former Public Enemy Joseph Cretzer, Coy smeared axle grease over his chest, head and extremities, and started climbing the West End Gun Gallery from the juncture at Times Square and Michigan Avenue. Climbing hand over hand, he scaled the barred gallery until he reached the top.

Clinched in his teeth was a small cloth bag that contained a crudely fashioned bar spreader device that was made from toilet fixtures in one of the prison workshops. The device was firmly set between the two bars (approximately 5 inches), and by using a small wrench, Coy was able to exert enough force to effectively spread the bars to create an opening nearly ten inches in width. It was believed that Coy had also been limiting his intake of food to reduce his body mass. With Cretzer eagerly watching his progress from below, Coy painfully squeezed his body through the opening and made entrance into the West Gun Gallery.

Philip Bergen later provided his perspective on the progression of events:

"Coy's experienced escape prone eyes, noticed what he thought to be a weakness in the physical structure of one of the gun gallerys. The only thing that he had to do, in order to put his escape plan in motion, was to distract the attention of the armed officer in the gallery, which he was able to do by creating with the aid of an accessory in the treatment unit, a disturbance which drew the officer off-post. When the officer did return a few minutes later, [Coy] was ready for him. He pounced on him, overpowered him, knocked him unconscious and took his weapons."

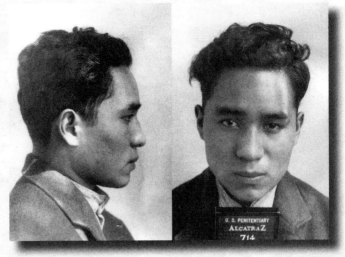

Clarence Carnes, at 18-years of age was the youngest inmate incarcerated at Alcatraz as a federal penitentiary.

The convicts now armed were able to capture nine unarmed guards and lock them into #402 and #403, which were the end cells located at the juncture of Seedy Street and Times Square. Their escape plans soon folded when they were unable to locate the key that would unlock door leading to the recreation yard. The key was bravely concealed by Correctional Officer Bill Miller who had surrendered all of his keys except the most critical. Miller was able to quietly hide the key in the cell toilet where he and the other correctional officers were held hostage.

Coy & Cretzer had also released three other accomplices from their cells. Clarence Carnes (the youngest convict ever sent to Alcatraz), Sam Shockley, and Miran Thompson, were serving sentences for violent crimes. The distress sirens of Alcatraz wailed, indicating grave trouble and could be easily heard from the shores of San Francisco. The Coast Guard and Marines were mobilized, furnishing support of demolition and weapon experts and all off-duty correctional officers were brought in to help take back the cellhouse.

Since the takeover occurred after lunch, the majority of inmates were in the industries and the cellblock was largely empty. Marines assisted correc-

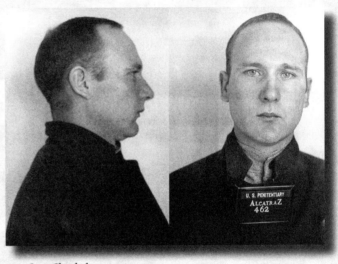

Sam Shockely

tional officers in assembling all of the industry workers into the recreation yard and helped to gather blankets and jackets for the inmates unable to return to their cells. Inside the cellblock a battle was raging. The inmates, realizing that they were unable to gain access to the recreation yard, became desperate. In a violent rage, cheered on by Shockley and Thompson, Joseph Cretzer took his revolver and leaning against the bars of cell

Battle of Alcatraz

#403, started unloading rounds into the cramped cell. Officers fell in the gunfire, some now critically wounded.

The warden had called together his lieutenants and formulated a strategy to send in strike teams to rescue the guards held captive. Lt. Philip R. Bergen was assigned to lead for the first team into the cellhouse through the West End Gun Gallery. Led by Bergen, two guards fired several rounds to clear the corridor. The team rapidly made their assault into the gallery and up the stairs to the first level. As one of the inmates fired rifle rounds at the assault team, Bergen and fellow officers worked feverishly to rescue the officer that had been ambushed by Coy.

Harold Stites was also part of Bergen's team and courageously returned fire, attempting to suppress the barrage. Stites was no stranger to this type of scenario. In 1938, three inmates rushed him while on post in a guard tower. In an attempt to stop them from securing firearms, he was forced to shoot two inmates, one fatally. The 1938 break attempt was one of the most violent in the Island's history. The tragedy resulted in the death of a correctional officer who had been fatally assaulted with a hammer by inmate named Rufus Franklin.

As Bergen rendered care to a downed officer, Stites continued to lay rifle fire into the cellhouse. In a sudden flash, Stites was struck, yelling out that he'd been hit. Three other officers were hit by gunfire during this assault. Stites was carried unconscious out of the gun gallery and laid onto a couch. He was quickly examined by the prison's physician and pronounced dead. Stites would be the first causality. The other officers were quickly transported by boat back to the mainland to be transported by ambulance to a local hospital.

Bergen and four other officers returned to the gallery and communicated information from one of the gallery phone lines. It appeared that an inmate was running from cell-to-cell firing random shots into the gun gallery. A little after 10:00 p.m., the associate warden took a group of fourteen officers and burst into the cellhouse, looking to rescue their fellow officers. The team fell under heavy gunfire from the inmates who had positioned themselves on top of C-Block. One of the officers was able to close the D-Block access door, and then was immediately struck in the shoulder by

Officer Donald Martin's entries in his personal journal relating to the 1946 "Big Break."

Amid the smoke in the aftermath of the battle, the United States flag was brought down to half-mast in honor of the officers who lost their lives during the siege.

Scenes of Alcatraz at war. Armed with field guns and mortars, the United States Marines used heavy artillery to barrage the cellhouse in an effort to regain control.

WARNING
KEEP OFF

Letters from Alcatraz

193

gunfire. After realizing their chances of escape were past, Shockley and Thompson retreated back to their cells to contemplate how to defend their involvement.

Not knowing the origin of the barrage of gunfire, the Marines started bombing D-Block with explosives as the cellblock filled with dense smoke. Coy, Cretzer, and fellow conspirator Marvin Hubbard retreated in the utility corridor as the bombing continued. The Marines drilled holes in the ceilings, lowering hand grenades attached to wire and then detonating them. The concussions were fierce and the prisoners in D-Block hid behind soaking wet mattresses with little protection. The barrage of gunfire, mortars, and teargas was ceaseless. Water from the broken plumbing started flowing from the tiers and flooding D-Block.

Robert Stroud (a.k.a., Birdman of Alcatraz), made efforts to end the battle. At fifty-six years old, he climbed over the railing of the third tier and lowered himself to the second tier, then dropped onto the floor of D-Block. In what seemed to be a valiant move, he started closing the front solid steel doors of the six isolation cells to protect the helpless men. Stroud yelled up to Bergen, explaining that there were no firearms in D-Block and that those involved had retreated to another section of the prison. He made it clear that many innocent men would die if they continued to barrage them with gunfire.

After nearly 48 hours of battle, the gunfire ceased. In the violent aftermath, Cretzer, Coy, and Hubbard were killed in the corridor from bullet wounds and shrapnel. The mastermind Coy, was found dead wearing a guard uniform. Officer Bill Miller later died from his injuries. A second officer, Harold Stites, was shot and killed during an attempt to re-

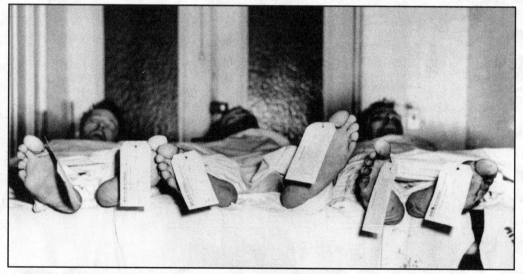

The lifeless bodies of the inmates presented by the medical examiner to the press. Clarence Carnes later commented in a documentary interview: "When they decided to die, I was there… It was on the bottom steps of C-Block, and they were talking about it like ordinary conversation. That struck me… I didn't know what I expected but I didn't expect them to casually talk about dying. Coy said, "Well… they're not going to get me…" Hubbard then said, "Well… they're not going to get me either…." Cretzer then said, "Well, we better save some bullets for ourselves…"

Battle of Alcatraz

Letters from Alcatraz

194

Warden Johnston showing members of the press the blood-stained wall of cell #403, where four officers were shot in cold blood by Joseph Cretzer.

Hand drawn diagrams by Philip Bergen which chronicle the violent events.

Letters from Alcatraz

Clarence Carnes, seen here as a tourist at Alcatraz in 1980.

gain control of the cellhouse. Thompson and Shockley were later executed sitting side-by-side in the Gas Chamber at San Quentin for their role in the murders of both officers. Clarence Carnes received an additional 99-year sentence and was eventually released into free society. He found life on the outside difficult and ultimately died in a federal prison hospital in 1988 at only 61-years of age.

It would take months before the cellblocks returned to any normalcy and the scars on the cement and cell walls would remain strong reminders until the closure of the prison of the consequences of attempted escape.

Bernard Paul Coy

READING Coy's letters from the years prior to his Alcatraz escape attempt, it would be nearly impossible to predict his violent and premeditated break for freedom. His letters articulated what appeared to be a true desire to reform, as is illustrated in these excerpts written to the superintendent of the prison where he was incarcerated on August 30, 1936:

August 30, 1936

Mr. James Hammond:

I regret that this request must be made under the present unfavorable conditions, rather than under circumstances relevant to the continued progress of some noble social service. Please believe me sincere in my regret, Mr. Hammond; and if there is a loyalty of promise incapable of future betrayal, you may be assured, Sir, that your confidence in me, however great or small, shall never be abused.

I become eligible for parole, under the present stature governing similar cases, in October of this year. I should like to go home at that time, Mr. Hammond. I have a position awaiting me in Detroit, Michigan; also one in Elizabethtown, Kentucky. I shall take either of the two, at your discretion. However, I do hold preference to the former named. Without your recommendation, I can hope for little to be done. Won't you do this for me?

It is true, I have served "Time" in other prisons than

Bernard Paul Coy was the primary architect of one of the most ingenious escape plots ever implemented at Alcatraz. He would be the only inmate in the prison's history to successfully secure prison firearms.

this one. I served - from 1 to 3 years - in the Wisconsin State Reformatory, at Green Bay. I also served a 5 year sentence in the Wisconsin State Prison, at Waupun. I was paroled on the first sentence and made good. On the latter sentence, however, I could obtain no consideration, due to the fact that I refused to change my plea of Not Guilty, to one of, Guilty, after arriving behind walls. It is a rare occasion when a man is paroled from Waupun unless he changes his plea of Not Guilty. I served the full five years. I was not guilty, and could not plead guilty. The reformatory sentence, on the other hand, was different. I was guilty as charged. And I plead guilty. These former counts, because of my attorney's refusing to take the stand at the time of trial, were not used against me. This would have been unconstitutional had it come to pass. And I am of the opinion that what is unconstitutional in court is also unconstitutional at any other time or place. The parole board will not further punish me for offenses paid in full. Of this, I am sure.

Since my incarceration, I have made a record which is the envy of everyone. Not one time have I been disobedient, or sullen, nor have I set an example which would not be commendable in the best society. I am a firm believer in discipline, and regulate my actions according to my belief. I believe I have proved myself trustworthy. I am president of the Holy Names Society here inside the prison, a Catholic society, and I know that I have acquitted my office satisfactorily every moment. I do know right from wrong, and certainly try to be well thought of by everyone I meet. The Army and the World War, at age seventeen, gave me a background upon which to build a life equally as remarkable as your own; and I may yet put the right foot first. I am not too proud to ask for help, nor too weak to win if refused. I am not guilty of any crime and have nothing of which to be ashamed. Your will is my determination, Sir, in prison or, at home. More than this no man can promise.

And I am,

Yours very truly,
Bernard P. Coy

Only six months after composing this letter, Coy was released from prison. He was soon involved in more crimes which would eventually lead to his incarceration at Alcatraz.

Wisconsin Rapids, Wis.
July 3, 1937

Dear Sir -

In reply to your questions, we were married April 3, 1923 at Milwaukee Wis. He was a painter & decorator and at that time - a very good worker. He was, at all times good to me - but he got involved with an Under Sheriff & 2 older men and that was his bad start. We were neither of us married before - and the past 5 years he has lived in & near Ky. I truthfully can say that if I had not of failed him when he needed me most - things might have been a lot different.

I hope this answers all the questions necessary.

Mrs. Bernard Coy

U.S. PENITENTIARY
ALCATRAZ ISLAND, CALIF.
REC'D.
OCT. 26 1938

Hillsboro, Wis.
Fri Eve - 8:45

Dear Bernard:

Spose you got my card from Rochester. Well they sent me home for three weeks to continue the treatment. I have to go to the hospital and have one of the nurses give it to me hypodermically. I can do it now as I'm pretty good with a hypo, but that is supposed to be in the hip and that's hard for me. I take my own morphine, when I need it, and lots of times when I don't. That is a habit that is easy to acquire and darn hard to quit.

I can get all I want, as there are some real addicts in this town. I'm alone tonight, with

Kakomo, Nan and Jerry went to the show and Henry is to the farm yet. Have a good program on. They just played SLEEPY TIME GAL sort of brings back memories and I hate to think. If things go O.K. I'm pretty liable to see you before too long, but can't plan too much yet. The fellows I worked for at Cicero are planning on a shot at Las Vegas, Nevada and I can work there. A gambling house. Will see how my health holds out. It's plain H to be sick all the time, but physically I'm better.

Austin's Dolly is sure growing and she's the sweetest baby I've ever seen, and he is wild over her. I'm anxiously awaiting her snapshots. Hope they are good.

Dolly is fine. She sure makes a good mother, but I hope they don't go in for too big a family.

Maxine just sent Nan her birthday present, a house coat and a hat. She (Max is fine - and Dot is OK. She is at Rose's. Jerry is getting real big. He's going to be a big man if he keeps on. About the picture, Bernard I have it framed and hanging in the dining room. I sort of hate to part with it. Just heard a report, the Forest Fires in Northern Minn. and Ontario are bad. The worst in years.

Well Bernard, gotta go and get Nan and Jerry, so I'll say good night and the best of everything to you.

With love until later. How long will it be?

Peggy Coy
Hillsboro, Wis.

(RECEIVED HERE AT ALCATRAZ Oct. 26, 1938)

Alcatraz, Calif. May 30, 1939
To Mrs. Edward Long
Louisville, Ky

Dear Anna:-

Although your letter has been here since last week, this is the first chance I've had to answer it. Thank you very much. And I am well and back to work now, as you must have imagined I would be.

We have a fine show coming up tomorrow and I am anxious to see it 'You Can't Take It With You' is the name of the show. And I might say, here that it has been a long, long time since I even imagined that you could---that is that you could take it with you. So many seem to think you may though. And if someone also seems a bit careless with life, it is never forgiven them. But what of it?

Listen, Sis, I want you to forget about Aunt Maggie. Don't ever as much mention my name in her presence again. I will like it better that way. But in the meantime you'd better have attorney Duffy go see Judge Mix about

Dick's liquor case. Dick needs all the help he can get now. And now is the time to help him. If help is postponed until he comes home, then it is too late. Don't think that I am saying some thing just to be saying it. I know what I am talking about. In the first place Dick is not the guilty man in the Meyer case. The ones who robbed the Meyer whiskey store are Delbert Lee Stiles, Ernie Wymann and myself, Dick was not even in Louisville at the time. He was either in Detroit or Greenfield, one of the two places. I don't just remember which one. Paulie Long doesn't remember either and if he doesn't no one does.

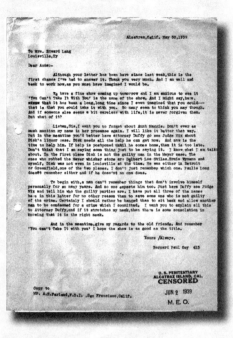

To begin with, a man can't remember things that don't involve himself personally for so many years. And no one expects him too. Just have Duffy see Judge Mix and tell him who the guilty parties are. I have put all three of the names here in this letter for no other reason than to save some one who is not guilty of the crime. Certainly I should rather be hanged than to sit back and allow another man to be condemned for a crime which I committed. I want you to explain all this to Attorney Duffy, and if it stretches my neck, then there is some consolation in knowing that it is the right neck.

And in the meantime, give my regards to the old friends. And remember 'You can't Take It with you' I hope the show is as good as the title.

Yours Always,
Bernard Paul Coy 415

Copy to
Mr. A.E. Farland, F.B.I., San Francisco, Calif.

Oct. 5, 1939
From Bernard Paul Coy
To The Dentist

Dear Sir:

On the 6th of April you extracted the last tooth preparatory to making new plates for me. At that time you assured me that by July the 15th, I could expect the new plates. I haven't heard from them yet. Roasting ear season is passed and the same rations of meat and other solids consumed

by the then inmates, have done me no good to speak of. I can't eat with the few teeth now remaining. I would appreciate it very much if you would either extract the few teeth I have left or fix me with the new ones.

I sent you a request for interview two weeks ago. But I suppose it got misplaced.

Yours Respectfully,
Bernard Paul Coy 415

May 11, 1946

Mr. James E. Fahey
Kentucky Home Life Building
Louisville, Kentucky

Dear Mr. Fahey:

Responsive to your communication of May 6, 1946, I give you the following:

Bernard Paul Coy, who was inmate Reg. No. 415-AZ, was a ringleader of a group of prisoners in a daring and spectacular attempt to effect a mass or group escape. Coy succeeded in securing a officers uniform and firearms. He helped to arm other prisoners. He and other prisoners were responsible for the wounding and killing of officers. At about 9:45 A.M. the morning of Saturday, May 4, 1946, he was taken from a cellblock utility corridor and the officer's rifle and some ammunition were alongside of him. The Chief Physician who examined the body believed that he had been dead several hours, but could not fix the exact moment of death.

I believe the above information will be sufficient for you in your purpose to file the motion for certiorari.

Sincerely, J.A. Johnston, Warden

May 16th 1946

Mr. Johnston,

Please send No. 415's personal property if any to me. And tell me where he
was buried. I have not been notified in
any way except what I read in papers.

It was impossible for me to claim
[the] body. Any information about him
would relieve me a lot. I was told by
his attorney it was best not to have
him brought back here.

If he has anything at all, such as
pictures, letters, paintings, please send
them collect.

Thanks,

Mrs. Anna Long
821 Racine
Louisville, Ky

P.S. I am his sister. Bernard P. Coy. 415-AZ

May 31, 1946
Mrs. Anna Long
821 Racine
Louisville, Kentucky

Dear Madam:

In response to your note of May 16, 1946, I give you the following:

After the death of Bernard Paul Coy, who was Reg. No. 415-AZ, we checked
the record and found that the nearest of kin to be notified in the case of
death was that of his wife, Mrs. Peggy M. Coy of Hillsboro, Wisconsin. Accordingly we notified her and told her that if she claimed the body we would
ship it for burial in accordance with her instructions. The telegram was
undelivered and returned with the remark that Mrs. Coy is now known as
Peggy Grant and could be located c/o Post Office, Markesan, Wisconsin. We immediately send a telegram to Peggy Grant at that address, but it was undelivered and returned to us.

Immediately after death we turned the body over to the Coroner of San
Francisco, who later released it to the Godeau Undertaking Parlors. Inasmuch as no one claimed the body, the Godeau Company buried it in San Francisco, California.

So far as personal property is concerned, we have made a check and find the following:

He had to his credit in the Prisoners Fund the sum of $6.16. He also had in his belongings a small cloth container containing a few photos which appear to be family pictures. In accordance with the required procedure the above listed personal property is to be turned over to his nearest of kin upon proper claim. Since your brother listed his wife, Mrs. Bernard P. Coy as his nearest of kin and the one to be notified, she should make the claim and if she does we will turn the above property over to her. If she does not desire to make claim and states that you are the next nearest of kin and wishes to turn the belongings over to you, we will then forward them on to you. The sun of $6.16 has already been sent to Mrs. Bernard P. Coy, c/o Henry Walker, Hillsboro, Wisconsin by our disbursing office.

Sincerely,
J.A. Johnston
Warden

The corridor known as Seedy Street, located between C and D cellblocks.

Marvin Hubbard

LETTER WRITTEN by Hubbard's wife to the Warden at the Atlanta Penitentiary on October 17, 1942, provides unique insight into his personal history and upbringing. Herein are excerpts from her letter:

Marvin Hubbard in the 1930's while an inmate at Kilby Prison in Montgomery, Alabama.

Dear Warden,

In answer to you letter received this week, I hardly know where to begin, I did not know where my husband was at, at this present time until I received your letter, it came as a quite a surprise, or rather a shock, as we had not been corresponding lately, I'm afraid I don't know very much of anything that would be of help to you, but will give you my best.

We were married at my mother's home in DeKalb County, on January 8, 1928. Neither of us were previously married, this being for the only marriage for either of us. We only have one child… My husband's attitude towards me and the child, were very fine at times, he didn't ever mistreat us in no-way except staying away from us for so much of his time, that he could have been with us, the harm he done was more of his own self than any-one else, only heartbreaks and sorrows, I had a fair share of that at an early age, my life has been filled with disappointments and heart aches. My husband has taken the responsibility of his family serious at times, and other times, he would leave us for a long time, as much as five or six months at a time, during this time he would never give us any support.

He was born and raised in Alabama, in Boaz, Route #3, we have lived out there part of our time together as well as here in Georgia. As far as where we have lived for the past five years is rather hard to explain, he spent a large portion of it in Kilby Prison as you no doubt already know, and the other part just here and yonder. His occupation has mostly been a bricklayer since I have known him, he does beautiful brickwork. Although he had farmed some during times when that trade was dull. His greatest handicap during these years, have been having no education, he was raised by a dear old mother who was left a widow with five children to raise, she did the best she could but could not educate the children. My husband's difficulties he has faced in recent years, I think depends on him getting started with the wrong kind of characters at a early age, which gives him the wrong opinion of life, before life was hardly started for him. Before he got started with the bad characters he was very kind and generous hearted, made good friends with all of whom he met, was well thought of in the community which he lived.

I just wish to say here, that anything you can do for him to make his stay in your institution, profitable to him, and as comfortable as possible, will highly be appreciated by me, although we have been separated a large portion of our time, it didn't take away the love and care I have for him. He was once good and kind and made home a place worth living for. I shall like very much to visit him as soon as possible, as I have not seen him since one year ago, last July 18th, 1941. Trusting this will be of some help to you in preparing my husband for his stay there.

Yours Very Truly,
Mrs. Lola Belle Hubbard

Ellenwood - Ga.
Dec - 6 - 1944.

Joseph W. Sanford, Warden
United States Penitentiary

Re: Hubbard, Marvin Franklin
Reg. No. 62398-A.

Dear Warden,

I regret that my husband the above named, have forfeited his privileges, however I don't feel that he really meant to do such but by some slip of thought are misunderstanding his why he did, for I know his visiting and writing privileges meant a lot to him as well as it did me. That was about

all the bright spots in my life I had to look forward to was my visits to
see him and letters from him, so if you will see that he has every chance
to make up this, I feel that he will and I know it will be highly appreciated by me. I understand by his letter that he is no longer in the industries,
so now he won't be able to help me along. Will you please tell me why he
was taken out? I need his help very much, even though I do work and make
a little my-self. I don't make much and in this day with living expenses up
so much, I don't see hardly how I can make out with what I have and live
comfortable. Another thing my health isn't so good, and I don't expect to be
able to work out very long. So if you will consider my welfare as much as
my husband and put him back in the industries at an early date I will be
grateful to you for that.

Please let me see him at an early date as possible.

Very Truly Yours, Mrs. Lola Belle Hubbard

Ellenwood, Ga.
July - 17 - 1946.

James A. Johnston, Warden.
United States Penitentiary.
Alcatraz, California.

Dear Warden:

Please let me thank you again for all
you have sent me as my husband personal
things. Also for all your kindness and
words of sympathy which are needed so much
in times like this.

Remember me as a true hearted friend.

Sincerely,
Mrs. Lola B. Hubbard,
Ellenwood, Ga.
Route #, 1

Joseph Paul Cretzer

June 4, 1940
To: Edna Cretzer
Berkeley, Calif.

My darling wife:

I was notified today that the Warden received a letter from you. He was kind enough in granting me the privilege in answering. I believe its best that you make no plans on coming here, because I'll probably be unable to greet you.

The charge is not serious and nothing to be become alarmed over. We are being treated exceptionally well and feeling in fine spirit. In a few months I'll be permitted to write and explain everything. I do hope you didn't become ill and upset over this trouble. I was certainly happy the night of the 27th when I knew you were home. It seems I continually keep you underweight by causing you so much worry. Perhaps after this affair is over you can regain your lost weight and health. Maybe someday I'll wake up and realize the sorrow and grief I've caused the one I love so dearly. There's one thing I'm certain of. My mind guides my body not my heart, I love you too much to cause you sorrow.

I imagine the little man keeps you well occupied and leaves little time for thinking, is he still the man of household and can he still outrun sis? I'll be very much relieved and settled after I receive a letter from you. It seems like years since I've received a letter. I would rather visit the dentist

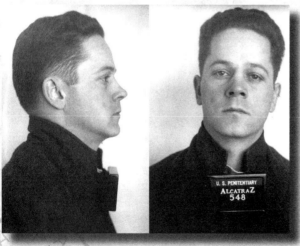

Joe "Dutch" Cretzer

three times daily than miss your letters. The time will pass very quick and I'll be writing regularly again. Tell all hello. I am certain everything here isn't as serious as it appears. All my love for only you.

Your Husband,
J.P. Cretzer

U.S. Penitentiary
San Francisco
Alcatraz Island, Calif.
June 11, 1941
REC'D
JUN 12, 1941

Warden Johnston
Alcatraz Island
Calif.

Dear Sir:

I am writing you to beg of your permission to write my husband Joseph Cretzer 543 Az. I realize of course that according to your rules he must be punished but it is so very diffi cult not to hear a word from him as to whether he is well or not. I do not of course fully understand the conditions over this, but surely the mental torture of being confi ned alone in solitary is very severe and in itself should be punishment enough. Do you not think you could please grant me the privilege of hearing from him once a week in allowing me to write him once in awhile? You do not realize the torture and punishment which of course, we the relatives of those we love, must undergo not even hearing one line. It is just as though they were buried alive. After all regardless of what he has done he is still a human being and I love him dearly. Couldn't you please fi gure out some way that I could write and hear from him just once in awhile so that I could know that he is alright. I would deeply appreciate any thing that you could do.

Sincerely,
Edna Cretzer
P.O. Box 1305
San Francisco, Cal.

Edna Mae Cretzer

San Francisco, Ca.
June 18, 1941

Warden Johnston,
Alcatraz, California
Dear Sir:

I wish to thank you from the bottom of my heart for the privilege you have accended me in permitting me a letter to my husband Joseph Cretzer No. 548 Az. I did so appreciate your kindly and humane attitude as expressed in your letter.

I am afraid that I have allowed my imagination to run away with me in trying to vision his punishment. Perhaps I have been unduly influenced by the recent newspaper publicity which certainly did not picture the confinement in any pleasant aspect. However, I do feel more assured after reading your letter that my husband is not being mistreated or harmed in any way. It is as you state hard for some people to adapt themselves to a prison routine and my husband seems to be such an individual.

If you will be in your office in San Francisco any time in this month I would appreciate it if you would let me know as I would like to talk over a few things with you. I feel that I know the reason underlying my husband's reputed attempts to escape. Perhaps, if that could be removed he could reconcile himself to his fate. I do appreciate and thank you for your letter. It was very kind of you to grant me permission to write occasionally.

Sincerely,
Edna Cretzer

P.O. Box 1305
San Francisco, Cal.

248

DEPARTMENT OF JUSTICE
UNITED STATES PENITENTIARY
ALCATRAZ ISLAND, CALIFORNIA

February 6, 1945

Mrs. E. Cretzer,
1021 - A Thaw Way,
Alameda, California.

Dear Mrs. Cretzer:

If you will bring this letter with you, it will serve as a pass for you to visit your husband Joseph Cretzer, Reg. No. 548-AZ, and your brother Arnold Kyle, Reg. No. 547-AZ, on Thursday, February 15, 1945.

Take the boat which leaves Dock No. 4, known as the Fort Mason Dock, at the end of Van Ness Avenue, San Francisco, promptly at 10:00 A.M.

When you get off the boat at Alcatraz, hand this letter to the officer at the Registration Office and he will arrange for your visit.

It is not customary to allow visitors to see two different inmates on the same day, but in the circumstances if you are willing to divide the time that you have between the two we will first arrange a visit with your husband, and, after that visit is concluded, we will arrange for you to see your brother Arnold Kyle. You must understand, of course, that the visiting time will be the same as usual, and, therefore the time that you have must be divided between the two of them as they will not be at the visiting panel at the same time.

Sincerely,

J. A. JOHNSTON,
Warden.

May 26, 1945

Warden Johnson
Dear Sir:
    Would you please reconsider my
request in wanting to go to work.?
you may rest assured that, considering the time spent in lock-up, I
will not become involved in any
future mischief.
    wherever Mr. Miller wishes to work
me, will be okay. I will feel very
much obligated to you, and will show
my appreciation by conducting myself in a favorable manner.

                    Respectfully yours
                    J. P. Cretzer
                    No. 548 - Icel.

Associate Warden Miller
Dr Ritchey
Capt Weinhold   For consideration
Lieut. Simpson   of recommendation
S.O. Frank Johnson

                    Released from.
             Isolation D Block
          to Idle in cell   5-23-46

San Francisco Cal.
May 28, 1946

Dear Mr. Mills.

Would you please be kind
Enough to Send me any
pictures. letters or personal
effects of Joseph Paul Cretzer.

Thank you for your
kindness.

U. S. PENITENTIARY
ALCATRAZ ISLAND, CALIF
REC'D
MAY 29 1946

Sincerely,

Edna Benedetti

175 Blythdale Av.,
San Francisco
Calif.

Miran Thompson

September 10, 1946

Horace S. Thompson
Mobile, Alabama

My dear brother:

I received your letter of September 6th tonight; I was more than glad to hear form you. I wrote you last week, I hope you have my letter by now. Horace, I am feeling pretty good now, I guess about as well as I could feel where I am. I hope you all are well and having lots of fun, someone needs to enjoy my part of life's pleasure, so maybe you and the rest can.

Don't worry about me brother, I don't worry so I don't think you or any of the rest should, because I realize none of you did not get me here, and if I would have had a good strong mind I would not of been here, although no one can beat a frame-up and you and all the rest know, that is why I am here, not because I committed a crime, but because some people needed a little more money for their self. Well Horace, the trial starts the 17th if I can't get it put off. I can't seem to get my lawyer to do what I want him to do, although I know he has been paid some money, by some people, he told me so one time, but he didn't say who gave it to him, the people must have told him not to let anyone know who paid him, but I haven't gave him any money personally and he wouldn't conduct my defense like I ask him to, and it is just like I told him, I am on trial for my life and I have a right to have it defended in any way I want to, you see there is several different kinds of plea I wanted him to, and I talked to another law-

Miran "Buddy" Thompson

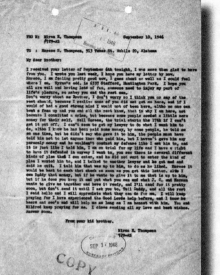

yer and he got mad and said he quit. I told him that was up to him, to do as he liked.

Tell Daddy, and all the rest I said hello and I will appreciate what they can do for me. I will keep praying for I have experienced the good Lords help before, and I know he hears and see's and will help me as long as I am honest with him. You and Mildred keep praying for me. I close sending all my love and best wishes. Answer soon.

From your kid brother,
Miran E. Thompson, 729-AZ

Senior Warden,
Name M. E. Thompson,
U.S. Penitentiary
Box No. A-5140, San Quentin, Calif.
Alcatraz Island, Calif.

Dear Sir:

I would appreciate getting my pictures that were taken away from me on May 4th 1946. I know some of them have been given to a certain Detective Magazine Co. and one of them has been published and my Sister has a couple of copies of the Mag. If I don't get my pictures, I am going to court with it & so is my people.

I have wrote you one letter since I have been here and three before I left the Island. I will appreciate your giving me the pictures, it is a violation of the U.S. Const. to take private property and I am sure you are aware of same.

M. E. Thompson
A-5740

FROM: Miran E. Thompson
Sept. 18, 1946
729-AZ

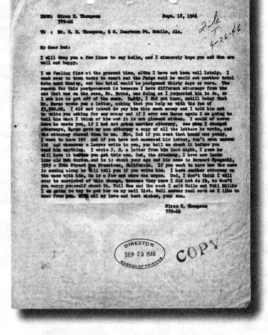

TO: Mr. R. E. Thompson, 6 S. Dearborn St.
Mobile, Ala.

My dear Dad:

   I will drop you a few lines to say hello, and I sincerely hope you and Mom are well and happy.

   I am feeling fine at the present time, although I have not been well lately. I went over to town today to court and the Judge said he would set another trial date next Monday, and the trial would be postponed thirty days or more. The reason for this postponement is because I have different attorneys from the one that was on the case, Mr. Burns, was doing as I requested his to do, so I ask him to get off the case. Daddy, I did not know, until today that Mr. Burns wrote you a letter, asking that you help me with the fee of $3,500.00. I did not intent to pay him this much money and I told him not to write you asking for any money and if I ever see Burns again I am going to tell him what I think of him and it is not pleasant either. I would of never knew he wrote you, if I had not gotten another attorney, see when I changed attorneys, Burns gave my new attorney a copy of all the letters he wrote, and the attorney showed them to me. Now, Dad if you sent that hound one penny, I want to know it? And if you have not answered his letter, don't even answer it: And whenever a lawyer writes to you, you tell me about it before you send him anything. I wrote J. C. a letter last night, I guess he will have it before you get this one. Dad, the Attorney, I have now looks like old Bob Gordon and he is about your age and his name is Earnest Spagnoli, 3305 - 20th Street San Francisco, California. If you want to know how the case is coming along he will tell you if you write him. I have another attorney on the case with him, he is a Jew and sure can argue. Dad, I don't think I will ever be convicted of this charge, because they know I did not do it, so don't you worry yourself about it. Tell Mom and the rest I said Hello and Tell Billie I am going to try to get her on my mail list. Well answer real soon as I like to hear from you. With all my love and best wishes, your son.

   Miran E. Thompson
   729-AZ

Mr. James A. Johnston,
Name M. E. Thompson
Warden,
Box No. A-5140, San Quentin, Calif.
Alcatraz Island, Calif.

Feb. 12, 1947

Dear Sir:

I am writing you in regards to some pictures that were handed to you or Mr. E. J. Miller on Sat. May 4th, 1946, in an envelope, the type inmate's mail reaches them in, it was wrote on the outside of the envelope in big red letter's, photograph's of family & friends, please do not destroy. There were ten (10) photo's for sure, and maybe (12).

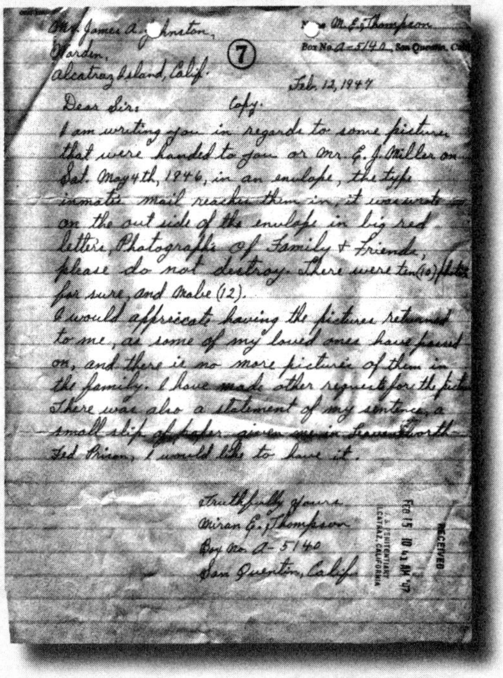

I would appreciate having the pictures returned to me, as some of my loved ones have passed on, and there is no more pictures of them in the family. I have made other requests for the pictures. There was also a statement of my sentence, a small slip of paper given me in Leavenworth Fed Prison, I would like to have it.

Truthfully yours
Miran E. Thompson
Box No. A-5140
San Quentin, Calif.

Mr. James A. Johnston,
Warden.
Alcatraz Island, Calif.
7
Name M. E. Thompson
Box No A-5140 San Quentin, Calif.
Feb. 12, 1947
Dear Sir: Copy
I am writing you in regards to some pictures that were handed to you or Mr. E. J. Miller on Sat. May 4th, 1946, in an envelope, the type inmate mail reaches them in, it was wrote on the out side of the envelope in big red letter's, Photograph's of Family & Friends, please do not destroy. There were ten (10) photo's for sure, and mabie (12).
I would appreciate having the pictures returned to me, as some of my loved ones have passed on, and there is no more picture of them in the family. I have made other request for the pictures. There was also a statement of my sentence, a small slip of paper given me in Leavenworth Fed Prison, I would like to have it.
Truthfully yours
Miran E. Thompson
Box No A-5140
San Quentin, Calif.
RECEIVED FEB 15 '47
U.S. PENITENTIARY ALCATRAZ, CALIFORNIA

COPY

Mr. J. C. Thompson
#65 Oaklawn Apts.
Mobile, Alabama

August, 1948

My dear Brother:

Just a couple of lines to say hello and get my business matters
straight. I hope all are well, I am, I guess.

J. C., there will be a slip of paper in this letter, there will
be a name and address of a friend who has did me a good favor; please
send ten dollars ($10.00) to that name and address on the slip of
paper - do not mention the person in any letter or to any one -
you understand! Don't say anything to me about other than just
saying " you took care of the business matter" - nothing more. Do
this at once - the person needs the dough - the favor has been done
for me - in past - send cash - not money order.

Best wishes & love to all,

Your brother,

Miran E. Thompson

STANDARD FORM No. 14
APPROVED BY THE PRESIDENT
MARCH 10, 1926

FROM _____

BUREAU _____

CHG. APPROPRIATION _____

TELEGRAM

OFFICIAL BUSINESS—GOVERNMENT RATES

U. S. GOVERNMENT PRINTING OFFICE   10—1728

C O P Y

SAN QUENTIN, CALIF.
AUGUST 12th, 1948

MR. M. M. BELLI
ATTORNEY AT LAW, TWA BLDG.
240 Stockston Street
San Francisco, California

I AM NOT ALLOWED TO FINISH MY PETITION.   I ONLY HAVE THREE DAYS LEFT TO FILE
IT.   PLEASE DO SOMETHING.

M. E. THOMPSON
A-5140

Record Form No. 8
(July, 1936)

CONDUCT RECORD

DEPARTMENT OF JUSTICE
Penal and Correctional Institutions

U. S. PENITENTIARY   ALCATRAZ, CALIFORNIA
(Institution)   (Location)

Record of THOMPSON, Miran Edgar   No. 729-AZ
FPI—LK—4-7-43—6M—588-5

Date	Prison Violations	Days Lost
5		
5-4-46	Joining in desperate escape attempt, and riot with other inmates attacking officers, with use of firearms & other weapons, causing death to officers & wounding others, May 2, 1946. TO SOLITARY A-BLOCK, 5-4-46.	
5-10-46	OUT OF SOLITARY INTO SEGREGATION D BLOCK	
12-21-46	FOUND GUILTY OF MURDER IN FIRST DEGREE BY JURY AT SAN FRANCISCO, CALIFORNIA AND SENTENCED TO DEATH, SAME DAY. 12-27-46 TRANSFERRED TO SAN QUENTIN, CALIF. ST. PRISON.	

Date of Execution set for Sept. 24, 1948, by Judge Louis Goodman,
    on June 29, 1948.
             Executed 12-3-48
                  S.Q. gas chamber

Offi cer William Miller

FOR THE officers working at Alcatraz, keeping the public safe from the nation's most notorious inmates sometimes came with the ultimate sacrifice. Officers were forced to work side-by-side with some of the nations most violent and vicious inmates unarmed and often outnumbered.

The Battle of Alcatraz was a clear reminder of the dangers encompassing their duties. Over the course of the prison's history, three officers would lose their lives at the hands of violent inmates desperate to escape. Numerous other officers were shot or injured during altercations and escapes, and sometimes forced to place themselves in harms way to protect even other inmates from peer violence. Some of these men were left permanently disabled and never able to return to work. Officers Royal Cline, Harold Stites and Bill Miller all heroically put themselves

William and Betsy Miller on their wedding day (date unknown). Officer Miller was a graduate of the prestigious Wharton School of Business at the University of Pennsylvania. During an era of scarce employment prospects, Miller took a job with the Bureau of Prisons to support his family.

Alcatraz Officer William A. Miller, circa 1945. Miller was credited for foiling the desperate 1946 escape by concealing the key that would have allowed inmates to breach the cellblock. Despite enduring fierce brutality while held hostage in a cramped cell with other officers, Miller heroically resisted the inmates. He was shot and killed by inmate Joseph Cretzer on May 3, 1946 in a fraught attempt to kill all of the officers being held hostage in fear they would later serve as adversarial witnesses to the events.

in harm's way and gave their lives. These men left behind friends, wives, children and loved ones who in turn were left to survive on small pensions and in many cases forced to find other means of support.

Officers William Miller and Harold Stites were the two officers fatally wounded during the Battle of Alcatraz. Their families suffered immensely as a result of their untimely deaths. The writings of Miller's wife remind us of their tragic sufferings and sacrifices. Her letter written only weeks after the incident is a portrait of genuine courage.

May 30, 1946
Department of Justice
Bureau of Prisons
Washington, D.C.

Dear Mr. Bennett:

Just want to say thank you very much for your very nice letters to me, they help to give me courage and strength to carry on.

My problems right now seem very heavy, and I am sorry that I made my plans to come back East, if only I could have had an opportunity to talk to Warden Johnston or yourself. My parents are dead, and my sisters are single, and they want me to stand on my own, of course I don't blame them, as my children are young and only God knows what is in front of me. Of course I am not afraid, my children are good and very smart. I can only live one day at a time.

Letters from Alcatraz

Letters from Alcatraz

Of course Mr. Bennett, I don't want to rush into things, and then wonder what it's all about. I prefer to stay at home, and take care of my children, you know, no mother can truthfully take on two jobs, and you also know what happens to youngsters when they are raised on the streets.

I think my best bet would be to settle in the country somewhere. Do you know whether I could have a small home built, the old houses are bring such high prices.

I am sorry that I had to write to you like this, but I haven't been able to sleep very much, and it is getting me down, if you can advise me in any way I sure would appreciate it. Do you know whether I could live in the Apt. at Alcatraz?

Thanking you for your kindness to me and my family, I remain

Yours truly,
Mrs. Wm. A. Miller

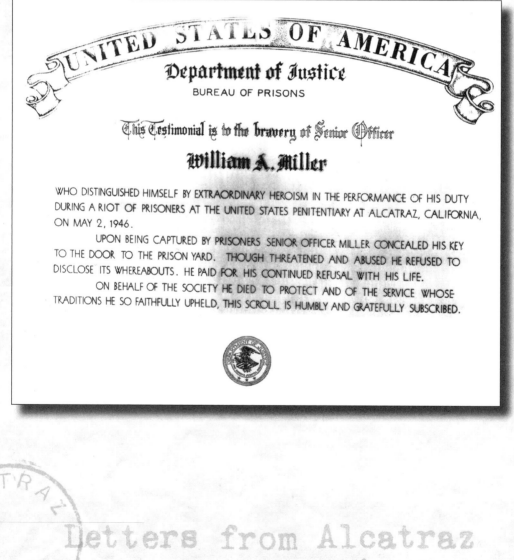

UNITED STATES OF AMERICA

Department of Justice
BUREAU OF PRISONS

This Testimonial is to the bravery of Senior Officer

William A. Miller

WHO DISTINGUISHED HIMSELF BY EXTRAORDINARY HEROISM IN THE PERFORMANCE OF HIS DUTY DURING A RIOT OF PRISONERS AT THE UNITED STATES PENITENTIARY AT ALCATRAZ, CALIFORNIA, ON MAY 2, 1946.

UPON BEING CAPTURED BY PRISONERS SENIOR OFFICER MILLER CONCEALED HIS KEY TO THE DOOR TO THE PRISON YARD. THOUGH THREATENED AND ABUSED HE REFUSED TO DISCLOSE ITS WHEREABOUTS. HE PAID FOR HIS CONTINUED REFUSAL WITH HIS LIFE.

ON BEHALF OF THE SOCIETY HE DIED TO PROTECT AND OF THE SERVICE WHOSE TRADITIONS HE SO FAITHFULLY UPHELD, THIS SCROLL IS HUMBLY AND GRATEFULLY SUBSCRIBED.

Henri Young

IN 1941, Alcatraz inmate Henri Young went on trial for the murder of Rufus McCain, a fellow prisoner and accomplice in a failed escape attempt. Young's attorneys claimed that Young was the subject of continual beatings by guards, and extensive periods of extreme isolation. The Rock fell under political siege for its confinement practices of inmates.

The trial became a worldwide media spectacle as defense strategies focused on prison conditions, working to pry off the heavy veil that the government had thrown over Alcatraz. *San Francisco Examiner* reporter Alvin Hyman highlighted in an April 1941 article the emerging trial themes set by the attorneys:

"Sleepwalking and dual personality, irresistible impulse and dissociation of ideas, strange psycho-physiological states in which the body acts while the mind sleeps–all these were briefly described in the court of Federal Judge Michael J. Roche yesterday as Henri Young went to trial for murder–for murder on Alcatraz."

In a letter to Bureau of Prisons Director, James Bennett, dated April 23, 1941, Warden James Johnston wrote:

I have just returned from Court and want to advise you that at the opening of the morning session the defense put Associate Warden Miller on the stand and gave him a lengthy and detailed examination, questions relating to routine, discipline, treatment, punishments, deprivations and explanations of regular cells, isolation cells, solitary cells and what they referred to as the "Spanish Dungeons," their express purpose being to show that the de-

Henri Theodore Young

Rufus Roy McCain

interview, MacInnis commented about his selection and the trial:

"I was flattered, of-course, thirty-five years ago when the federal court appointed me to defend Henri Young, who at that time was one of the fabled names of Alcatraz. Alcatraz had the same macabre fascination for people in the 1930s and 1940s as it does in retrospect for people today. And, the Young case was a marvelous vehicle because it could be presented so simply. The whole theme was the utter brutality of the treatment of prisoners at Alcatraz. Young had a different kind of psychiatric drama in his own prison background, because on the day he killed McCain, he had been released only 11-days from the hole... He had been kept in solitary confinement for the incredible stretch of three-years and two months..."

fendant Young having been subjected to imprisonment and while in prison isolation, solitary, so forth reached a mental state that they described as "psychologically unconscious." While that was the intention, the form and manner of the questions were clearly intended to impress the jury with the rigorous discipline, severe punishments and bad treatment of prisoners at Alcatraz. In other words, put the prison on trial instead of Alcatraz.

Attorney James MacInnis would instill in the minds of the jurors and public that it was Alcatraz, not Young who was on-trial for the murder of McCain, and his defense would ultimately make courtroom history. MacInnis had only been out of law school for four years, and it had been Henri Young himself, who sought young and inexperienced attorneys to handle his case. In a later documentary

The trial theme was a staccato of terms like "psychologically unconscious" and "legally irresponsible." MacInnis was a dynamic public speaker who held fast the attention of the courtroom shouting allegations of barbaric practices by prison officials. "It was Alcatraz who killed McCain. It was the cold, sadistic logic that some men call penology that killed McCain" MacInnis roared to the jurors made up of an insurance man's wife, a publisher's representative, a railroad man's wife, a couple homemakers, a steelworker, and other professionals.

Henri Young was a habitual criminal with a long record of violent crimes which included strings of bank robberies, kidnapping and murder. At Alcatraz he was considered a difficult inmate who challenged

No. 27107 R.

UNITED STATES DISTRICT COURT

Northern District of California

Southern Division

THE UNITED STATES OF AMERICA
vs.
HENRY YOUNG

INDICTMENT

18 USCA Section 452; Murder

PRESENTED IN OPEN COURT
AND ORDERED

FILED

DEC 18 1940

WALTER B. MALING, CLERK
By _____ Deputy Clerk   Bail, $

STATE OF CALIFORNIA,
City and County of San Francisco

THE PEOPLE OF THE STATE OF CALIFORNIA TO Henri Young # 244 az
Alcatraz Island

We command you, that all business and excuses being laid aside, you be and appear, before the undersigned, Coroner of the City and County of San Francisco, at Coroner's office, 850 Merchant Street, between Kearny and Montgomery Sts., on
TUESDAY 10th day of DECEMBER 1940 at 9 45 o'clock a. m,
to testify upon an inquest then and there to be had on the body of Rufus Roy McCain, Deceased, and hereof, fail not at your peril.
WITNESS THE HAND OF THE CORONER,
this 4th day of DECEMBER 1940   JOHN J. KINGSTON, M. D. Coroner,
By V. A. Dinsmore, Deputy.

and provoked fights with several of his fellow prisoners and officers. Young and fellow inmate Rufus McCain, who would eventually become his murder victim, had both spent nearly twenty-two months in solitary confinement for a failed escape that had resulted in the shooting death of the famous gangster Doc Barker.

After Young and McCain returned to the normal prison population, McCain was assigned to the Tailor Shop and Young was sent to work at the Furniture Shop, which was located directly upstairs. On December 3, 1940, Young waited until just after the ten o'clock count, and then when a guard's attention was diverted elsewhere, Young ran downstairs and plunged a knife into McCain with violent force. McCain rapidly fell into shock, and died just a few hours later from the stab wound. Young refused to disclose his motive for the murder

During Henry Young's trial, his attorneys made the claim that because their client had been held in strict isolation for three years, he could not be held responsible for his violent action, due to the influence of what the attorneys considered "cruel and unusual punishment." They alleged that because he had been tormented for so many years, his response to hostile situations had turned desperately violent.

Warden Johnston was brought to the trial under subpoena to testify on prison conditions and policies. Several inmates were also subpoenaed to describe the environment at Alcatraz, and many recounted "rumors" they had heard of inmates being locked in dungeons and severely beaten by guards. They also testified that they knew of many inmates who "went crazy" because of such treatment.

During trial, Young publicly testified on the extreme conditions he endured while being confined in isolation. While on the stand he offered the following testimony on the solitary confident conditions at Alcatraz to jurors:

"The cell was all black…It was nine by five by seven feet high. I was placed there in the nude. After my clothes had been searched for particles of tobacco, they were thrown-in to me. But not my shoes. I had no tobacco, no soap, no toothbrush. Because of the foul smell, it was like stepping into a sewer and was terribly nauseating. Two blankets were thrown into me at five o'clock in

Letters from Alcatraz

Attorneys James MacInnis (left) and Sol Abrams (right) with client Henri Young (middle).

eaten for fifteen days. I could hear (Associate Warden) Miller cursing and raging like a mad man. I was scared to death…"

The jury sympathized with Young, and he was ultimately convicted of manslaughter, a charge that would add only a few years to his sentence. He continued to be a difficult inmate following his trial, and was eventually transferred to the Medical Center for Federal Prisoners at Springfield, Missouri. After serving out his Federal sentence, he was transferred to Washington State Penitentiary in 1954, and was released on parole in 1972 after spending a total of nearly forty years in prison. He finally jumped parole, and vanished without a trace. Henri Young emerged only as a legendary crime figure and was never seen or heard from again.

the evening. There was no bed or mattress, and no fixtures. The cell I was in was called the ice box. There was an old type ventilator in the wall that was always open. I shivered all the time. I was in my stocking feet on the cold concrete. At times I would get into a corner and put my coveralls around my head to keep warm."

"When you walk into a black cell, you have to keep one hand on the wall so you won't hurt yourself… I'd sit in one position until my legs went to sleep, then I'd move and lie on the hard cement floor. The concrete was cold and always damp. You never have a bath in solitary. All the time I was there I only saw one man get a bath. He had a bucket of water thrown on him."

"You hardly ever slept, only cat naps. You wake up shivering, hardly able to move. You ache. Men were beaten into unconsciousness. I could hear their yells and screams. One boy was beaten after he hadn't

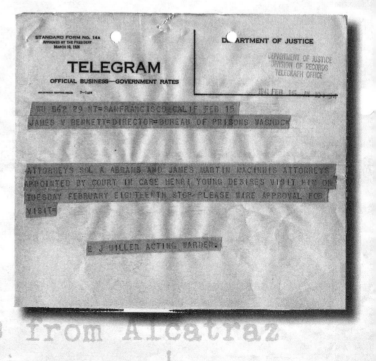

STANDARD FORM No. 14a
APPROVED BY THE PRESIDENT
MARCH 10, 1926

DEPARTMENT OF JUSTICE

TELEGRAM

OFFICIAL BUSINESS—GOVERNMENT RATES

WD10 95 NT=SANFRANCISCO CALIF APR 30 1941
HON JAMES BENNETT= FEDERAL DIRECTOR OF PRISONS

IT IS MY DUTY TO INFORM YOU, ON BEHALF OF THE TWELVE JURORS
WHO FOUND HENRI YOUNG, AN INMATE OF ALCATRAZ PENITENTIARY
GUILTY OF INVOLUNTARY MANSLAUGHTER AFTER OUR DELIBERATIONS
TONIGHT UPON THE CONCLUSION OF HIS TWO AND ONE HALF WEEKS
TRIAL FOR MURDER OF A FELLOW PRISONER THAT IT IS OUR
ADDITIONAL FINDING THAT CONDITIONS AS CONCERN TREATMENT OF
PRISONERS AT ALCATRAZ ARE UNBELIEVABLY BRUTAL AND INHUMAN,
AND IT IS OUR RESPECTFUL HOPE AND OUR EARNEST PETITION THAT
A PROPER AND SPEEDY INVESTIGATION OF ALCATRAZ BE MADE SO
THAT JUSTICE AND HUMANITY MAY BE SERVED=

PAUL VERDIER FOREMAN CITY OF PAIRS DRY GOODS CO SANFRANCISCO.

U. S. District Court, Northern District California,   Division

United States of America,
vs.
Henry Young.

Frank J. Kennessy, U. S. Attorney
Louis R. Mercado, Asst. U. S. Atty.

No. 27107-R.

Sol A. Abrams
James Martin MacInnis
Attys for Defts.   (E. W. Lehner, Reporter)
                     & C. P. Wight.

1. Moses W. Altmayer.	7. Mrs. Constance C. Foss,
2. Mrs. Ruth Packscher.	8. Frank H. Atwater,
3. Mrs. Marguerite Nicholson,	9. Edward W. Long,
4. Mrs. Grace Cody.	10. Paul Verdier,
5. Mrs. Rene H. Thompson,	11. William H. Caruthers,
6. John M. Glennan.	12. Mrs. Vera Meierdiercks,

Letters from Alcatraz

January 21, 1945
Miss Amelia Young
Kansas City, Missouri

Dearest Aunt Amelia:

I don't at all understand how the mix-up came about that you should have been told that I am in our church formally. Father Lyons has never had the opportunity to take me into our church. I have all the time been in isolation and cannot go to church…

Aunt Amelia, my dear, the fact that I am a true conversionist is definitely why I know I am going to be out of prison and a priest within five years. It is all a miracle I grant you, but one that your prayers helped obtain for me. I never would have been a Catholic, or even religious, were I not a true conversionist. And do so wish you would question your priest as to what a true conversionist is even after I give you these details. A priest can make it so clear by many illustrations that I haven't the paper to draw out. A true conversionist is a person who re-lives every one of his sins. He is a made to do this by God so that he will be clean-souled enough to work for God on some specific task that God has in mind for that person to do. It is a miracle, a miracle of a human being going through Purgatory here on earth. Even your priest will tell you that I am the only human on earth who will know that I am a true conversionist until God chooses to reveal it to His Church, and I know that I am a true conversionist who will be free and with you and a priest within five years.

That was ever so good of you to renew my name at Saint Jude's Shrine. I hope some day to visit there with you. Then we can pay our respect to Saint Jude in-person and have long talks with the priests at His Shrine.

Just as you have done in the past, Aunt Amelia you might do now, send the prayer book and calendar you have for me directly to me here. But wait until I let you know about the "Register" before you send them. They may have to go direct to Father Lyons. Yet I wish I had them now to turn to as a religious discussion. I know they are pleasing to God, Mother, and to Saint Jude.

Lovingly yours,
Henri Young, 244-AZ

C O P Y   May 15, 1946

Mr. & Mrs. Ruckman Ward,
4060 Brown Ave.,
Oakland, Calif.

Dear Bob & Naomi:

        This is the first time I have had an opportunity to write to you
since the awful escape attempt of May second. I am now cold. All the windows were bombed and shot out, and all the radiators were broken up by shells.
Workmen are laboring to get the place warm again. And I am writing this on
a Life news magazine held on my knee.

        When that terrible escape attempt started I was writing a letter to
Aunt Amelia. A while later I tore it up because if I didn't come through all
the shooting I didn't want anyone else to read it. At first the shooting was
light. Another fellow and I sat on the floor until he caught a deflected shell
in his shoulder. He wasn't hurt badly. We however grabbed some mattresses and
built a barricade at the front of my cell door. Then we stacked all my books
up behind that. Things got hotter. The noise of gun firing was terrific. We
crawled under my steel bunk and stayed there nearly all the time. Those anti-
aircraft and anti-tank bombs the Navy and Marines threw into isolation lifted
my cell up and crashed into my eardrums with an awful din. I'd lay there and
wait to feel the pain from a fragment or a shell. But I never even got touched.

        Two real close calls scared me. One came at the very first and one
at the last. But after I got used to the firing I slept a while over different
periods. I raised up to take a look around the cell block during some of the
heaviest firing. The place was truly beautiful. There was a steady stream of
brilliant white and red flares casting their lights over every thing. Tracer
bullets were lancing through the smoke. Actually the worst of the whole thing
physically was that pungent smoke from smoldering mattresses. I could hardly
breath and my eyes ran a steady stream.

        When I wasn't sleeping or talking I was praying for all of us fellows,
the officers I knew were in danger of getting killed, and that the officials
and guards would have the courage to come on in and capture those who had caused
such horror. It was a sheer miracle that so few innocent inmates were slightly
wounded. Even the guards couldn't hardly believe their own eyes when they saw
us all walking.

        There is a big colored fellow among us who was through the Italian
campaigns during the recent war. He laughed aloud and said that even Italy
was never so bad as what we went through.

        Yours, with love,

                        /s/   Henri Young   244-AZ

September 30, 1947

To: Attorney General Tom Clark, Washington, D.C.

Dear Sir:

I am writing to you concerning a hunger strike, which is now going on here at Alcatraz, California. I want to present our just grievances to you in hope that you will require this Warden to act as he should. This hunger strike is taking place in isolation, where there are about 27 men, 22 of us began it, now we are down to 15 men, all of whom I expect to remain on it since the weakest ones have fallen out.

Here is the reason for the hunger strike. The two orderlies who attended to our wants in isolation which we others remain locked in our cells, are two men no came to isolation for protection because they had caused so much trouble for themselves out in the main cellblocks. They have caused so much trouble here in isolation for themselves that they refuse to go to the isolation recreational yard. These men are John Davis #557, and Ramos Nemine, whose number I don't know. Both of these men are sarcastic and swearing to most of us. Both of these men have committed petty acts against us that hardly a normal person would do.

And John Davis #557 is now in the district courts on petition to prove himself insane. He is in truth for the man has been in several insane asylums. I have read his psychiatric record. He is a confirmed liar, as his psychiatric record will show.

And, you know that no person should be in a position to handle the wants of others who are so afraid that they refuse to accept the normal privileges of others, the main cellblocks or of isolation. That alone proves that the men are unbalanced.

This is now the 5th day of the hunger strike to have these men removed from their positions. No one wants to hurt them, simply to require them to cease handling our food and our other necessities.

It is peculiar that Warden Johnston has refused to remove these two men from their position in the light of similar past events.

Four men have been removed from the food job alone for getting into trouble with only one inmate. These two men are protected on it when 22 out of 27 men object to them.

Why Warden Johnston acts in this manner only he has the answers.

Will you therefore please investigate this matter and require that we isolation men obtain justice?

Very sincerely yours,
HENRI YOUNG 244 AZ

September 30, 1947
From Henri Young 244 AZ
Alcatraz, California
To Mr. James V. Bennett
Washington, D.C.

Dear Sir:

In this letter I am trying to obtain your help in relieving a couple of almost unbearable burdens from inmates of this institution. We are now on the fifth day of a hunger strike in protest against Warden Johnston's unjust actions.

First, Warden Johnston has forced us to accept as an orderly an insane man, John Davis #557. This man is in position to foul our food, clothing, and the toilet necessities we require. He entered isolation for the reason that he could not get along with the inmates in the main cell blocks. He refuses to go to the yard in isolation for the same reason. He sneers and snarls at us as he passes our cells; he has been in several insane asylums; he is an escapee from the last one in which he was confined; and, now he is in the district court on petition to prove himself insane. You know that a man of such character should not have power over other inmates, and it is desired by us inmates that you require Warden Johnston to remove this man.

Second, Warden Johnston has sometime ago taken a great deal of our yard privilege. This was unnecessary. We receive only three hours of yard privilege each week now, and with hardly no change whatsoever from the administrative viewpoint, we could as easily receive eight hours of yard each week. This lack of yard has contributed immensely toward the cracking of men in isolation. There are two men here short-timers both, who hear voices - pure delusion. These men are Willie James Westley and Clifford Owens. Nothing at all is done for them, but soon they will go out into society with your permission and that of Warden Johnston. When the insane orderly we have now first came over to isolation he believed that many of us were "talking" about him when that was not true. If we can receive a longer yard privilege, even what has been taken away from us, we can cooperate to better the mental condition of these men who are cracking up.

These hunger strikes are not pleasant experiences. But as Warden Johnston has never indicated any desire to negotiate on such wrongs, we must use as severe means against ourselves as this. I am therefore seeking your aid, as a delegated representative of the group, to bring about a just conclusion to our grievances.

And may I hope that this letter finds you willing to help us?

Very sincerely yours,
Henri Young 244 Az

December 20, 1947
To: Warden Johnston

Sir:

We isolation inmates are making arrangements to protect your refusal to permit us a different yard status.

We see no reason why all of us cannot be in the yard at one time, especially when you can lock up any chronic troublemaker on any yard day, for example, Basom. And this separate yard basis is a constant source of agitation for the reason that it gives no inmate an opportunity to prove to the officials that past feuds are over.

No one would protest if you would give us all the yard on a three-day two-hour period week. We have discussed it and think that a six-hour week would be sufficient. At the same time, that would save your personnel expense, and the trouble of letting us in and out on the fourth day.

I hope you won't refuse us this reasonable request. More of us want to buck you on this question; none of us enjoy a non-cooperative protest.

May we hope that you will give us a least the three-day, two-hour yard period?

Very sincerely,
HENRI YOUNG

This statement was made in response to the request for an investigation of Alcatraz, made by the jury that tried Henri Young for the murder of Rufus McCain.

Statement of James V. Bennett
Director, Federal Bureau of Prisons
May 1, 1941

I am firmly convinced that the jury which tried Henri Young for murder of another inmate in the Alcatraz Penitentiary has been misled about conditions at the prison. It has been impressed by tactics which sought to free Young through disparaging and attacking a public institution performing humanely and intelligently a most difficult task of protecting the public from hardened and unregenerate criminals. Young has been described by former United States Attorney Simpson and Federal Judge Stanley Webster of Spokane, Washington, as "the worst and most dangerous criminal with whom they ever dealt" and as "one who would not hesitate to kill anybody who crossed his path." He has been permitted to go virtually unpunished on the basis of inferences and innuendoes made by inmates whose criminal records and life histories show them to be wholly unreliable and who were able to commit deliberate perjury with impunity since they could not be reached by any effective legal process. From such information as I have about the trial, it is apparent that the Jury had before it no first-hand information or reliable evidence as to the policies or methods followed in the management of the most difficult and desperate group of prisoners ever assembled.

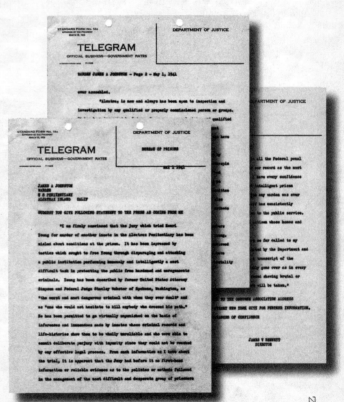

Alcatraz is now and always has been open to inspection and investigation by any qualified or properly commissioned person or groups. It has been inspected by Judges, Congressmen, penologists and qualified private citizens and has been approved as a modern and intelligent method of protecting the public from those desperate criminals who have proved themselves to be wholly intractable.

The institution, for instance, was recently inspected by experts of the Osborne Association of New York, a private philanthropic organization devoted primarily to the investigation of prisons, and was pronounced by them as well managed and operated and as using no improper system of discipline. Members of the Appropriations Committee of Congress in the course of their examination of our estimates also recently inspected the institution and made no criticism of its methods or operations.

I have visited Alcatraz frequently as have various members of our staff and know personally most of the inmates, including Young. As a matter of fact, I have on several occasions personally interviewed Young and done everything possible to obtain his cooperation. I have never found or had called to my attention any authentic case of brutality or inhumanity at Alcatraz.

Corporal punishment is prohibited in all the Federal penal institutions including Alcatraz. We stand on our record as the most modern and humane penal system in the world. I have every confidence in Warden Johnston. He is a just, humane, and intelligent prison warden capably performing the most difficult job any warden was ever asked to assume. The entire institutional staff has consistently displayed their courage, patience, and devotion to the public service. They deserve the support of every fair-minded citizen whose homes and safety they have helped to protect.

The statements made by the prisoners so far called to my attention have already been carefully investigated by the Department [of Justice] and found to be wholly unfounded. When, however, a transcript of the testimony has been received, it will be carefully gone over as in every other case, and if any evidence or facts are found showing brutal or inhuman treatment, vigorous corrective measures will be taken.

Richard Neumer

FORMER ALCATRAZ Officer Al Bloomquist once described convicted bank robber Richard Neumer, AZ-286, as "Neumer the Nuisance," an inmate who exhaustively complained about the conditions at Alcatraz. Neumer was a very close friend to Robert Stroud the "Birdman of Alcatraz," and had a reputation for inciting fellow inmates and scheming against the administration. He was characterized by officers as an abrasive personality type who could never be trusted, even by his fellow inmates. Neumer was one of the prisoners barricaded in D-Block during the *Battle of Alcatraz*, and wrote prolifically to federal officials and as illustrated here even the President of the United States seeking intervention on the strict confinement practices on the Rock.

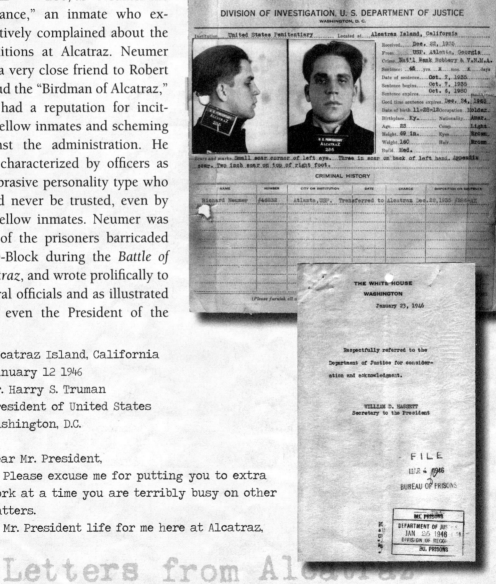

Alcatraz Island, California
January 12 1946
Mr. Harry S. Truman
President of United States
Washington, D.C.

Dear Mr. President,
 Please excuse me for putting you to extra work at a time you are terribly busy on other matters.
 Mr. President life for me here at Alcatraz,

under Warden James A. Johnston, and Associate Warden E. J. Miller is getting to a point where it is double jeopardy, and causing me great mental strain.

I do not wish to cause myself any trouble by doing as others had to do to get medical treatment and other privileges due them. A fellow that fl ares up and losses all his good time gets treated better than those that do not.

Sir, truly, I can prove to you I am receiving unjust treatment through the prejudice of the Associate Warden, Mr. E. J. Miller.

Mr. President, I pray you will order an investigation concerning my treatment before my mental strain forces me to do acts beyond my control and against my will to do.

Sir, we have recently received a very fi ne doctor, Dr. Rochek, I feel he will or could help me if Mr. Miller would allow me to go to the hospital for the treatments that has been recommended for my trouble.

Thanking you in advance and promising to be a future good citizen I remain

Yours Respectfully
Richard A. Numer
Inmate #286

January 27, 1946
From Richard Numer
Alcatraz Is., California

To Mrs. R. G. Oliver
854 Woodhaven Ave.
Memphis, Tennessee

My Dear Sister & Family,

It is Sunday afternoon and a very nice sun-shiny Sabbath. Wish we could all go for a drive in the country or perhaps to the Memphis Zoo. Do you take the children out to Overton Park very often? I use to get a big thrill watching those silly monkeys. Ha.

Certainly glad you received and enjoyed the poem - "Ode to God." I hope Mrs. Coons will enjoy reading it. I am ashamed of myself because I didn't send Thelma a copy of it! I will yet.

Darn it, of all the swell sisters I had, it seems as though my life should have been differently woven. No one to blame but Poor Richard Acough! I had a swell opportunity from a swell Uncle and Aunt to gain a good education. That golden chance was thrown to the four winds. And of all the places to be chosen along life's pathway to stop to realize - It had to be prison! Ha Poor me!

A bright light shines on the horizon! Hopes of my near freedom exists with me. Yes Linnie, I really believe something will turn out for my good. And if I must continue to serve the term to its long end; I only hope my mind stays together.

Through sending some letters to Washington and putting in some writs for Medical Treatment and yard recreation unusual punishment is being inflicted upon me. I am in the right Sis, and recently I wrote President Truman a letter asking for his help. If I don't get the letter through to his personal attention then it must be that my letters are not convincing and God is not answering my prayers.

I could write you all about my recent hardships and undue punishments how long it took me to get proper eye glasses, how I have been trying to get the dentist to fix a bad tooth. How I've tried to get an English Course to better my self mentally. All about why I am not getting due recreation etc. I wrote it all to the Attorney General! I can't yet see why he hasn't sooner investigated. Try, Try Again is my Dutch motto. And keep your chin up!

Well I know Honorable Thomas C. Clark is a good man and we have the best President in the world. And also I have a Sister that can and will word to either if that time comes - which appears to be peeking around the corner. And Linnie I'll assure you I have a legitable complaint!

Sister I don't say prisons are not needed and that criminals should not receive punishment. Far from it! But that punishment in prison should be just punishment. Filing writs in a United States District Court trying to get what you think is rightfully yours is surely no grounds to punish one. Discrimination!

Well Linnie Pray for me, that all will turn out right, and that official-dom performs their sworn duty as taxpayers and laws insist. I'll say a a prayer tonight.

    With love to all.
    Your Brother Richard Numer

From Richard A. Numer

Letters from Alcatraz

February 24, 1947

Inmate No. 286
To   Warden James A. Johnston
Alcatraz, California

Dear Sir:

I have been told that I stand a good
chance of being placed back in population
if I would write and ask you to do so.

Sir, I am now asking you to consider placing me back in population. I feel I can, and
will, meet all rules and follow them.

I have been in Isolation now for nearly
twenty-two months, lost all my statutory
good time, and I have did my health no good.
I think you will find out that I can, and
will, do all right in population, and, after
I am out, I think I can get your permission
to have an interview with you. I wish to convince you, Sir, that I have something wrong with me.

My case rest with you - I hope you can, and will, accommodate.

Respectfully yours,
Richard A. Numer
Inmate No. 286

"D" Block
3-19-47

To: Associate Warden

I understand that #286 Numer is going to court next week. His plans of
campaign is being masterminded by Stroud, and goes something like this:
Numer is to ask for a certain lawyer when he gets to court. The lawyer is
then to ask the Judge to issue an order for the immediate production of
certain papers which Number will say he left behind here. Stroud's idea is
that there will be so many pages and the time so short that the officials
will not have time to examine them thoroughly. For the past few nights
Franklin, Fleish, Stroud, Sharpe, Davis, and possibly others have been busy
working on stuff which they apparently hope to get to the lawyer in this
manner to be passed on to others.

The above plan may be changed to have Numer bring the papers over with
him. In any event any papers going out in this case will bear careful examination. It appears that some of them succeeded in getting some papers

out in similar manner during the recent trial. For example, Fleish got some stuff out which his sister picked up at Spagnoli's office. All papers will probably be in Stroud's handwriting.

Respectfully,
J. Mullan
3-20-47

To the Warden
/s/ J. Muller
/s/ JAJ

From *Richard A. Numes,*   *April 19, 1947.*
(Date)

To *Warden Johnston,*
(Name)   (Address)

Dear Sir:

    After our talk Saturday noon this date, I meditated over what you told me, and I am willing to accept full responsibilities of all my past actions, and I feel that I have received just punishment and wish to show you that my future conduct will meet your approval.

    As you said you did not wish or expect any sweet talk or begging or getting down on my knees— I hope you accept my promise to abide by the rules, and that you will soon release me from D. Block.

    With kind regards, I am

            Yours sincerely,
            Richard A. Numes,
            Inmate No. 286,
            Alcatraz, California.

Theodore Audett

THEODORE AUDETT held the sole distinction of being the only inmate ever sent to Alcatraz three times under three separate convictions. Audett, a convicted bank robber a record of escape from U.S.P. at McNeil Island, was the only inmate to have been issued three separate Alcatraz register numbers.

In 1954, Audett published his memoir entitled Rap Sheet: My Life Story with a foreword by Gene Lowall, a prominent crime writer and editor for the Denver Post. His book enjoyed strong sales in both the United States and Europe, and sensationalized some of the escape stories along with his views on life served inside the walls of Alcatraz.

AUDETT	Record Form No. 36 **1217** Rev. Oct. 1940	ASSOCIATE WARDEN'S RECORD CARD		

Offense Bank Robbery		ce White	Age 1-19-03
Sentence 20 yrs Begins 4-10-56		Married yes	Deps. none
Date Imp 4-10-56 At Idaho-Moscow		Citizen USA	Relig Catholic
Date Rec'd 4-13-56 from court		Physical Cond. fair	
Par. Elig. 12-9-62		Mental Cond. criminalism CPI	
C. R. 9-13-69 9/9/ Max. 4-9-76		Education: S. A. T.	
Comm. Fine G. T. 2400		G.S. 6th grade	

PREVIOUS RECORD:

Jails several Ref. no	PSYCHOLOGICAL and APTITUDE TESTS:
Pens: Fed. 4 prior State 1 (2 Canada)	I.Q. 95 M.A. 14 plus
Detainers: Fed. State	Occupational Skills:
Escapes: Fed. 2 State 1 Canada	machinist, cook, culinary
CUSTODY: maximum	work.

Crimes Involved: (Enumerate)
NMVTA, false pretenses, escape, Enter bank to commit Larceny, Bank burglary, possess. stolen money, CRV. PV
Former #551-AZ & 208-AZ

Avocational Interests:

History of Occupational Experience

Occupations	No. Yrs.	Verification of Performance	
		Quality	Dependability
Cook	10	good	o.k.
M.C. + G.T. 15°°			

Former Nos. 208-551 AZ

Aliases:
T. J. Audett, Theodore James Audett, L. A. Elders, George Pitman, etc.

30114-M 60

Name	Number	Residence	Occupations		
AUDETT, James Henry	1217-AZ	Oregon	cook	machinist	laborer

Prisoner's Mail Box
May 15, 1932

Hon. W. D. Mitchell, Attorney Gen.
Washington, D.C.

Dear Sir,

    I am J. T. Audett, No. 32137 and am writing you concerning the restoration of my good time which I am now serving and have been ever since the first of April this year, I claim I am entitled to my good time under the condition I was not responsible at the time I escaped having been pronounced insane by Government Drs. At McNeal island and it was during the transfer to St. Elizabeth. I escaped therefore under these conditions I am asking you to consider this and if I am entitled to my good time would appreciate very much to get it restored, would like for you if in doubt to communicate with Dr. Bennett of this place in regard to this hoping to hear from you soon with a favorable reply I remain Resp.

    T. J. Audett

Alcatraz Is., Calif.
August 9, 1939

Hon. Frank Murphy,
Attorney General
Washington, D.C.

Dear Sir:

    I was sentenced to a term of five years, on the 14th day of February, 1934, for the offense of the Dyer Act. And was immediately confined in the penitentiary on McNeals Island.

    On the 14th day of June, 1934 I escaped. And was apprehended during the month of August, 1934, and transferred to Leavenworth, Kansas.

    During the time that I was at the U.S. Penitentiary at Leavenworth, Kansas, Four-hundred eighty days good time was taken, the punishment for escaping.

I was transferred to Alcatraz during the month of September, 1934.

During the June term of court, 935 at Tacoma, Washington, I was tried and convicted for the offense of escaping from the U.S. Penitentiary on McNeals Island, and received an eighteen mo. Sentence, which runs consecutive with the five years that I was serving.

It is my understanding that I only have a very short time left to serve. Because of this fact and of my physical condition, I am writing this plea for your sincere consideration.

I was wounded during the World War, 1917. Since that time I have undergone a number of operations. And have been forced to use certain medicines, constantly, to feel well, and to have bowel actions.

Immediately after arriving here at Alcatraz, I made my condition known to Dr. Hess, a physician in charge of the hospital. But he failed to administer me any medical attention in any manner. His comment to my requests for medicine and help, was, that there was nothing wrong with me and that I was only gold-bricking.

During the latter part of 1934, Dr. Hess was forced to operate on me for lock-bowels. This operation done by him was a very crude piece of work, as he replaced my intestines, etc., in the wrong way.

Just recently the physician who is in charge of the hospital took pictures of my stomach, which plainly show the awful disarrangement and the cause of my present illness. Since the operation done by Dr. Hess I have suffered continually.

I have been advised that a major operation is necessary.

I sincerely feel that the present physicians are doing everything possible to help. But since the nature of the operation is very dangerous, I would like to have it done in a hospital outside and by certain physicians that operated before.

Every one in charge seem very interested in my welfare and show me every consideration.

I hope you are able to help me in this matter, by recommending enough time to cause my discharge. So that I can get the very needful operation before it is to late.

I sincerely hope that you will give this matter your earnest consideration, I am

Very respectfully
T. J. Audett

From T. J. Audett   2-24-41
    #57948
To Hon. R. H. Jackson
U.S. Attorney General, Wash. D.C.

Hon. R. H. Jackson,	T. J. Audett, 57948
U.S. Atty General,	U.S. Penitentiary,
Washington, D.C.	Leavenworth, Kan-
	sas

Dear Sir:

I am writing you in regards of my case, and asking for your help and advice if it is possible. I sincerely do hope it is possible for I am now acting on your advice that you gave me when you visited Alcatraz. Your advice was to contact the U.S. Atty General, if things should go wrong.

Sir after being released from Alcatraz the 5-30-40 my intentions were to go straight and was succeeding in doing so; also making my monthly reports, I seen the Parole Offi cer several times about getting a job for me but he was unable to get work for me, and I was unable to get a job in Calif. So I left Calif. To try and fi nd work. And was arrested, 8-25-40 and held in custody untill the date of my trial 12-3-40 without being allowed to contact anyone to prove my innocence.

I was charged with entering the First State Bank of Whitman, Nebraska with intent to commit larceny, (and was tried under Section 264 of Title 12) and also tried and found Guilty of the above charge and sentence to ten years in imprisonment.

Sir that brings me to the object of this letter and asking you for your help for I am not guilty and during the time I was held in custody, waiting for trial I could have proven my innocence. For on the night the said Bank was entered, I was no where near that vicinity and never have been to the said city where the Bank was said to be entered and I could have proven it but I was

Theodore Audett and Warden Madigan greeting a VIP guest during the grand opening of the Officer's Dining Hall located in the upstairs administration area of Alcatraz, 1961.

not allowed to see or contact no one. Also during the investigation before the trial I was told by the F.B.I. agents that there were finger prints found in the said Bank and that they had sent them to Washington to prove they were mine but they were not my finger prints, and the F.B.I. agent testified that they were not mine. There was no evidence at all against me only my previous record, and the jury that tried my case was told at the opening of the trial that I just got out of Alcatraz, (it was persecution and not justice) and since I have been here at Leavenworth Penitentiary I haven't been allowed to write no letters which will enable me to prove my innocence so that is why I am asking your help. I am thanking you in advance if you will investigate.

Very truly yours,
T. J. Audett

Miss Grant

Audett, T. J.
408 Ay

July 27, 1939.

Mr. James A. Johnston,
Warden,
United States Penitentiary,
Alcatraz Island, California.

My dear Warden Johnston:

I am returning the letter written by T. J. Audett to his mother, Mrs. Anna Wineland, which you forwarded with your note of July 20, 1939.

I wish you would be good enough to talk this matter over once more with Audett and tell him that I think he is causing his mother unnecessary worry and mental anguish by sending her such letters as this. He makes no specific request other than that she not permit a post-mortem to be made upon his body in the event he dies. You may tell Audett that we can assure him that no such post-mortem will be made in view of his request, and we shall respect his wishes just as we would his mother's. Under the circumstances, therefore, I think it is hardly the manly and courageous thing to do to worry his mother about his physical condition, which at least according to the doctors is now not serious. If it does become serious, we shall reconsider his request to write his mother along the lines he has indicated.

Sincerely yours,

Director.

JVB/te

FILE
JUL 27 1939
Bureau of Prisons

John & Clarence Anglin
The Great Escape from Alcatraz

BROTHERS JOHN and Clarence Anglin were destined to become central figures in one of the most spectacular prison escapes in American history. With fellow accomplices Frank Lee Morris and Allen West, the inmates devised a cunning escape plan from America's most secure and ultimate escape proof prison. The concept was to escape through the ventilation shaft onto the roof of the pris-on and then swim to shore using flotation devices. The escape took over a year to design, and it would necessitate the fabrication of clever decoys and water survival gear.

Accomplice Frank Morris and alleged mastermind had spent a lifetime navigating the prison system before his arrival on Alcatraz. Morris's criminal record would include a multitude of crimes ranging from narcotics possession to armed rob-

Escape accomplice and alleged mastermind, Frank Lee Morris. His Alcatraz inmate record documented his mental condition as having "superior intelligence" with an IQ of 133.

Letters from Alcatraz

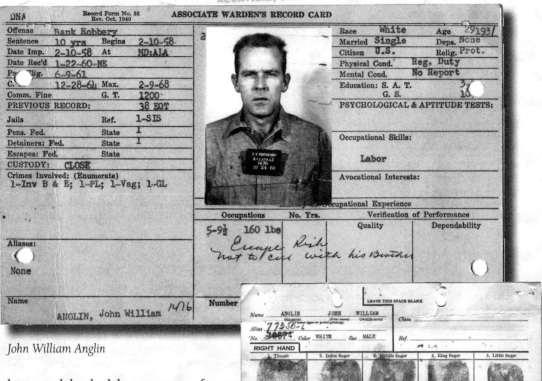

DNA

DNA	Record Form No. 36 Rev. Oct. 1940	ASSOCIATE WARDEN'S RECORD CARD

Offense: Bank Robbery
Sentence: 10 yrs Begins 2-10-58
Date Imp. 2-10-58 At MD:ALA
Date Rec'd 1-22-60-NE
Parole Elig. 6-9-61
C. 12-28-64 Max. 2-9-68
Comm. Fine G. T. 1200
PREVIOUS RECORD: 38 EQT
Jails Ref. 1-SIS
Pens. Fed. State 1
Detainers: Fed. State 1
Escapes: Fed. State
CUSTODY: CLOSE
Crimes Involved: (Enumerate)
1-Inv B & E; 1-PL; 1-Vag; 1-GL
Aliases:
None

Race White Age 29 1931
Married Single Deps. None
Citizen U.S. Relig. Prot.
Physical Cond. Reg. Duty
Mental Cond. No Report
Education: S. A. T. 3
G. S. 10
PSYCHOLOGICAL & APTITUDE TESTS:
Occupational Skills:
Labor
Avocational Interests:

Occupational Experience

Occupations	No. Yrs.	Verification of Performance	
		Quality	Dependability

5-9½ 160 lbs
Escape Risk
not to cell with his Brother

Name: ANGLIN, John William 1476 Number

John William Anglin

LEAVE THIS SPACE BLANK
Name ANGLIN JOHN WILLIAM Class.
Alias 77356-L
No. Color WHITE Sex MALE Ref.

RIGHT HAND

1. Thumb	2. Index finger	3. Middle finger	4. Ring finger	5. Little finger

LEFT HAND

6. Thumb	7. Index finger	8. Middle finger	9. Ring finger	10. Little finger

bery, and he had become a professional inhabitant of the correctional system by his late teens. Morris was credited by prison officials as possessing superior intelligence, and he earned his ticket to Alcatraz by building an impressive résumé of escapes. He arrived on Alcatraz in January of 1960 as inmate AZ-1441.

Brothers John and Clarence Anglin were also serving sentences at Alcatraz for bank robbery, having been convicted along with their brother Alfred. All three had been incarcerated at the Federal Penitentiary in Atlanta when they first became acquainted with Morris, and John and Clarence were eventually sent to Alcatraz following a sequence of attempted escapes.

Alcatraz inmate Allen West, who occupied an adjacent cell, was also brought in on the scheme. He was serving his second term on the Rock and carried a reputation as an arrogant criminal, and he knew

John Anglin from the State Penitentiary in Florida. The escape plan started to take shape in December of 1961, beginning with a collection of several old saw blades that West allegedly found in one of the utility corridors while cleaning. In later interviews, West credited himself for masterminding the clever escape.

The plan was extremely complex and involved the design and fabrication of ingenious lifelike dummy heads, water rafts, and life preservers, fashioned from numerous rain coats that had been acquired from other inmates—some donated and some stolen. They would also require a variety of crudely made tools to dig with, and to construct the acces-

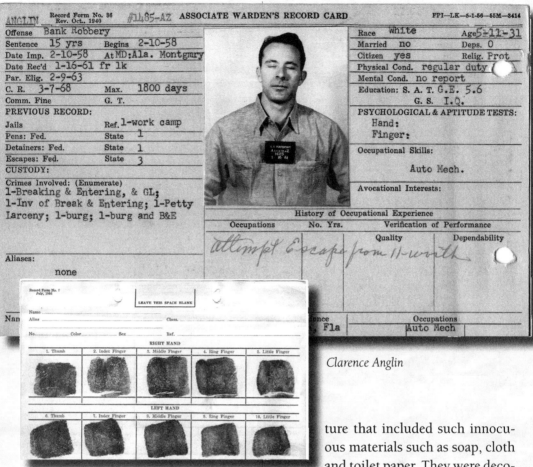

| ANGLIN | Record Form No. 36 Rev. Oct., 1940 | #1485-AZ | ASSOCIATE WARDEN'S RECORD CARD | | FPI—LK—5-1-56—55M—8414 |

Offense	Bank Robbery
Sentence	15 yrs	Begins 2-10-58
Date Imp.	2-10-58	At MD:Ala. Montgmry
Date Rec'd	1-16-61 fr 1k
Par. Elig.	2-9-63
C. R.	3-7-68	Max. 1800 days
Comm. Fine		G. T.

PREVIOUS RECORD:

Jails		Ref. 1-work camp
Pens: Fed.		State 1
Detainers: Fed.		State 1
Escapes: Fed.		State 3

CUSTODY:

Crimes Involved: (Enumerate)
1-Breaking & Entering, & GL;
1-Inv of Break & Entering; 1-Petty
Larceny; 1-burg; 1-burg and B&E

Aliases:
    none

Race	white	Age 5-11-31
Married	no	Deps. 0
Citizen	yes	Relig. Prot
Physical Cond.	regular duty
Mental Cond.	no report
Education: S. A. T.	G.E. 5.6
	G. S.	I.Q.

PSYCHOLOGICAL & APTITUDE TESTS:
  Hand:
  Finger:

Occupational Skills:
    Auto Mech.

Avocational Interests:

History of Occupational Experience

Occupations	No. Yrs.	Verification of Performance	
		Quality	Dependability
attempt Escape from 11-work			

| Nan | | | | | ence ,Fla | Occupations Auto Mech |

LEAVE THIS SPACE BLANK

Name				
Alias		Class.	
No.	Color	Sex	Ref.

RIGHT HAND

| 1. Thumb | 2. Index Finger | 3. Middle Finger | 4. Ring Finger | 5. Little Finger |

LEFT HAND

| 6. Thumb | 7. Index Finger | 8. Middle Finger | 9. Ring Finger | 10. Little Finger |

Clarence Anglin

sories necessary for the escape. By May of 1962, Morris and the Anglins and had already dug through the cell's six-by-nine-inch vent holes, and had started work on the vent on top of the cellblock. The Anglins inhabited adjacent cells, as did West and Morris, who also resided nearby. The inmates alternated shifts, with one working and one on lookout. They would start work at 5:30 P.M. and continue till about 9:00 P.M., just prior to the lights-out count. Meanwhile John and Clarence started fabricating the dummy heads, and even gave them the pet names of "Oink" and "Oscar." The heads were crude but lifelike, and were constructed from a homemade cement-powder mix-

ture that included such innocuous materials such as soap, cloth and toilet paper. They were decorated with flesh-tone paint from prison art kits, and human hair from the barbershop.

Using glue stolen from the glove shop, the inmates also started working to cut and bond the raincoats into a makeshift raft and life preservers. Each evening following the completion of their self-imposed work detail, they would hide the materials on top of the cellblock to minimize any chance of being caught with the contraband materials. The inmates also acquired an elaborate array of handmade tools. West was able to lift an electric hair clipper while working on a paint detail in the barbershop, and he used the clippers, along with drill bits stolen from the

Industries by another inmate, to fashion a makeshift motorized drill. However the motor proved be too small, and thus the project would require more effective equipment.

By a stroke of good luck, West had recently learned that the prison's vacuum had broken. He was permitted to attempt a repair, and while inspecting the machine, he found that it had two motors. He carefully removed one, and was able to get the other working, thus deflecting suspicion. Morris and the Anglins were then able to use the vacuum motor for their drill. They attempted to drill out the roof ventilator, but with only limited success. The motor proved too noisy, and it was not very effective.

After months of long preparation the inmates had completed fashioning all of the gear they needed for their escape, and they then continued working to loosen the ventilator grill on top of the cellhouse. John Anglin carefully completed the valve assembly on a large six-by-fourteen-foot raft, while Morris modified an accordion-like musical instrument called a concertina, which would be used to rapidly inflate the raft. But while the others had progressed well in their various preparations, West had fallen behind in digging out the ventilator grill at the rear of his cell. His primary role had been to construct the life preservers and special wooden paddles for the raft, tasks which didn't require him to leave his cell. On the night of June 11, 1962, Mor-

ris indicated that the top ventilator was loose enough, and that he felt that they were ready to attempt the escape.

At 9:30 P.M., immediately after lights-out, Morris brought down the dummies from the top of the cellblock and announced that the escape would be staged that very night. Clarence Anglin attempted to assist West in removing his ventilator grill by kicking at it from outside of the cell in the utility corridor, but his efforts were unsuccessful. Morris and the Anglins would have no choice but to leave him behind. The inmates made their final thirty-foot climb up the plumbing to the cellhouse roof, traversed 100 feet across the rooftop, and then carefully maneuvered down fifty feet of piping to the ground near the entrance to the shower area. This would be the last anyone ever saw of Morris and the Anglin Brothers.

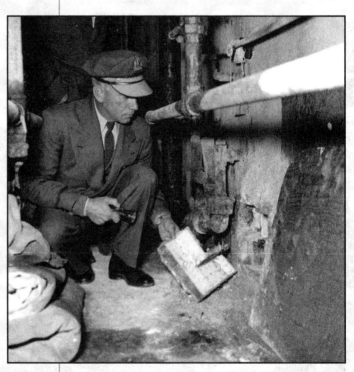

An officer examining the false grill sections behind Allen West's cell (B-152).

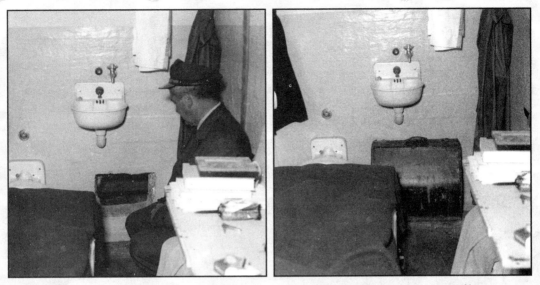

Frank Morris succeeded in covering the ventilation grill inside his cell (B-138) with the case of his concertina, thus diverting any suspicion from the planned escape. The inmates emerged from the tunneled openings in the back of their cells, and ascended through the maze of plumbing to the top of the cellblock. Their final exit was through a rooftop ventilator. As quiet as possible, they trekked across the rooftop of the cellhouse before making their descent down a pipe along the west wall of the prison.

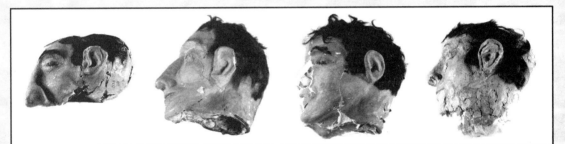

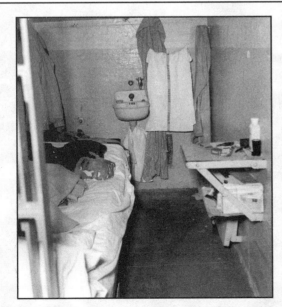

(Above) The inmates used clever decoys to fool the guards during the late night counts. The amazingly detailed and lifelike dummy heads were fashioned primarily from scrap bits and pieces. The materials included soap chips, concrete, wire, plaster, glue, paint, and hair that had been smuggled from the prison barbershop.

(Left) John Anglin's cell (B-158). The towels and clothing were used effectively to hide the ventilation grill.

Letters from Alcatraz

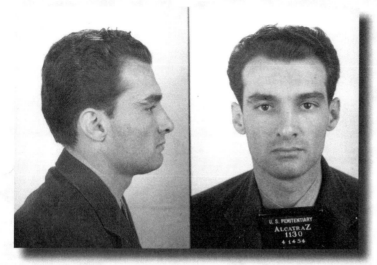

Allen Clayton West

no raft or other means of escape, he was forced to return to his cell.

For decades speculation abounded as to whether this famous escape attempt had been successful. The FBI spent several years investigating, and later resolved that the inmates' plan had failed. The families of the Anglins stated that the escape had been a topic of family discussions for several years. None of them had ever been contacted by the brothers, and they felt that the men would have made contact in some form if they had survived. The Anglins' third brother, Alfred, was electrocuted on security fence while attempting to escape from Kilby Prison in Montgomery Alabama just two years after his brothers' escape from Alcatraz.

In a later interview, West said that their plan had been to use their raft to make their way to Angel Island. After resting, they would then reenter the Bay on the opposite side of the island and swim through a waterway called Raccoon Straits, then on into Marin. They would steal a car, burglarize a clothing store, and then venture out in their own separate directions. West had finally been able to complete the removal of his grill and climb to the rooftop, but by then all of the other inmates had disappeared. With

The mysteries are still being explored decades after the escape, and it remains as one of the most intriguing unsolved mysteries surrounding the world famous prison.

Warden,

   I think I've done as much as any man can do to keep a clean record here. I worked as hard as I knew how. I have went out of my way to avoid trouble when I seen it coming my way. I worked very hard on my job over in Industry and liked it. I had worked my way up to a second grade job and pay. It took me two long years to get there and I would like to say that it meant plenty to me. No one has spoke up for me or did anything in my favor.

   I feel that my two years here has been in vain to all of you. I think that I have earned the right to let all of you know how I feel. I'm not guilty of the charge against me and I want my job back. I've got thirty five years hanging on me and I can't do it over here in A-S. I'm being punished for something I knew nothing about and I wish that some of you would come up with that same idea. I can't just sit here and watch everything that I've worked for go down the drain without saying something.

   This might not sound like much to you but here is one of my main reasons for trying to keep a clean record here.

   I wrote my mother last year and told her that I would have a photo made to send her. I lacked just a few days having in enough time to qualify. So I wrote and told her that I would have to wait until next Xmas. She asks me about that in her letters. It doesn't mean all that much to me, but it do to her. I haven't had a visit since I've been here. My people don't have that kind of money. I was planning on sending her a photo this Christmas and make a phone call.

   I would like to know how and where I stand, on all this. I'm only asking for what I have earned here. I would also like some kind of consideration on my case. Please.

   Yours Truly,
   John William Anglin
   25034

   United States Penitentiary
   RECEIVED
   NOV 30 1959

c

From Clarence Anglin   5/58
75H56
To James V. Bennett
Dir. Bureau of Prisons
Washington D.C.

Mr. James V. Bennett
Dir. Bureau of Prisons

Dear Sir.

I am writing in regard of transfer to Atlanta
U.S.P.

I was transferred here to Leavenworth from
Atlanta but not by my request. If I had broken their rules or done something wrong I could understand being here, but I was getting along real
good there. My Mother and Family were visiting me. And everything was ok.

Now I am fifteen hundred miles from home and no chance of even getting
a visit.

I have a long time to stay in prison. I would appreciate it if you let
me visit them while they still live. They are not in good enough health to
travel so far or afford such a trip.

For consideration I thank you in advance.

Clarence Anglin
75456

June 6, 1958

Dear Sir

I've got two boy one in Kansas & one in Pennsylvania their in Prison there & their names are Clarence
Anglin & John William Anglin & I would like to get
them brought back to Atlanta Ga. so I can go to see
them, they are two far away & I can't go to see them, &
me & their Daddy are getting old & we're not able to
make a trip like that even if we had the money witch
we don't have. I would like very much if you would
give them a transfer to Atlanta Ga. as we can visit
with them once in awhile, as we are about 500 miles
from Atlanta, we could go once in awhile.

    Mrs. G. R. Anglin
    Ruskin, Fla.

Ruskin, Fla
Oct 28, 1960

United States Dept of Justice
United States Penitentiary
Leavenworth, Kansas

Dear Sir:

    I am writing you in regards to my Son - John William Anglin. I would like to have some information concerning his removal from there to the Penitentiary in Alcatraz California. I know there must be something wrong and I would like very much to hear something about this. I would like to know also about my other son Clarence Anglin. Is he alright? I thank you for your help.

    Mrs. Rachel Anglin
    Route 10 Box 205
    Ruskin, Florida

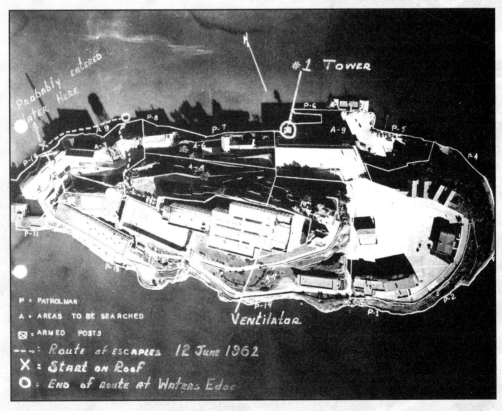

The perimeter search map utilized by prison officials and the FBI. Investigators charted the path of the escapees down to the water's edge. Once the inmates entered the water, they were never seen or heard from again. They are presumed dead.

Letters from Alcatraz

Alvin Karpis

LVIN KARPIS, would hold the exclusive distinction of serving the longest single term on Alcatraz, nearly 26-years on the Rock. Alvin Karpawicz was born in Montreal, Canada in 1908, and his father moved the family to Topeka, Kansas when Alvin was still a young boy. It was an elementary school teacher who decided to shorten his name to simply Alvin Karpis, and later while at Alcatraz he was tagged by fellow inmates with the nicknames of "Creepy Karpis" and "Old Creepy."

Karpis would live a quarter of a century in a place where he would never be allowed to walk astray, and would never see many areas that were only a few yards from his cell. In his memoir published in 1980, Karpis claimed that his first encounter with crime had occurred when he stole a gun at only ten years of age, beginning his lengthy crime pursuit during his formative years as a youth. Like many other criminals of his era, Karpis' first arrest was for illegally hopping trains. He was sentenced to a Florida chain-gang, and after his release he was again arrested for robbery. He subsequently escaped from prison, and became a fugitive.

Karpis joined the Barker gang after meeting Fred Barker in 1930 at the Kansas State Penitentiary in Lansing and embarked on a long and violent crime spree consisting of bank robberies, kidnapping and several murders including the slaying of three police officers. Karpis had also been one the architects of the famed kidnapping of the Hamms Brewery heir William A. Hamm in 1933. His vicious crimes earned him his designation as one of America's most wanted public enemies, and an equal billing as a leader of the Barker-Karpis Gang, which became one of the most formidable criminal gangs of the 1930s.

J. Edgar Hoover who had personally designated Alvin as "Public Enemy

Number One" initiated an intense pursuit to capture Karpis and his associate gang members. On May 1, 1936, under Hoover's personal direction, the FBI descended on Karpis and Fred Hunter, another alumni of Alcatraz in New Orleans. Hoover was on hand to command the squad of FBI agents who performed the arrest. Karpis would later mock Hoover's claim that he had been present for the arrest, stating that Hoover was actually nowhere to be seen until Karpis and his accomplice had already been cuffed, when he quickly emerged for the photo opportunities. He would later credit FBI Agent Clarence Hurt with the famed arrest. His capture would signify the end of the gangster driven public enemy era, and elevated J. Edgar Hoover and the FBI to national prominence by taking back America.

Sentenced to life imprisonment, Karpis was incarcerated at Alcatraz from August 1936 to April 1962, although he did enjoy a short absence from Alcatraz during a

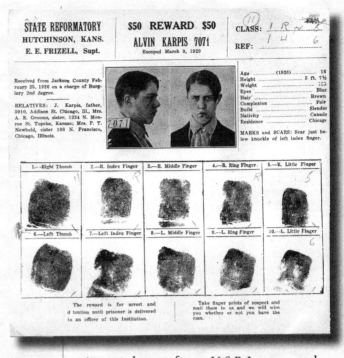

six-month transfer to U.S.P. Leavenworth in 1958. Karpis served his time quietly at Alcatraz, though he was considered far from being a model inmate by correctional officers. Former Alcatraz Officer Al Bloomquist called Karpis a mild nuisance, and described him as an inmate who complained frequently about the conditions, and one who fought constantly with fellow inmates. He was known as an obsessive reader and held numerous positions in the Alcatraz industries and a kitchen assignment. It is rumored that when baseball games were broadcasted inside the cellhouse in the late 1950s, Karpis would bellow in laughter when the Hamm's jingle played during commercial breaks.

He remained at Alcatraz until his transfer to McNeil Island in 1962, was released on parole in 1969, and then

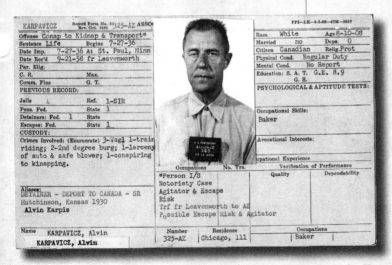

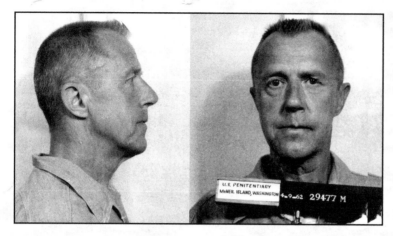

about his life at Alcatraz, including one bestseller, and would thus acquire enough funds to fulfill his longtime dream of moving to Spain in 1973. His life in Spain is largely undocumented, but on August 26, 1979, Karpis was found dead from what was originally ruled suicide by

he was deported to Canada, although he initially had difficulty obtaining Canadian passport credentials, on account of having had his fingerprints removed by the well known underworld physician Joseph Moran in 1934.

Karpis would later write two books

authorities, as sleeping pills were found by his body, but later it was modified to death from natural causes. It was suggested that Karpis had become dependent on drugs and alcohol, which may have influenced his death. Karpis wrote prolifically during his incarceration at Alcatraz.

July 30, 1942
To: Mrs. Emily Janke
Alcatraz, California
1456 W. Cuyler
Chicago, Illinois

Dear Sister:

An hour or so ago the Assoc. Warden came up to my cell and told me to be sure and write a letter to you tonight as you are worried about not hearing from me for so long. Well, kid, it's a long story but I will try to explain it provided I am permitted to do so.

On April 20th I was informed that the mat shop, where I am working, would be closed due to lack of material, etc., and that I would have to go to the laundry to work, which was agreeable, provided I wasn't put in a certain Dept. as things were rather unsettled there. It was insisted upon that I work in that Dept. "or else." I chose the "or else" and when the "or else was over with, on or about May the 7th, I was put in the cell without any privileges except to take a bath once a week, a shave three times a week, and a hair cut once a month and all other privileges taken until I knuckle under and do as I am told naturally my mail privileges were taken right along with my exercise, sunshine, fresh air, reading material, tobacco, personal property, etc., so I had no way of answering your letter. Now as to how long it will be until this situation will be straightened out will be strictly up to the officials for the only thing they can possibly accomplish by keeping me locked up in a cell without fresh air, sunshine or exercise, is possibly a breaking down of my health, and if by being able to do that they can derive any personal satisfaction from it, more power to them. You see Emily when I chose the "or else" I feel as though I paid in full for my refusal even though under the circumstances I considered my refusal un-wholly justified due to existing conditions at that time, so as far as I am concerned I just have no way of knowing when I will be able to write again for I have no intention of going to work down there in view of the fact that I have already paid for my refusal with "or else". I realize that what I have already written in this letter will come as a shock to you since in my mail to you in the past I have always covered up the more unpleasant things that have occurred since I have been out here, but I for some unexplainable reason find myself unable to go on using such hypocrisy this time. Maybe I should have let you know about these things long ago but I just didn't care to bother you. There isn't anything that I am able to do about except explain it to you as I have done on the other side of this paper. Oh I guess I could have done as I have in the past, give you a line of bull as to why I wasn't writing etc. but it would have been the same old thing over again. Oh I could probably get permission to write by asking for permission every time I intended to write but you can imagine how that works out the first time you get in some scrape it was "or else" so until I am given back my mail privileges by them on their own account why I won't be writing to anyone for awhile. Now Emily what ever you see fit to do, don't you dare let the folks know about all this you know how upset they get. After this whenever you want to get information and aren't getting it why you know you can always get it thru your Senator Brooks or someone like that you know who to see about matters of that kind. I think he is working on the Chicago Tribune. Well I sure have my doubts as to whether you will receive this as the truth sure hurts some people but I have read it over carefully and I am sure there are no military secrets in it so maybe it will pass. Well the above just about covers it. Now once more don't say nothing to the folks. How is Betty? Tell her I said hello. I received a letter from Father the other day and one from Mother a week or so ago. For some reason or other they allow me to receive mail sent to me. I am getting short of paper, so I may as well close. Now that you understand what is what there isn't any use in you worrying—I will write to you when my mail privileges are restored, so pay it no mind if you don't hear from me for a few years.

Alvin Karpawicz, Reg. No. 325-AZ

Letters from Alcatraz

AUGUST TWELFTH 1 9 4 2
Mrs. Emily Janke
1456 W. Ruyler Street
Chicago, Illinois

Dear Madam:

Responsive to your letter of August 5, 1942, regarding your brother, Alvin Karpavicz, Reg. No. 325-AZ, I want to tell you at the outset that there is not any person here, certainly not any officer, who is putting any pressure on your brother for any personal reason. Of course, it may be that he may consider that an order in accordance with regulations is pressure, for it sometimes happens that while the officers endeavor to carry out their duties in an impersonal way and without any prejudice, the inmate who is subject to the order and the regulations may view it differently because he is in a different position with different ideas.

As you stated in your letter, your brother seemed to be getting along quite well for a long time, and I was glad to see him make what appeared to be a fair adjustment to his difficult position. The facts with regard to his loss of privileges to which he refers are as follows:

He was working in the Mat Shop and seemed to be getting along quite well until we reached a situation where we ran out of rubber, couldn't make any more mats for the time being, and were obliged to close the Mat Shop and to transfer the inmates who were working in that shop to the laundry, where we were very busy. Your brother seemed to think that since he was assigned to the Mat Shop that was his place and therefore it was unfair for us to send him to the laundry just because the Mat Shop was closing, and he refused to obey the order or take the assignment in the change of work.

As a fair-minded person, I am sure that you will see the reasonableness of the order, and I am sure you would if you were in my position. I think it would be better for your brother if he accepts the order and goes about the work to which he has been assigned, using what few privileges it is possible for us to grant. Although his privileges have been restricted, he has been advised that he could write to you, and he availed himself of that privilege and probably told you about his trouble in his own way, so that now you have his point of view as well as the facts which I have given in response to your request.

Sincerely,

J. A. JOHNSTON, Warden

Sept. 1945
From Alvin Karpawicz No. 325
Alcatraz California

To The Warden
Alcatraz Island California

Dear Sir:

As the time available for personal interviews is somewhat limited, I thought it best that I explain what I have in mind in form of a letter.

I would like to find out what my chances are, in getting transferred to one of the other institutions by the end of 1946, preferably Leavenworth.

While I am satisfied with this place in most ways my reasons for wanting a transfer, are as follows;

I have been working in the Bakery for over 26 months and I would very much like a chance of doing the same kind of work where modern bakery equipment is extensively used so that when I am eventually deported I would feel confident in being able to get and hold a good paying position in the Baking industry.

My parents and son reside at Topeka Kansas which is about 60 miles from Leavenworth. It is now over nine years since I have seen anyone of my family and as my parents are getting pretty old I think them being able to visit me once a month would be a very nice thing.

By the 26th of July 1948 I will have 10 years served, which would leave me 5 years more to serve before becoming eligible for deportation. I could learn a great deal working 5 years in a large Bakery.

As to my prison record, I can't honesty say that is any too good except in way of performing well any work that I have undertaken. I have been reported perhaps a dozen times in the nine years that I have been here in the past 3 years. I have been reported only once it is my opinion that when my past conduct in prison is reviewed, due consideration should be given to the fact that where - as almost all the inmates in here had a chance to become accustomed to prison routine and discipline, I was one might say, practically taken right from the freedom of the streets and put in here as I was in Leavenworth only 6 days.

Of course I also realize that the unpleasant notoriety in my case isn't helpful in this matter but I feel that I should at least inquire as to what chances are or might be in the next year or 18 months.

Naturally I would be highly pleased to receive an encouraging answer to all of this but in the event that my hopes are a bit premature I would still appreciate knowing just where I stand at present. Your advice in this matter would be helpful to me in planning for the future regard of a favorable or an unfavorable answer.

I believe the above just about covers my case at the present time. Thanking you in advance for your consideration in this matter.

Respectfully

Alvin Karpawicz
No. 325

[Handwritten Note] Interviewed. Told him I could not give him any definite date when his application would be acted on but if he made good record it would taken up for consideration before his parole date - J.A.J-3yrs.

May 8, 1948
From Alvin Karpawicz No. 325

Alcatraz California

To Warden Swope
Wardens Office

Dear Sir:

Not knowing just when you will begin granting interviews, I decided to write this letter hoping that it will serve, at least partially, the same purpose that a personal interview would. As I understand it Paul Ritter is scheduled to be transferred soon. In that event I would like very much to have the job he now has.

I have cooked for the officers mess 3 different times, for the main line twice and for 3 ½ years was in charge of the bake shop. I believe my work record, my conduct for the past 5 years and the monthly work reports will prove satisfactory.

Before asking you for this job I first discussed the matter fully with both Mr. Madigan and Mr. Scanland as I realize that if either one or both considered it ill advised I best not bother asking but as both spoke favorably in regard to the matter I feel that I owe it to myself to try for it.

At the present time I am the printer and also do clerical work for Mr. Scanland. I am serving a life sentence for kidnapping. July 26th I will have in 12 years. I have in my possession a warrant calling for me deportation. I will be eligible for deportation July 26, 1951. I have several detainers on me which I could get lifted without too much effort but haven't tried as I feel they will be dropped automatically at the proper time.

I have several reasons for wanting that job. The most important one being that, if I could work for you satisfactorily for 2 or 3 years, it would go a long long way in giving the proper Authorities a fair idea as to my future conduct in the event they were to deport me. Another reason is that I like that type of work. I also believe the change would be beneficial to me as I have been inside a long time.

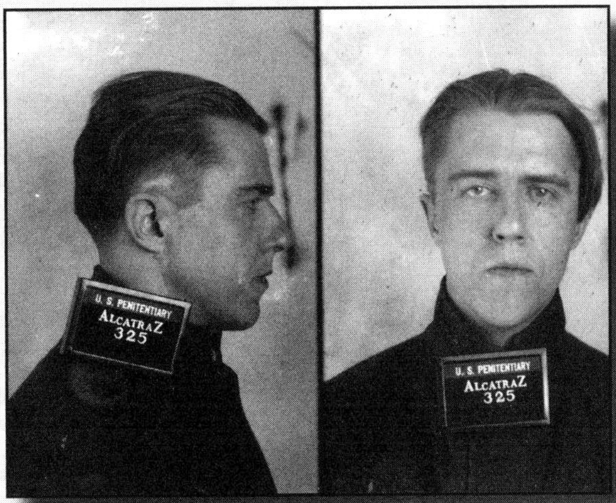

About 3 years ago I asked Warden Johnston about a transfer but I now believe that job means more than a transfer in regards to me getting deported. I believe that the above just about covers it. Hoping that you can and will give this matter favorable consideration.

Respectfully yours

Alvin Karpawicz

[Handwritten Note] told no

May 21, 1953
FROM: Alvin Karpawicz, 325
Alcatraz, California
TO: Mrs. Emily Janke
3644 Diversey, Chicago, Ill.

Dear Sister:

I just received your letter and sure was glad to hear you are all alright, now about Mother, frankly I expected to hear much worse news, even though it is bad enough. Let's hope she snaps out of it. She is Lucky to have you looking out for her. I am glad that, Clara is acting decently for a change hope she keeps it up. Well Emily I am writing this from S.T.U. I've been locked up since Monday Morning, on the flimsiest of pretences. I won't go into details but locking me up was such obviously apparent act of frustration on an officials part that he

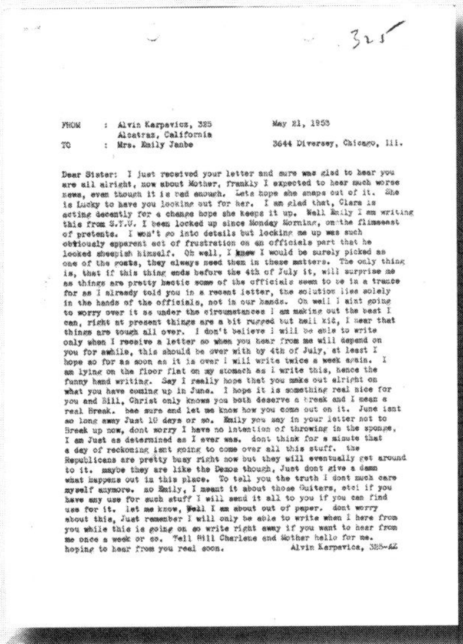

325

FROM : Alvin Karpavicz, 325 May 21, 1953
Alcatraz, California
TO : Mrs. Emily Janbe 3644 Diversey, Chicago, Ill.

Dear Sister: I just received your letter and sure was glad to hear you are all alright, now about Mother, frankly I expected to hear much worse news, even though it is bad enough. Lets hope she snaps out of it. She is Lucky to have you looking out for her. I am glad that, Clara is acting decently for a change hope she keeps it up. Well Emily I am writing this from S.T.U. I been locked up since Monday Morning, on the flimseest of pretents. I won't go into details but locking me up was such obviously apparent act of frustration on an officials part that he looked sheepish himself. Oh well, I knew I would be surely picked as one of the goats, they always need them in these matters. The only thing is, that if this thing ends before the 4th of July it, will surprise me as things are pretty hectic some of the officials seem to be in a trance for as I already told you in a recent letter, the solution lies solely in the hands of the officials, not in our hands. Oh well I aint going to worry over it as under the circumstances I am making out the best I can, right at present things are a bit rugged but hell kid, I hear that things are tough all over. I don't believe I will be able to write only when I receive a letter so when you hear from me will depend on you for awhile, this should be over with by 4th of July, at least I hope so for as soon as it is over I will write twice a week again. I am lying on the floor flat on my stomach as I write this, hence the funny hand writing. Say I really hope that you make out alright on what you have coming up in June. I hope it is something real nice for you and Bill, Christ only knows you both deserve a break and I mean a real Break. bee sure and let me know how you come out on it. June isnt so long away Just 10 days or so. Emily you say in your letter not to Break up now, dont worry I have no intention of throwing in the sponge, I am Just as determined as I ever was. dont think for a minute that a day of reckoning isnt going to come over all this stuff. the Republicans are pretty busy right now but they will eventually get around to it. maybe they are like the Demos though, Just dont give a damn what happens out in this place. To tell you the truth I dont much care myself anymore. so Emily, I meant it about those Guitars, etc! if you have any use for such stuff I will send it all to you if you can find use for it. let me know, Well I am about out of paper. dont worry about this, Just remember I will only be able to write when I here from you while this is going on so write right away if you want to hear from me once a week or so. Tell Bill Charlene and Mother hello for me. hoping to hear from you real soon. Alvin Karpavicz, 325-AZ

looked sheepish himself. Oh well, I knew I would be surely picked as one of
the goats, they always need them in these matters. The only thing is, that
if this thing ends before the 4th of July it, will surprise me as things are
pretty hectic some of the officials seem to be in a trance for as I already
told you in a recent letter, the solution lies solely in the hands of the
officials, not in our hands. Oh well I ain't going to worry over it as under
the circumstances I am making out the best I can, right at present things
are a bit rugged but hell kid, I hear that things are tough all over. I don't
believe I will be able to write only when I receive a letter so when you
hear from me will depend on you for awhile, this should be over with by
4th of July, at least I hope so for as soon as it is over I will write twice
a week again. I am lying on the floor flat on my stomach as I write this,
hence the funny hand writing. Say I really hope that you make out alright
on what you have coming up in June. I hope it is something real nice for
you and Bill, Christ only knows you both deserve a break and I mean a real
break. Be sure and let me know how you come out on it. June isn't so long
away Just 10 days or so. Emily you say in your letter not to break up now,
don't worry I have no intention of throwing in the sponge; I am just as determined as I ever was. Don't think for a minute that a day of reckoning
isn't going to come over all this stuff. The Republicans are pretty busy
right now but they will eventually get around to it. Maybe they are like
the Demos though, just don't give a damn what happens out in this place.
To tell you the truth I don't much care myself anymore. No Emily, I meant
it about those Guitars, etc., if you have any use for such stuff I will send
it all to you if you can find use for it, let me know. Well I am about out
of paper, don't worry about this, Just remember I will only be able to write
when I hear from you while this is going on so write right away if you
want to hear from me once a week or so. Tell Bill Charlene and Mother hello
for me. Hoping to hear from you real soon.

Alvin Karpawicz, 325-AZ

Administrative Form No. 16
May 1937

UNITED STATES BUREAU OF PRISONS

INTRA-BUREAU CORRESPONDENCE

February 17, 1938

TO: Warden Johnston, Alcatraz

RE: Correspondence between an inmate and his wife confined in one of our institutions

IN REPLY REFER TO: 726

Thank you for forwarding to me the letter from Alvin Karpis written to Dolores Delaney.

It was my understanding that correspondence between a man and his wife was permitted but that not more than two letters a month could be written to the wife or husband confined in another institution, and I see no reason to make an exception in Karpis' Case. I believe that he claims Dolores Delaney for his wife, and even if she is not his legal wife, it is clear that she is his common law wife and, therefore, comes within the rule.

I do not think that a similar privilege ought to be denied the others. If, for example, Volney Davis desires to correspond with a bona fide common law wife, I see no reason why she should be barred so long as the correspondence otherwise is in accordance with the rules.

Director.

P.S. The letter from Alvin Karpis to Dolores Delaney has been forwarded to Milan.

ALCATRAZ ISLAND, CALIF.
RECD.

FEB 23 19

March 19, 1957
From Alvin Karpawicz

Alcatraz California
Mr. P. J. Madigan, Warden

Cell C-140

Dear Sir:

In the more than 20 years since my arrival here I have occasionally received postal cards from relatives on my approved correspondence list but today Mr. Ringwald informs me, cards that have accumulated in the mail office from my niece down in Miami are not to be given me and that furthermore, I should notify her to cease sending cards.

Mr. Madigan, surely you realize that after all the years I've spent in this place there are very few things left to me from which I can derive any pleasure. The cards I occasionally receive from various localities with which I am familiar have always been a great source of pleasure to me and why after twenty years of them, which has resulted in harm to no one, they should now be suddenly prohibited beats me. Naturally I will survive it if this privilege is to be taken from me, just as I out rode the other vindictive petty persecutions shot at me in the past around this place, but I find it hard to believe that you would acquiesce to seeing me deprived of a privilege I have had for 20 years or more, one which I have at no time abused or attempted to take advantage of. In the remove event that I am mistaken tho, then I believe that at the very least, the cards, either should be promptly returned to the sender or else to my sister for after all they were purchased and sent in good faith and the money they cost should not be wasted as the result of a capricious whim on the part of some official connected with this place.

Respectfully yours,

Alvin Karpawicz 325 AZ

Elliott Michener

WHEN NOTORIOUS inmate Roy Gardner wrote in his memoir: "The very word "Alcatraz" has struck terror into the hearts of the underworld gangsters." it couldn't have applied more aptly to Elliott Michener. But Elliott would also become a man of redemption, proof that Alcatraz didn't mean the final chapter in one's life, but rather a chance at a new beginning.

Elliott Michener was an elite class counterfeiter who had landed himself on Alcatraz following a desperate escape attempt at Leavenworth Prison. Michener clamed that it was his fear of transfer to Alcatraz that prompted him to build a makeshift weapon (a homemade handgun) to aid in his escape. His inmate file contained the following excerpts from an interview transcript conducted by Associate Warden Cecil Shuttleworth, who had also once served as Associate Warden at Alcatraz:

Q: What was your fear of Alcatraz that was so great that you would have been willing to almost take your own life in preference to being transferred there? What is there about Alcatraz that you fear so much? I can show you letters from Warden Johnston of ten days ago in which he listed 12 men for transfer back here from Alcatraz and enclosed copies from men who preferred to stay there. Have you ever talked to any of the men from Alcatraz?

A: *What I heard from Alcatraz has been unpleasant. I still believe it is like Wisconsin State Prison. I done time there. I do not want to do no time like I done in Waupun and thought it was like it was there.*

Q: The silent system at Alcatraz is in the cellhouse. All men are in single cells and all men prefer to read and write and do not make a lot of noise in their cells, and do not want to be disturbed. Do you prefer to cell alone?

A: *Yes.*

The gun, "home-made" found in possession of inmate Elliott Michener, 55506-L, on Saturday; July 12, 1941 by Lt. Concannon.

This inmate admitted he intended using this in an attempt to escape through the South Gate, using Mr. O. N. Shelton as a shield.

C. J. SHUTTLEWORTH
Senior Associate Warden
U.S.Penitentiary
Leavenworth, Kansas

Letters from Alcatraz

DEPARTMENT OF JUSTICE, BUREAU OF INVESTIGATION
IDENTIFICATION DIVISION, WASHINGTON.

CRIMINAL HISTORY

Q: When did you think up this idea, how long have you been working on this idea?

A: *As soon as I thought I was going to Alcatraz.*

At Alcatraz Michener gained the trust of the administration and worked as both a gardener and a passman. The passman assignment was one of earned, a special assignment to aid the Warden and his wife inside their home, with duties ranging from basic housekeeping and cooking, to complex maintenance duties. Michener developed a passion for gardening, and was believed to have introduced many botanical varieties to Alcatraz. Michener was also close friends with John Giles, who would later become famous for a failed escape attempt where he assembled an Army uniform over a ten year period and gain entrance onto a military boat which performed a laundry exchange. He was quickly noticed missing and captured.

Michener was released from prison in 1952 and successfully integrated back in society. As illustrated in his letters following his release, he maintained a close affinity with Warden Swope and his wife with frequent correspondence. Michener died in Los Angeles in May of 1997 at 90-years of age.

Q: The only other place there is silence is in the Dining Room. You cannot hold a conversation in the Dining Room, but you can ask somebody to pass you something. At work they talk to each other and when in the yard they are allowed to talk. Alcatraz is one of the cleanest and most sanitary places in the United States and one of the most orderly run prisons.

A: *Many attempts of escape have been made with something that looks like a real gun that cannot be fired and there have been some successful escapes. The now deceased (John) Dillinger made his escape with a wooden gun.*

Letters from Alcatraz

Aug. 14, 1939
From Elliott Michener
#55506

To James A. Bennett
Leavenworth Penitentiary
Superintendent of Prisons

Dear Sir:

This is a request that you investigate and change some of the unhealthful conditions existing here.

There are, in "C" cell-house here, a number of long-timers awaiting transfer to other penitentiaries. They have broken no rules, and yet are subject to harsher discipline than men in the punishment gang. The latter, for instance, are allowed to go out to work everyday; but long-timers like myself are kept locked up, two men to a stuffy cell, for twenty-three hours a day.

The cells are hot, stuffy, and crawling with bedbugs and cockroaches. The narrow space beside the double-deck bunks is not wide enough to walk in. The result is that we must spend our days lying on our bunks, dull-minded and dispirited, and wishing we had a little exercise. At present, the only "exercise" we get is at noon, when we are turned out for a short period in the cell corridor, which is then too crowded for walking.

I have been here for a little more than a month, and have felt half-sick from want of exercise every day of the time. The doctor tells me I need more ventilation-fresh air.

I understand that I am slated for Alcatraz. I do not mind that so much - there, we will at least be given something to do; what I and all the other men awaiting transfer hate, is the five or six months we must lie idle in our cells.

Is there any reason why we couldn't be given an hour or two of active physical exercise in the fresh air everyday? Lord knows there are enough guards to watch us! Or is there any reason why those of us who wish it could not be given a chance to go out and do manual labor with the "punishment" gang? The punishment gang is closely watched.

My outside record may be bad but my inside one is excellent. During the last three-and-a-half years I have been editor of the prison magazine and school teacher at Waupun, Wisconsin prison (which I come direct). Having been trusted with this work there, when I had twice as much time as I have now, it would seem that I could be safely trusted to work under supervision here, until the time of my transfer. <u>Cannot something be arranged</u>?

Respectfully,
Elliott Michener

From Elliott Michener   Feb. 26, 1951
55506

To Warden E. B. Swope

Dear Sir:

A couple of days ago I received a slip from the Parole Board saying that my application had been denied.

As you may recall, I wrote to Mr. Bennett a few months ago to the effect that I'd prefer to stay at Alcatraz unless, in the event I should transfer here and be denied parole. I could then be sent to a minimum security institution in order that I might have a chance, as Franseen had at Sandstone, to show dependability and after a couple of years earn a parole. Mr. Bennett didn't answer so I can't know what his attitude is. The outlook seems bleak, however, and after thinking the problem over for a couple of days I believe that my best and only practical course is to get back to Alcatraz.

You will understand, I think, that after sixteen years in prison I just haven't the stomach for eight more of the discipline and close confinement that are standard here. At Alcatraz I could at least grow Bell roses and delpheniums seven days a week and enjoy considerable freedom and trust, and in general make the best of things. I haven't the fortitude for a long and weary pull here, with repeated disappointments regarding parole. I'd much rather forget the whole thing and content myself with what privileges as can be had there, even if they must be earned all over again. Of course, prisoners are usually not returned there except for cause, and that is the reason for this letter. Will you help me in this, please? A letter of explanation from you to Mr. Bennett would do more to help me get back than would anything else. I'd be _very_ grateful.

Mr. Madigan would be glad to know that Franseen is doing very well and was allowed to make a plane trip to Los Angeles to visit old friends there. The only news I have to report of myself is that I've been assigned to the shoe factory.

Will you give my respects to Mrs. Swope, please, and to Wesley, and thank the Magruders for their cheerful card at Christmas?

Respectfully,
Elliott W. Michener
#55506

From E. Michener   Jan. 10, 1952
55506
To Warden E. B. Swope

Dear Mr. Swope -

The seven (or seventeen) lean years are past, and there are, it seems, some fat ones ahead. The Board has just granted me a parole and I'm due to go out within a week or so. Mr. Charles Ward, of Brown & Bigelow, has assured me a job as clerk at the St. Paul plant, at a starting wage of $200 a month, and indicated that later I may have a choice of occupation. Needless to say, I'm as happy as Pat is when he sees you coming in the front door!

This letter is to thank you for the help and consideration which you and Mrs. Swope have given me. I enjoyed working for you, was grateful for the trust you showed, and appreciate your efforts on my behalf. You may be sure that I'll do nothing to make you regret it.

If you have time would you tell me how the orchids came out? And would you tell my friend Giles of my good fortune and that I wish him good cheer? Thank you.

With respect to you and your family,

Elliott W. Michener
#55506

(General Delivery, St. Paul)

January 15, 1952
Elliott W. Michener
PMB 55506
Leavenworth, Kansas

This will acknowledge your letter of January 10, 1952, and we are quite pleased with the fact that the Parole Board has seen fit to grant you parole, and that Mr. Charles Ward of Brown and Bigelow, has assured you a position as Clerk in the St. Paul Plant with a starting wage of $200.00 with every indication of advancement. I understand that he has, in times past, been of material assistance to other men who have been paroled or discharged from prison, and feel quite sure he will give you every consideration.

I, also, am convinced that you will certainly adjust yourself to conditions on the outside and be successful in fitting yourself back into a po-

Alcatraz Warden Edwin B. Swope served from 1948 to 1955.

sition in society, which will bring you a great deal of joy and pleasure in the future.

With reference to the orchids, these plants are still growing, but very slowly. A great many of them perished along the way, however, there will be plenty perhaps in the next four to five years.

With reference to Giles, he has been transferred to McNeil Island, and I am sure would have been very happy to hear about your good fortune.

Again, hoping for your every success.

Sincerely,

E. B. SWOPE
Warden

January 24, 1952
Mr. Elliott Michener
c/o Mr. C. Buckley
Probation Officer
Federal Building
St. Paul, Minn.

My dear Michener:

This will acknowledge recent of your recent letter. We are all happy for you and there is no question of doubt in my mind but what you will make good. Do not become distressed when it is necessary for you to meet adversities. The only thing that will ever get you into difficulty is your temper and acting on the impulse of the moment. We all must go through life and meet many disappointments. I am sure you will overcome all of the many trying situations that you will be confronted with.

It certainly was a good thing that you worked in Industries and earned the $250.00 price to your parole from Leavenworth. I am so happy they gave you a nice suit of clothes which made you feel you were presentable.

Mr. Ward will no doubt give you every opportunity to make good. The Probation Officer in that District is a very capable man and he has a very excellent organization. Don't hesitate to discuss your trouble with him as I am sure he will help you.

The value of the dollar unquestionably has decreased and you will find that it is a little more difficult to stretch it than it was seventeen years ago.

It is certainly encouraging to be informed that Franzeen is making good. He has been out quite a little while now and we all have a feeling he will conduct himself in the future as he has in the past, that is, since his release. It is also encouraging to know that you will, no doubt, be as proud of your conduct as we will be. Anything we might have done for you while you were committed to this institution was done because you earned the right to our confidence by your conduct and application and we are quite sure that our confidence was not misplaced and the proof of that is you earned the parole and that the board could see you were determined to prove your eligibility for release.

I hope you will not hesitate to write to me whenever you feel in the mood to do so. If there is anything we can do to assist you in your adjustment on the outside, please do not hesitate to call upon us. As I told you in the previous letter, the plants are all doing fairly well, although it is quite a chore to take care of them, as very few people have the interest that you had in the flowers and garden.

Looking forward to your continued success.
Sincerely,

E. B. SWOPE
Warden

August 21, 1952

Dear Mr. Swope -

Thought you might be interested in the enclosed clipping....

Dick and I are getting along well and for the first time I'm learning how much better one can do living honestly than by, say, counterfeiting! We have cars & fat bank accounts; and have two patents (one for a soap dispenser that fits into packages) which Brown & Bigelow is going to manufacturer and pay us royalties on.

And we have a favor to ask: will you send us a bush of our old 'gardener' rose? It is not 'Mrs. Charles Bell' as the rosarian in Berkeley told Mrs. Swope. We have ordered 'Mrs. Charles Bell' and it is considerably different from, and inferior to, the 'Gardener.' We'd like very much to have one, or even cuttings from one, and have no idea of where else to get one. In return we'd be glad to send you any named variety you'd like. Do you have 'Peace'? Good luck to you and your family.

Respectfully,

Elliott W. Michener

September 2, 1952

My dear Michener:

We were very happy to hear from you and appreciate your sending us the clipping. Everyone is indeed gratified to know that you and Dick are getting along so well. Mr. Ward must be a fine person to give you boys the opportunity he has to readjust yourselves.

That seems to be some car you are driving and of course I know you feel very happy over the fact that you have freedom of action and it certainly must give you a great deal of pleasure to own an automobile.

Your patents must be good or Mr. Ward wouldn't handle them. I do hope you make a lot of money out of them. Brown and Bigelow are a big outfit and can be of lot of help in selling your soap dispensers, etc.

I would be very happy to do something about sending you the rose bush but we just can't identify it. As you know, Wesley when he purchased a house, we gave him some of the plants and it might be the rose you want was given to him. I see you are still interested in fl owers - this is commendable.

It is indeed a great deal of satisfaction to all of us to know you are doing so well.

With kindest regards.

Sincerely,

E. B. SWOPE

THE RYAN HOTEL
SIXTH AND ROBERT
SAINT PAUL 1

RECEIVED
JAN 24 8:52 AM '5
U.S. PENITENTIARY
ALCATRAZ, CALIFORNIA

Dear Mr. Swope -

Just a note to let you know that I'm out! Everything worked out for the best - during the year in Leavenworth I earned about $250, and that comes in handy now. Furthermore I got a very nice gray suit and overcoat, and look quite presentable. The world doesn't seem to have changed so very much during the last 17 years, except that a dollar sizzles out as fast as a drop of water on a hot stove. And the girls look prettier.

Parole is not going to be hard to keep. The probation offi cers here have made it plain that they're on my side and will give me all possible help provided I just play fair. My boss, of course, is to be Mr. Charles Ward. He's at his Arizona ranch now but will be back here in a few days and I'll then learn defi nitely where I'm to work - in the big plant, or out on one of his farms.

Franseen is working in Mr. Ward's home, and has about the same work there (except for cooking) that I had with you. He's very happy, well-liked and trusted, and the proud possessor of a new Oldsmobile. You may put it down on the record that he's one Alcatraz man who has made good - and that I'm going to be another.

Much of my good fortune I owe to you - first for giving me the chance to work at your home (when it must have seemed to most of the officials there a risky thing to do), and later for your active help in getting me a transfer and a parole. I know now that your recommendations carried the day. I'm grateful.

Please give my regards to Mrs. Swope.

Respectfully,

E. Michener

c/o Mr. C. Buckley
Probation Officer
Fed. Bldg., St. Paul

11601 Brockway St.
El Monte, Calif.
June 19, 1954

Dear Mr. & Mrs. Swope -

This letter has a dual purpose. The first is just to let you know that I was married over in Yuma about five weeks ago, and that we're living in El Monte. Dick Franseen was also married, back in Hudson, Wisc. Mr. & Mrs. Ward, and the elite of Hudson, attended their wedding and reception. Both the Franseens and the Micheners got presents from the Wards - a check apiece for $1000.00, and the most gorgeous sterling 4-piece coffee services. My wife and I are very happy and look ahead to happy years.

The second purpose of this letter is to ask a favor that may be a bit presumptuous. Dr. Newton of Hudson is in San Francisco for the A.M.A. convention, and would like more than anything to see Alcatraz. He has been mayor of Hudson for fourteen years and is a close friend of the Wards. He is also the doctor for whom my wife, Lucille, worked as receptionist, and has of course heard all about the Rock and

Warden & Mrs. Swope. If you can manage it, would you extend him an invitation to see the Island? He is staying at the Hotel Shaw, or could be reached through his son George F. Newton, 131 Waltham Rd., Concord.

It continually amazes me that so many good things can have happened, beginning with the day when you gave me a job at the house. I have a fine job, financial security, a nice home and a lovely wife. We even have an invitation out to dinner with the Wards next week, when they will be in Los Angeles. Ain't that sumpin'!?

Please give my respects to the Schroeders, etc., and all of your friends who were so kind to me, and my very best wishes for you and Wes and Family.

Respectfully,

Mickey

June 24, 1954

My dear Michener:

This will acknowledge your letter of June 19, 1954, and we are so happy to hear that you are now married. We certainly wish the utmost happiness to both of you. I am sure you must have married a very lovely girl, and of course we know you will make her a good husband. Also, thanks for the information that Dick Franzeen is married and living in Hudson, Wisconsin.

Mr. and Mrs. Ward must, indeed, be fine people to have treated both of you boys so elegantly. A check for $1000.00 - just think of how nice it is to have this nest egg to start your married life on. They are certainly wonderful people and we are so happy for you both.

With reference to Dr. Newton of Hudson. I am extremely sorry that we are unable to comply with your wishes, but we had so many Doctors in town during the American Medical Association Convention, and our visiting arrangements, as you know, are so that only a few can go through the institution, that it was necessary for us to turn down a great number. In fact only this morning our Chief Medical Officer wanted to bring four Doctors over today and we had to turn him down. Will you please advise your good doctor if he is ever in San Francisco again to please drop us a line and we will try to take care of him. I am awfully sorry we can't do it at this time.

Sincerely,

E. B. SWOPE
W a r d e n

RECEIVED
SEP 10 1957
CRESCENT Engineering & Research Co.
5440 North Peck Road
El Monte, California
TELEPHONE:
Gilbert 4-0528

Mr. J. V. Bennett
Director of U. S. Prisons
Room 554, HOLC Bldg.
Washington 25, DC

Dear Mr. Bennett:

As you may know, both John K. Giles and I are now employed as technical writers. Giles has just finished a two-year job with American Pipe and Steel, working with Air Force refueling systems. He is largely concerned with hydraulics. My work has so far been with the above company, which designs and manufacturers transducers and other electronic sensing devices, and carrier systems.

To progress as technical writers, we have found, and to get the pay checks that go with important work, it is often essential to have security clearance. Do you know of any way or avenue which we could use to get this clearance? Have any ex-convicts that you know of been able to get clearance?

My job is secure, but has its limitations. The work which Giles has now, however, seems somewhat temporary.

We are both doing well, and feel a great sense of gratitude for the help which you and other prison officials have given us.

Respectfully,

/S/ Elliott W. Michener

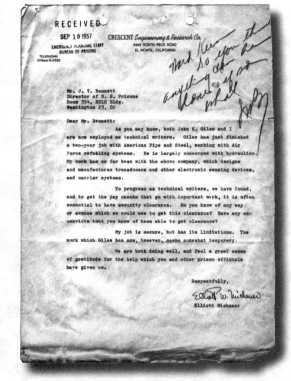

Rufus Franklin

IN THE DARK CLOAK and dagger underworld of Alcatraz, Rufus "Whitey" Franklin held a high-ranking status within the inmate population for his role in the vicious and violent murder of senior correctional officer Royal Cline. He would spend the longest term in a closed front solitary cell of any inmate in the history of Alcatraz.

On May 23, 1938, inmates Thomas Robert Limerick, James Lucus and Rufus Franklin executed a desperate plan to escape using a few simple tools coupled with deadly force to break out of the prison industries. The escape would rank as one of the bloodiest chapters in Alcatraz history (rivaled only by the Battle of Alcatraz in 46'), and resulted in the tragic death of both a well-liked officer, and the shooting death of one of the inmate escapees. Franklin would suffer severe consequences for his role in the officer's murder and would be made an example to other inmates.

Rufus "Whitey" Franklin. He would spend nearly his entire adult life in prison.

While at work in the woodworking shop, located inside the model industries building, the inmates attacked senior custodial officer Royal Cline, who was patrolling the floor unarmed. The three men rushed the unarmed officer using a hammer and other blunt objects with brutal force, delivering fatal wounds in the aftermath. The three then went out of a window and crawled up onto the roof after cutting through barbwire in an attempt to disarm the correctional officer positioned in the Model Shop Tower and secure his weapons. While locked in the

tower behind shatterproof glass, the inmates in what was later described by the officer as an all out suicide charge, stormed the tower from various angles; hurling heavy metal objects which included hammers, drill chucks and wrenches against the shatterproof glass windows. The reinforced glass held up remarkably against the barrage and only one heavy metal fragment managed to break through the glass hitting the officer. The officer first fired warning shots, then began to fire at the inmates with the intent to kill. Limerick received a bullet wound to the head, and Franklin suffered moderate wounds from a gunshot which left him completely immobilized lying on barbwire. Limerick died later that evening in the prison hospital, while Cline died the following day at the Marine Hospital from the wounds inflicted by the convicts.

Alcatraz Officer Royal Cline was brutally murdered by Thomas Limerick during the escape attempt. In his final moment of bravery, Cline refused to aid the escapees, and subsequently was killed.

Thomas Robert Limerick

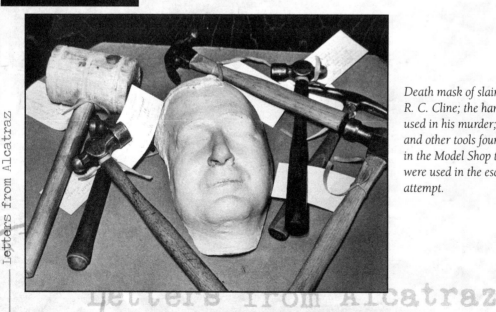

Death mask of slain guard R. C. Cline; the hammers used in his murder; and other tools found in the Model Shop that were used in the escape attempt.

letters from Alcatraz

Rufus Franklin (left) and James Lucas (right) and during their highly publicized court appearances. Both inmates were convicted of first-degree murder for their role in Officer Cline's death.

Officer Royal Cline tragically had been only thirty-six years of age at the time of his death. His wife Etta remained faithfully at his side in the hospital until he succumbed to his injuries. Fellow correctional officers were profoundly affected by Cline's death, which was especially sobering to the island's families since Cline left behind four young children. His death would emphasize the reality that convicts would commit murder in trade for potential freedom.

The trial of Franklin and Lucas lasted three weeks. It was an emotional process, due to the brutal circumstances of Cline's murder. The jury was forced to examine the grisly weapons used in the crime. They were shown graphic photos of the blood trail left behind when the body was dragged, the hammer which delivered the fatal blows, and the vivid death mask showing the viciousness of the attack. These factors contributed to the jury's quick decision. Franklin and Lucas were convicted of first-degree murder, and both received life sentences for Cline's death.

Franklin, who had been found with the bloodied hammer used in Cline's killing, would be sentenced to serve nearly fourteen years in a closed-front solitary confinement cell in D-Block. He would spend the longest term in a closed front solitary cell served by any inmate housed at Alcatraz. Nevertheless, Franklin was eventually extended a few special privileges. After a long period, he was allowed to keep the door front open and to enjoy a non-restricted diet. His long-term isolation status made him an underground hero among his fellow inmates. Even while being held in the most controlled cell row, he was able to communicate with others in the general population via orderlies, and thus to obtain contraband.

Franklin was released back into the general population in 1952. Because he refused to participate in a culinary strike that lasted from March 18th until April 4th, Franklin was forced back into the Treatment Unit for protection from the hostility of other inmates. He was allowed to continue work, and was permanently returned to the general population on February 12, 1954. Records show that Franklin readjusted easily to the normal prison routine. He increased his reading habits and was noted to take special interest in spiritual and philosophical subjects. Franklin gradually became more trusted by the custodial staff, and was later awarded a privileged position in the prison's hospital. He was trained as an X-Ray technician and later qualified as a surgical assistant, and was even allowed to prepare and handle the surgical instruments during operations.

After spending twenty years at Alcatraz,

Franklin was allowed to transfer back to Leavenworth Penitentiary for a brief ten-month stay, and then to Atlanta Federal Prison to be closer to his family. In one letter written in August of 1958, Franklin boasted about the train ride through New Mexico and Arizona in a Pullman car, and the emotion of seeing life outside of prison for the first time since the murder trial of Royal Cline. He wrote frequently to Warden Madigan and other friends at Alcatraz, keeping them up-to-date on his progress. Madigan seemed to reflect pleasantly on Franklin's progress.

Franklin would spend nearly his entire life behind bars. He was finally paroled on October 29, 1974, and died of lung cancer (as indicated on his death certificate) only a short time later on May 27, 1975 in Dayton, Ohio at 59-years of age. He was living with his sister Ruby Farrow at the time of his death, and was said to have enjoyed cooking every morning, and rode the bus into the city everyday to savor his freedom. He is buried at the Willow View Cemetery in Dayton, Ohio, with a simple gravesite marker.

His letters and writings reflect a life turning full circle.

August 9, 1959
From Rufus Franklin
Atlanta, Ga.

To Warden Paul J. Madigan

Dear Warden:

I am happy, sir, to tell you that I am here in Atlanta. It has been wonderful being here close to home and being able to have visits with the family and to get acquainted with them again. I told them all about you and they are as grateful as I to you for making it possible for me to be together again.

It has been an uplifting experience sir, and I can't describe the happiness we have felt at being reunited again. I was not quite prepared for the impact of meeting all my brothers' and sisters' children all of whom I had never met – they having been born since my incarceration, but it was all pretty wonderful and it seemed as though we had known each other all the time!

I was in Leavenworth a little more than ten months before I was transferred here the first of June. I have been trying to find time to write to you ever since I have been here, but there has been so much happening that I have just now been able to settle down and write to you.

I am working in the Hospital here for Dr. Pirkle, who is a very good friend of Mr. Cain. He is a fine man and it is a pleasure to be able to work for him.

All the officials here have been very good to me. They have been most helpful in any way they could be.

I feel, sir, that it might not be too much longer until I shall be paroled. I plan to apply in November. I am praying and hoping with all my heart that the Parole Board let me go home to the finest and best family any man could ever wish for.

I know I shall never violate another law. The only thing I have now is to go out and be a good, respectful, and loyal citizen and try to erase the black name I have placed on our family name. I feel a deep shame when I think of the pain I have caused them, and I intend to make it up to them and make them feel proud of me.

Please give my regards to Captain Rychner, and God bless you, sir, and all your family.

I will write you again when I hear from the Parole Board.

Most sincerely,

Rufus Franklin - #48531
October 15, 1959

Mr. Rufus Franklin
U.S. Penitentiary
Atlanta, Georgia

Dear Rufus:

Thank you for your letter of August 9, 1959. It was a pleasure to hear from you and I know it means a great deal to you to be in Atlanta so you can receive visits from your family.

You are in a good department and your training here at Alcatraz will be helpful to you in hospital work. No doubt the Atlanta hospital is a large operation.

It has been a long time since you first came to Alcatraz and you have been through many difficult years and trials. You were a young man when you first came to us and as many young men you possessed the fire that got you into difficulty. You grew out of those years and by application improved your education and work habits. It was not easy for you since there were many pressures brought to bear that made it most difficult for you to conduct yourself as you wished to do. At any rate you accomplished what you set your mind to do and are now in a position to accomplish still more.

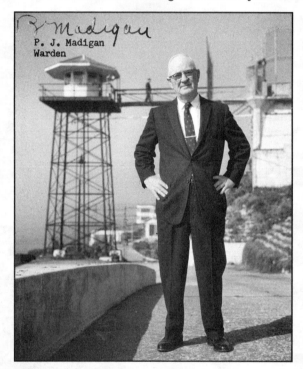

P. J. Madigan
Warden

Paul J. Madigan served as Warden from 1955 until 1961.

We hope you continue to get along well and take advantage of the many opportunities available for increased knowledge. You have learned to accept reverses gracefully and you can be a strong force in Atlanta for proper conduct and living.

I appreciate your remembering me and hope the future brings you the happiness you have missed for many years.

Sincerely,

P. J. MADIGAN
W a r d e n

Rufus Franklin - 48531-131
Jan. 9, 1974

Dear Brother,

Rec. your letter to-day sure was glad to hear from you. Hope you are doing fine, hoping you like being in Atlanta better.

I can line you up on a job, it will be a good job, with pretty good pay. I know the guy well. I want you to keep me posted on any-thing I can do as far as helping you. Are you aloud any visitors, if so let me know the day.

If I send you money will you be aloud to have it?

For me and the family just fine. Guess I will close for now & this is the mail.

Ans. soon

Love,

C. S. Franklin
Route 2, Box 60
Munford, AL 36258

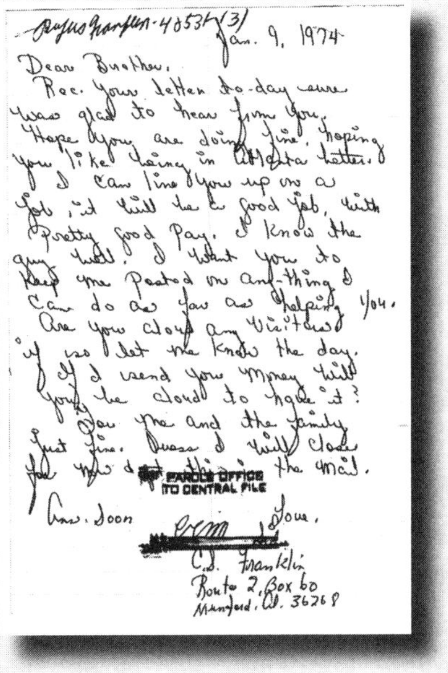

1974

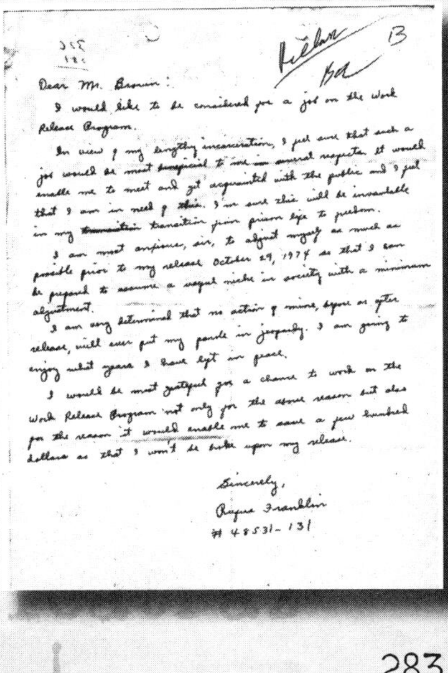

Dear Mr. Brown:

I would like to be considered for a job on the Work Release Program.

In view of my lengthy incarceration, I feel sure that such a job would be most beneficial to me in several respects. It would enable me to meet and get acquainted with the public and I feel that I am in need of this. I'm sure this will be invaluable in my transition from prison life to freedom.

I am most anxious, sir, to adjust myself as much as possible prior to my release October 29, 1974 so that I can be prepared to assume a useful niche in society with a minimum adjustment.

I am very determined that no action of mine, before or after release, will ever put my parole in jeopardy. I am going to enjoy what years I have left in peace.

I would be most grateful for a chance to work on the Work Release Program not only for the above reason but also for the reason it would enable me to save a few hundred dollars so that I won't be broke upon my release.

Sincerely,

Rufus Franklin

#48531-131

August 25, 1974

Dear Mr. Brown:

Sir, I would like to submit another Parole Plan.

After long consideration, I have come to the conclusion that my best parole bet is to go to Dayton, Ohio to live with my sister.

The employment situation around aviation is not good at this time and I can foresee that I am going to have difficulty finding work there.

Employment in Dayton is much better and my two sisters there are most anxious and willing to help me and they will submit a job to the Probation Officer just as soon as it is requested.

My sister, with whom I will be residing is: Mrs. Ruby Farrow, 172 Olive Rd. Dayton, Ohio 45427.

My sisters and I have always been very close and they both want me to come to Dayton.

You might have noticed in my file that I submitted a parole plan in 1959 when I originally applied for parole for Dayton.

At that time my sister had me a job lined up in a hospital there. Of course, that same job might not still be available, but my sister assured me today on the phone that a job would be no problem.

So, sir, I would be most grateful if you will send a request to the Probation Officer in Dayton asking him to contact my sister for a plan.

Sincerely,

Rufus Franklin

48531-131

Dorm. E

August 25, 1974

Dear Mr. Brown:
Sir, I would like to submit another Parole Plan.
After long consideration, I have come to the conclusion that my best parole bet is to go to Dayton, Ohio to live with my sister.
The employment situation around aviation is not good at this time and I can foresee that I am going to have difficulty finding work there.
Employment in Dayton is much better and my two sisters there are most anxious and willing to help me and they will submit a job to the Probation officer just as soon as it is requested.
My sister, with whom I will be residing is: Mrs. Ruby Farrow, 172 Olive Rd. Dayton, Ohio 45427. Telephone

48531-131
Dorm. E.

Inmate Petition

Alcatraz
Hon. Frank Murphy
U.S. Attorney General
Dept of Justice Bldg
Washington D.C.

Sir:

We the undersigned respectfully submit this petition for the purpose of obtaining your approval in granting we inmates the privilege of subscribing for the Nation's newspapers.

We do believe that if an unbiased analysis is made with a view of determining the amount of good contributed by a newspaper as compared with the theoretical harm that is alleged both from the Institution's point of view as well as the inmates a good deal of constructive good is to be concluded.

We do further believe that at this time World History is being written and destiny molded in a manner vital to the Nation as well as to the individual.

Heretofore we have been given to understand that we inmates have been denied access to the newspapers because of the crime news contained therein.

Incredible tho it may sound crime news to a man in this Institution is of less interest than it is to the man on the street.

A letter smuggled off Alcatraz to the Attorney General, requesting that inmates be allowed to read newspapers in order to keep up with current events. This letter, considered as contraband, was signed by numerous famous inmates at Alcatraz, but it did not reach its intended destination. A mail handler found the letter in Sacramento and turned it over to the authorities.

Letters from Alcatraz

There are at present in this Institution men whose Homelands, which are now the scene of the tragedy taking place in Europe and it so follows that it is a natural desire to wish to be informed of the events there taking place the same as if your Country or Home State wher to be invaded altho we hope that the latter will never occur.

We have it is true, weekly news-magazines but it can be readily seen these are of necessity limited in scope, accuracy and detail, it is also obvious that mail facilities are unable to cope with the present situation.

There are circulating in this Country many conservative newspapers of unimpeachable character many of which you are no doubt personally acquainted with and can vouch for as to their integrity and lack of sensationalism.

Doubtless these same newspapers assist you in your daily life and if contact with these newspapers were to be severed their value would be apparent.

The healthy minded person enjoys keeping pace with progress in the worlds of National and Foreign affairs with science and invention, history and civic life, industries and world markets, sports and modern trends to mention a few of the educational features to be found in the every day newspaper.

We inmates regret that we have no other means to employ in making this contact with you and wish to assure you that this petition will not be the forerunner of future attempts to petition your office with requests of this nature.

We also wish to assure you that we will deeply appreciate any consideration you may show us in regard to this request and remain

Respectfully yours,
/s/ The men of Alcatraz

Frank Weatherman

"Alcatraz was never no good for nobody."

—FRANK WEATHERMAN, 1963

FRANK C. WEATHERMAN, AZ-1576, would gain widespread notoriety as the last inmate to be issued a register number on Alcatraz, and additionally, one of the final inmates to depart on the day of the prison's closure. Weatherman, who was serving time for armed robbery from a conviction in August of 1960, was only 28-years of age when he boarded the prison launch, destined for transfer to U.S.P Atlanta from Alcatraz on March 21, 1963.

Originally from Alaska, Weatherman stated that the attention he received as the last inmate from Alcatraz placed him under considerable strain. One of the final reports in Weatherman's file indicated that he had alleged that the never ending barrage of questions from inmates and staff members had contributed to a withdrawn and reclusive state, much of which would endure for the remaining days of his incarceration.

A letter written just three months following the closure of Alcatraz is a fitting bookend to the closure of America's most famous prison. Like so many other inmates who served time on the Rock, Weatherman was desperate to escape the conditions of his confinement. Weatherman was finally paroled from prison in September of 1966, but continued to find himself at odds with the law. He died in California at only 64 years of age in January of 1999.

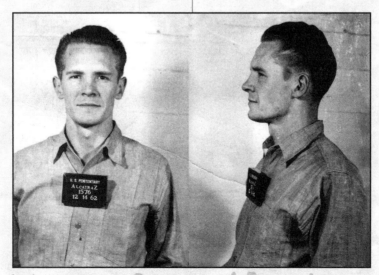

Letters from Alcatraz

June 19, 1963
From Mr. Frank C. Weatherman

To Mr. F. T. Wilkerson
Washington 25, D.C.

Dear Sir:

I am writing in regard to the difficulty I am having in seeking a job in the "Prison Industry" that will suit my medical conditions.

First I shall explain to you from the start to finish why I am being given a hard time. When I first arrived at this institution and being the last man to leave "Alcatraz" my nerves were on edge because I was confronted by so many people and ask so many questions as though I was a freak of some kind instead of a prisoner. This was my main reason for refusing work in Industry before the "Committee" in my first appearance.

They told me it would be six month's before I could have another chance to get into the factory.

After refusing an assignment in industry and reconsidering my action I called on my "Case Worker" two weeks later to seek another chance to be placed on the list for employment.

This was done and I made my appearance before the committee for the second time. I explained to said "Committee" that I'm a medical case to be placed on light duty by the "Doctor's" order. I have to work while it's cool and a job where I can sit down. I am allergic to excessive sweating and I can't lift anything heavy. They told me that the doctor would have to verify all of this, in which he did. The doctor sent a memorandum to the supt. of industry, Mr. Crowder. In turn Mr. Crowder sent it to the warden, "Mr. Herritage."

Mr. Herritage suggested that I be given a job change to something more suitable for my condition. This all took one week to check out and in the mean time I worked in the weave shed regular. I was taken out of the weave shed and placed in spin one where the heat is over 85° everyday. Aside from the heat I have to do a lot of walking since I'm employed as a sweeper.

One more thing I can't understand is why Mr. Crowder lied to me. He said there were no openings in any place but the card room and every week they put men in all the outher Industry's that have no medical condition. Sir, this job I have at present is defi nitely unbearable to my medical handicap.

Mr. Wilkerson, when I was at McNeal Island, my work record was very good and it goes to show that I am very will to work.

I went to see Captain Farr on the 7th of June and he also said that he could understand my condition and that adjustments should be made and he said he would talk to Mr. Crowder about it. Mr. Wilkerson I have not heard anything from the Captain or Mr. Crowder. Mr. Wilkerson you told me to write you if I had some problems at this institution, well this is the only one that has come up. I like this institution and want to stay here, you told all of us that we would be treated as all the others and that is all we can ask. Thanking you in advance for any consideration you may give me.

Sincerely yours
Frank C. Weatherman
#86238

Letters from Alcatraz

Epilogue

LCATRAZ had become one the most expensive facilities in the federal prison system by the time officials finally determined that the Rock had outlived its usefulness in 1962. But even as early as 1949, Attorney General Tom C. Clark had informed the United States Congress that closing Alcatraz was under consideration. The cost of running the institution was the reason most often citied by officials. In 1949, it cost $8 a day per inmate, while at other federal institutions it averaged only $3. By 1959, the cost at Alcatraz had risen to more then $10 per day, while parallel costs at other institutions remained at about the $3 rate.

Alcatraz continued to fall under extreme scrutiny in the press, and when the *San Francisco Examiner* published a feature article in February of 1962 entitled: 'The Rock' Is Crumbling; Alcatraz Is Reaching the End of the Line, the Kennedy Administration acknowledged its consideration for closure not only due to the extreme expenses required to maintain daily operations, but also the evident structural degradation from age and the

ocean's caustic elements. James Bennett had also provided a variety of other factors that made the prison difficult to maintain. The Examiner quoted Bennett as stating that Alcatraz had become an "administrative monstrosity" and that "Prison Bureau guards and staff do not like to be assigned to the barren island any more than prisoners like being sent there."

The last group of inmates being led down "Broadway" on March 21, 1963.

Alcatraz had been established in the 1930s to strike fear into the hearts of the American gangsters, and now more central and state-of-the-art facilities were being implemented to better serve the ever changing demographics of crime. When Alcatraz closed its gates for the last time on March 21, 1963, it never loosened its grip on public intrigue. During its twenty-nine years of operation, 1576 inmate register numbers were issued. 1546 men had served time on the Rock, 28 of those had returned twice, and as previously referenced in Theodore Audett's case, he had served three completely separate terms at Alcatraz.

In addition to the fourteen escapes, there had been scores of plots and schemes to escape that never materialized, and several men (and in at least one case a woman) lost their lives on the Rock, even before its tenure as a Federal Prison. As Erwin Thompson noted in his epic history entitled: The Rock: A History of Alcatraz Island: 1847–1972:

Births and deaths were a part of the fabric of Alcatraz's history. Between 1875 and 1891 and from 1893 to 1910, 35 garrison soldiers and general prisoners died on the island. Of these deaths, 20 were caused by disease, 9 were accidental, 5 were suicides, and 1 was a murder. In addition, two wives lost their lives: one who was killed (below), and a sergeant's wife who committed suicide.

One of the most tragic incidents of death involved the capable and conscientious post surgeon, Capt. William D. Dietz. On the morning of January 28, 1891, the 29-year-old captain and his young wife were found dead in their quarters. The terse medical report read:

"Mrs. Dietz came to her death at the hands of the Captain. Weapon used-- shot-gun, Caliber 10, subsequently the Captain killed himself with the same weapon. Insanity is supposed to be the cause of the tragedy."

The island experienced another act of violence in 1909 when Sgt. Roy Ford threw Pvt. Thomas Mullaly out of a third-story window in the barracks. The private fell 37 feet onto the iron grating and was killed instantly. Sergeant Ford then killed himself with a .38 caliber Colt.

Over the course of its history, the Rock has seen its share of tragedy and desperation. During its Federal term from 1934 to 1963, there were eight people murdered by inmates. Five men committed suicide, and fifteen died from natural causes. The highest number of inmates ever recorded at any single period was 302 in December of 1935, and the lowest number of 222 recorded in January of 1950. The average number of inmates during the 29-years of operation was 263.

While there were several men who tested their fate and plotted to escape the Rock, the reality was that most did their time uneventful. They lived their days on Alcatraz, enduring the iron rule against the painful landscape of the San Francisco shoreline.

Countered against the numerous tragedies were equal or greater numbers of victories for some men as illustrated in this letter to Warden Johnston following the prisoner's transfer to U.S.P. Leavenworth:

March 20, 1963.

TO: CONCERNED:

RE: Transfer of prisoners from Alcatraz, plane leaving from the S.F.I.A. 12 NOON, Thursday, March 21st. Captain furnish Lieutenant, who will be incharge of trip, and five officers. Two additional officers being sent in to assist. Chief Steward prepare eighty (80) lunches.

LEAVENWORTH (11)

Davis	1329
Evans	1287
Gandara	1461
Gill	1574
Lipscomb	1141
Nunez	1532
O'Brien	1447
Rixinger	1468
Romero	1436
Semien	1503
Young	1162

TERRE HAUTE (1)

Cain	1494

ATLANTA (8)

Johnson	1477
Massie	1515
Newman	1034
Nunez	1533
Reynolds	1539
Soviero	1380
Sprenz	1414
Weatherman	1576

LEWISBURG (7)

Donovan	1420
Duncan	1359
Hawkins	1245
McGraw	1406
Marcum	1407
Nicholson	1300
Pravato	1432

TOTAL 27

THESE TWENTY-SEVEN PRISONERS REPRESENT:

1	LIFE SENTENCE
471	YEARS of sentenced time
15	Detainers
3716	days of outstnding forfeited GOOD TIME

F I L E
MAR 2 6 1963
BUREAU OF PRISONS

A memorandum detailing the final transfer of remaining inmates during the closure of Alcatraz in March of 1963.

January 2, 1948
Mr. James A. Johnston
Alcatraz, California

Dear Sir:

I received a letter tonight from my brother, he wrote that you informed him that I was receiving 1095 days extra credits. I was notified of the extra credits here, some few days before Christmas.

I wish to sincerely thank you for this and the confidence you have shown and belief in my honesty. I shall always feel thankful and I can surely repay it in honest endeavor to do that which is right. I am working in the hospital here. I am satisfied with my work. I am going to church regularly. I like that too. I have found that to be truthful and honest is easier, and leaves one feeling good, undisturbed and sure of oneself.

I have heard the remark that "Alcatraz has served its purpose", for me it did serve a purpose-for it was there that I eventually found myself. I learned there that the criminal thought is the most repugnant thing in the world.

For you, in your thankless job, I feel most humbly thankful. I feel that I cannot be thankful enough. I shall ever be.

Most respectfully yours,

The closure of Alcatraz marked the end of an era. Now but a skeleton, it remains as an iconic symbol of America's ultimate escape-proof punishment. During an early reunion event I toured Alcatraz with Jim Quillen and Phil Bergen together. When a young girl asked Jim whether the island was haunted and inquired if he had ever seen any ghosts, he paused and then responded simply: "Every time I come back I see my own ghost...That is only ghost I've ever seen..."

The passage of time has softened the voices that once resonated from the cement cellblocks. As their voices pass from memory and into pages of history, their letters remind us of their thoughts and the struggles they endured while in prison, and of their dreams of recovery, redemption and ultimate freedom.

Tragically, Alcatraz's former Warden James Johnston wouldn't live to see the prison's closure. He died on September 6, 1954, in San Francisco at 80-years of age.

Epilogue

Letters from Alcatraz

Acknowledgments

THE LEGACY of Alcatraz has been defined in the strictest sense, by those individuals who lived the experience, and those who conserve and sustain the history. Whether they spent time on the Rock as an inmate, correctional officer, or even a child growing up on the island, the history of Alcatraz encompasses a variety of people and perspectives, all equally important to framing the history in its proper context. The primary research for this book was in many respects a crossover from my first book chronicling the history of Alcatraz. While the scope of research was more singular in focus, credit falls to those same people who were willing to share their time, knowledge, and memories of life on the island. Their contributions were every bit as significant to this work as to the former. The acknowledgements section could have easily been copied over into this book and have remained as accurate, since it was many of the same people who inspired and provided advice on the best avenues to explore with this material. There are still those who again deserve special mention as well as some new voices. Without their help and expertise, this book would not have enveloped the same level of genuineness to understanding the complex inter-workings of Alcatraz.

Joseph Sanchez, Archivist with the National Archives continues to remain an enthusiastic supporter even after years of endless file requests. Along with Joseph, I remain thankful to all of the staff members at the National Archives who have always extended their support and assistance. Sam Daniel at the Library of Congress was key in helping locate specific elements for this collection. All of these people remained instrumental in offering advice and direction for materials in all stages of my research. I know that America's history is in very good hands with these people...

John Reinhardt, the extraordinary designer has become a very good friend over the past decade. His vision and passion for this history always make these pages come to life. Jim Zach, the brilliant designer of the cover is also an amazing and great colleague.

The National Park Rangers, Volunteers and Golden Gate National Parks Conservancy Staff are a group of dedicated individuals who continue to earn my sincere and deep admiration. Their passionate efforts to share this history with visitors from all over the world with such integrity and neutrality, is not only something to be commended, but a model for all interpretive museums and historic sites alike. They continue to approach the history in a balanced and dignified fashion, and make this history come alive for visitors on a daily basis. Nothing has been more rewarding than the friendships that have evolved from spending time on the Rock. Everyone at Alcatraz has been very supportive and encouraging. Namely but not limited to National Park Rangers: Ricardo Perez, John Cantwell, Lori Brosnan, Benny Batom, Jayeson Vance, Dan Unger, Al Blank, George Durgerian, Andrew Prys and Craig Glassner.

From the Golden Gate National Parks Conservancy: Linda Chalmers, Robert Lieber, Chris Warren, Lala Macapagal, Louise Audell, Wendy Swee, John Moran, Jim Nelson, Katherina Machwitz, Sharlene Baker, Drew Morita, Art Owen, Dan Cook, Angelita Cecilio, Eric Knackmuhs, Jude Savoy, John Donelan, Glenn Mullin, Phillip Griffiths, Tory Light, Heather Paris, Kristen Elford, Arman Safa, Jim Breeden, Dallas Fargo and all of the dedicated employees from this organization and also the staff at Alcatraz Cruises continue to do stellar service for this national treasure. Historians John Martini, Jolene Babyak, Phil Dollison, Anne Miller, Mario Gomes, Tim Brazil and San Francisco City Archivist Susan Goldstein also helped in providing additional material and perspectives. Also Stan Cordes, Tom Ryan, Lorie Johns, Petty Terry, Rick Roesch, Allen & Lisa Cress, Amanda Williford, John Weingardt, and Pete Dracopoulos have all been very supportive. Fern Price and Joan Santoro carefully transcribed the letters for this collection.

There are numerous Alcatraz Alumni who continue to keep the history alive.

Notably, Ernest Lageson, Father Bernie Bush; and Chuck Stucker, a man who I continue to maintain a deep respect for sharing his experiences and research with Alcatraz visitors. Former Alcatraz Officers George DeVincenzi, Frank Heaney, Patrick T. Mahoney, John Hernan, Ben Blount, Sam Hill, Ron Battles, Bill Long, Robert Sutter, Ned Ubben and especially Larry Quilligan, who have all helped me immensely by always taking time to answer my plethora of questions, many during the reunion events held on Alcatraz. Darwin Coon, former Alcatraz inmate, is also someone who I've known for several years now, and a person who I've come to admire and consider a good friend. I continue to deeply respect his willingness to openly share his personal experiences with the public, even in cases where the memories are not always pleasant. John Banner, John Dekker and Morton Sobell also deserve special mention for having shared perspectives of life on Alcatraz during initial interviews for my first book and richly shaped my understanding of some of the more complex issues of long-term confinement.

Tragically, in the time since the publication of my last work of the same theme, we've lost many of the prominent voices that were the architects of this history. It is their voices which have inspired the Alcatraz heritage. Philip R. Bergen, former Captain at Alcatraz, remains to me a lost friend. He long considered his 16-years on Alcatraz as some of the best years of his life. One very cold and early morning before visitors arrived, I experienced the audio tour in a completely empty cellhouse. As Phil's voice provided some of the narration for the tour, it was a profound experience to hear him even after

Acknowledgments

his passing recounting for visitors life on the Rock. There was no tougher critic than Phil when it came to documenting this history. He always inspired accuracy and encouraged me to leave no stone uncovered. Phil provided numerous letters, audio recordings, and diagrams to illustrate various events. The spirit of his devotion to this history continues as an inspiration to me, and I remain proud to pay forward his heritage. Clifford Fish, Irving Levinson and Al Bloomquist were also kind spirits who helped me immensely during my path of discovery.

Champion Open Water Swimmer Lisa Johnson is also someone who had a powerful impact on me. Lisa swam Alcatraz numerous times during her competitive career and in a variety of conditions. She was an enchanting soul, and there was no other person who offered a more valuable perspective on what the inmates faced once they entered the water to make their break to freedom.

The late former Alcatraz inmates: Jim Quillen, Leon "Whitey" Thompson, Dale Stamphill, Glenn Nathan Williams, Tom Kent, Elliott "Mickey" Michener and Willie Radkay are just a few people of whom I maintain a deep appreciation for sharing their experiences with me. Jim once pointed out to me that while in a dark isolation cell on Alcatraz, he had an epiphany. He realized that he had reached in the lowest point a human could reach. He was considered so unfit for society that he had to be confined in a pitch black steel reinforced cell. It was here that turned his rudder and plotted a course back to society. All of these men worked to become good men within their communities. I appreciate their willingness to share their stories and help others learn from their mistakes and the consequences of some of their choices. I don't believe it was an easy life for any one of them, even once released from prison, but I appreciate the openness and honesty. Their voices continue to educate and help others understand life at Alcatraz even after their passing. The real gift of my time studying this history has been the resulting and longstanding friendships. Getting to know these people and our talks over morning coffee on the boat to the island are the memories I will look back on and treasure most.

Finally, I wish to thank all the people I love most: My mother and father Theresa and Clyde Clabo, Temple and Jack, Linda and Steven, my wife Julie and three sons Forrest, Brandon, and Ross. Finally, my late terrier Luck, my lost writing partner who I miss deeply... My life has forever been enriched by all of you...

Thank you all,

Michael Esslinger

Photography and Illustrations Credits

Unless noted in the following source index, all prisoner catalog photographs, letters, documents and illustrations are courtesy of the National Archives and Records Administration and/or United States Library of Congress Historic Records Collection. Specific catalog collection numbers or facility locations for unique photographs are included in the source index below.

ABBREVIATIONS (t-top, b-bottom, c-center, l-left, r-right):

AAA	Alcatraz Alumni Association, Courtesy Chuck Stucker
AC	Author's Historical Artifact Collection
AM	Anne Miller Family Collection
AP	Associated Press Archives
BOP	Bureau of Prisons Archives
CSA	California State Archives
GGNRA	Golden Gate National Recreation Area, Parks Archives
GGNRA-DN	Don Denevi Collection, Golden Gate National Recreation Area, Parks Archives, Associated Press Photograph, GOGA Catalog Index number provided in description.
GGNRA-PD	Phil Dollison Collection, Golden Gate National Recreation Area, Parks Archives, GOGA Catalog Index number provided in description.
JMC	John Martini Collection
JRE	Julie R. Esslinger
LC	Library of Congress Historical Photograph Collection
ME	Photography by Michael Esslinger
MGC	Al Capone Museum, Mario Gomes Collection
NACP	National Archives and Records Administration, College Park, Maryland
NPS	National Park Service / Golden Gate National Recreation Area Museum Collection
PTWR	Patty Terry & William Radkay Family Collection
RC	Ronnie Comeau, iStock Photography
SFC	San Francisco Chronicle / San Francisco Call Bulletin / Examiner Photo Archives
SFPL	San Francisco Public Library, History Center Archives
USCG	United States Coast Guard Archives

V(t) AAA: 1 (t) ME; 6 (tl) PTWR; 7 (t-r) SFPL AAC-9430, 8-9 RC, 13(t-r) CSA, (l-c) SFPL, 13 (b) GGNRA TASC Collection, Box 22; 14 (t-c-b) CSA; 15 Harper's Magazine, May 1883, (c-b) NACP; 16 (t-c) CSA, GGNRA – Interpretative Negative Collection; 17 (t) LC; 18 NACP; 19 USCG; 20 (t) NACP, (b) JMC & National Archives; 21 (t) AC, (b) SFPL AAC-9265; 23 (tl) GGNRA-PD 17934, (b) Andrea Pistolesi, Image Vault; 24 SFPL; 25 (t) AC, (c) GGNRA-DN 17975.049; SFPL (c) AAC-9485 (b) AAC-9484; 27 AAA; 29 (t)(cr) AP, (bl) AAA; 30 (t)(c) ME, (b) GGNRA-DN 17975.050; 31 (tl) AP (wire photo), (cr) ME, (bl) ME, (br) AP (wire photo), 32 (tl) BOP; 33 Warner Brothers; 34 NACP; 35 ME; 37 (t) SFC, (b) Corbis / Time Life Images; 38 ME; 40 AC; 42 AC; 44 (t) AC, (br) Marc Fischetti Alcatraz Collection GGRNA-GOGA 18352.104; 56; AAA, 61 MGC; 62 (bl) MGC; 64 (b) ME; 65 (br) MGC; 67 SFPL; 72 SFPL; 78 (b) BOP-AAA; 79 (t) ME; 86 PTWR; 114 AC; 120:121 Paramount Pictures; 124 (tl) ME, (bl) BOP; 184 (tr) (bl) AAA; 188 GGRNA 18308; 189 AP (wire photo); 190 AP (wire photo); 192 AC; 193 AP (wire photos); 194 SFPL; 195 (t) AP, (bl) SFPL, (br) AC; 196 NPS GOGA-18261k; 204 ME; GGNRA-DN GOGA-18261m; 220 AM; 221 AM; 226 SFPL; 249 NPS GOGA 405, GOGA 406, GOGA 407, GOGA 408; 270 William Woodfield Collier's Magazine Proof Set AC; 278 SFPL, 279 SFPL, 282 BOP File Photo - Getty Images; 291 GGNRA-DN 18261.006; 294 LC; 311 JRE

Index

Index

Index

Letters from Alcatraz

Index

Index

Index

Index

Letters from Alcatraz

About the Author

LETTERS FROM ALCATRAZ is Michael Esslinger's second endeavor chronicling the history of Alcatraz Island. Esslinger is a historical researcher, whose acclaimed work has appeared in numerous books, film and television documentaries, including segments on the Discovery, National Geographic and History Channels. In 2003 he published: *Alcatraz—A Definitive History of the Penitentiary Years*. Hailed by the *San Francisco Chronicle* as one of the most meticulously detailed histories ever written the subject, it has remained a best selling reference since its publication.

He is also the author of the forthcoming reference chronicling the first expeditions to the Moon entitled: APOLLO—A Definitive History of the Apollo Lunar Expeditions. His research resulted in one of the most comprehensive assemblages of information on the Apollo Program, derived from intensive archival research and over a thousand hours of in-depth one-on-one interviews, which include the elusive Apollo 11 Astronauts Neil Armstrong, Michael Collins, and Buzz Aldrin. He remains one of the foremost historians on the Apollo Program.

Michael is currently collaborating with Julie Dawn Cole, the original Veruca Salt in the classic motion picture *Willy Wonka and the Chocolate Factory* on her personal memoir. The book entitled "I Want it Now!" chronicles her experiences during the entire epic production and also includes a fascinating portrait of her life and acting career.

Esslinger's academic background includes advanced studies in history and is also a graduate of the College of Recording Arts in San Francisco where he studied film and audio sciences. He is a native California coastal resident along with his wife and three sons, and frequently participates in the guest author program on Alcatraz Island. For more information on this and other projects visit www.historyarchive.com.

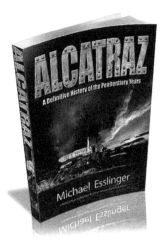

Also available from Ocean View Publishing:

ALCATRAZ—
A Definitive History of the Penitentiary Years

BY MICHAEL ESSLINGER

Paperback: 464 pages
ISBN-10: 0970461402
ISBN-13: 978-0970461407

• NATIONAL EDITORIAL REVIEWS •

"Michael Esslinger's steady gaze penetrates the Hollywood fog surrounding Alcatraz to find an even greater trove of historical riches and human drama than screenwriters could imagine, illuminated in meticulous detail."
—JEANNE COOPER, *San Francisco Chronicle*

"They're all here, from Capone and the Birdman to tough warden "Salt Water" Johnston and even the "Rock Islanders" inmate orchestra. "Alcatraz" delivers on its promise as a definitive history. Author Michael Esslinger balances the drama of his narrative with an earnest effort to let the facts speak for themselves. The result is a fascinating portrait, sprung from the heart of Devil's Island."
—GREG BURNS, *Chicago Tribune*

"This is a serious book, a comprehensive history of the island during its three decades as a federal penitentiary. At 451 oversized pages, including more than 1,000 pictures, it also represents a mammoth research undertaking... simply a terrific book, and an even better reference tool."
—SUE FISHKOFF, *Coast Weekly*

"I think you will enjoy reading Michael's book. Through meticulous research, he has captured the experience of Alcatraz with an authentic voice. It is a skillful blend of history and character study, and a compelling portrait of America's most notorious prison."
—Former Alcatraz Inmate DARWIN E. COON

"Historian Michael Esslinger offers readers an in-depth portrait of the intimidating and seemingly inescapable American prison in Alcatraz: A Definitive History of the Penitentiary Years. Black-and-white photographs enhance a detailed chronicle of this penal institution and its inmates, from its creation as a Mexican military fortress, to it's first use as an American Civil War facility of incarceration for prisoners of war by the Union in 1861, down to its final closure in 1963. A detailed, in-depth, definitive, informative, and superbly presented account of an infamous institution of American history, Alcatraz is a unique and welcome contribution to Penology Studies and American History reference collections."
—JIM COX, Editor-in-Chief
Midwest Book Review, KNLS Bookwatch

Available at reputable on-line booksellers including ParksConservancy.org, Amazon.com, Alcatraz.com, HistoryArchive.com and AlcatrazHistory.com.